THE
"LAST"
NAZI

ALSO BY GERALD ASTOR

AND A CREDIT TO HIS RACE
THE DISEASE DETECTIVES
HOT PAPER
THE CHARGE IS RAPE
BRICK AGENT

THE

"LAST"

NAZI

THE LIFE AND TIMES OF DR. JOSEPH MENGELE

by Gerald Astor

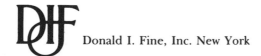

Donald I. Fine, Inc. New York

Copyright © 1985 by Gerald Astor

All rights reserved, including the right of reproduction in whole or in part in any form. Published in the United States of America by Donald I. Fine, Inc. and in Canada by Fitzhenry & Whiteside, Ltd.

Library of Congress Catalogue Card Number: 85–80628
ISBN: 0–917657–46–2
Manufactured in the United States of America

10 9 8 7 6 5 4 3 2 1

This book is printed on acid free paper. The paper in this book meets the guidelines for permanence and durability of the Committee on Production Guidelines for Book Longevity of the Council on Library Resources.

Auschwitz: True Tales from a Grotesque Land, by Sarah Nomberg-Przytyk, translated by Roslyn Hirsch, and edited by Eli Pfefferkorn and David H. Hirsch. Copyright © 1985 by University of North Carolina Press. Used with permission.

Aftermath, by Ladislas Farago. Copyright © 1974 by Ladislas Farago. Published by Simon & Schuster. Used with permission.

Black Sabbath, by Robert Katz. Copyright © 1969 by Robert Katz. Used with permission of Macmillan & Co., Literistic, Ltd.

The Deputy, by Rolf Hochhuth. Copyright © 1964 by Rolf Hochhuth. Published by Grove Press, Inc. Used with permission.

"Gizelle, Save the Children," by Gizelle Hersh and Peggy Mann. Copyright © 1980 by Gizelle Hersh and Peggy Mann. Published by Dodd, Mead & Co. Inc. Used with permission.

None of Us Will Return, by Charlotte Delbo. Copyright © 1968 by Charlotte Delbo. Published by Grove Press, Inc. Used with permission.

To the Victims and the Survivors

Contents

Acknowledgments

MANY PEOPLE HELPED ME gather materials for this book. In particular I would like to mention Moyra Ashford in São Paulo, Brazil; Wanda Menke-Glückert in Bonn, West Germany; and Alfredo Seiferheld in Asunción, Paraguay. Others whom I want to thank are Nina Lindley in Buenos Aires, Argentina; Bob Slater and Wendy Elliman in Jerusalem; Janet Stobart in Rome; Jan Rocha in São Paulo; Manfred von Conta of *Stern* in Rio de Janeiro; Brian Moser of British Central Television. I am also grateful to Iris Berlatsky and Dr. Israel Krakofsky of Yad Vashem in Jerusalem; Adaire Klein and others at the Simon Wiesenthal Center in Los Angeles, California; Rhonda Barad of the Simon Wiesenthal Center in New York City; the Beate Klarsfeld Foundation in Paris; the staff at the Yivo Institute for Jewish Research in New York City; the staff of the Leo Baeck Institute in New York City; and Bill Mader of *Time* magazine. Thanks also go to Pablo Weinschenk-Tabernero and Ruth Greenbaum for their translations.

My agent Toni Mendez was a steadfast support and the confidence given me by my editor and publisher Don Fine was gratifying. Most of all, my wife Sonia had faith in me.

The Phantom

TWO HUNDRED AND EIGHT BONES, assorted skeletal fragments, eight teeth, rags from burial clothes, the inevitable handfuls of dust; these were, in June 1985, the apparent remains of Dr. Joseph Mengele, a.k.a. The Angel of Death; The Angel of Extermination; Dr. Death; The Butcher; *Schöne* Joseph. The fossils of a man who had drowned more than six years earlier on the beach at Bertioga, Brazil, dug from a tomb in Embu, Brazil; thus ended the greatest manhunt in history.

Joseph Mengele's name has come to encapsulate the horror of the Holocaust in which the Nazi engines of destruction ground up six million Jews and wiped out untold tens of thousands of other human beings. Before the news of Mengele's death Simon Wiesenthal, hunter of war criminals, had pronounced: "He is the last living mass murderer from Hitler's and Himmler's death factories." By the time the corpse was disinterred, reward money for Mengele had totaled $3.4 million.

He soared above the other executioners for the quantity and quality of his crimes as well as his style. "He stood before us, the handsome devil who decided life and death. . . . He stood there like a charming, dapper dancing master directing a polonaise. Left and right and right and left his hands pointed with casual movements. He radiated an air of lightness and gracefulness, a contrast to the ugliness of the environs; it soothed our frayed nerves, and made whatever was happening devoid of all meaning . . . A good actor? A man possessed? A cold automaton? No, a master at his profession, a devil who took pleasure in his work . . ."

So wrote Frau Grete Salus, an inmate of the Auschwitz concentration camp, whose husband and family perished there. The "master at his profession," "the devil who took pleasure in his work" was Mengele. He was a physician who took a child from her mother, then returned the infant a few days later. In place of one eye was only a huge, ugly red mass. "What's the difference whether you make black eyes out of blue," said the doctor.

He was confronted by a prisoner who said he did not fear death. Mengele turned to an SS sergeant. "If this prisoner asks for it so much, then shoot him." The SS soldier pulled out his pistol and killed the defiant inmate.

As a doctor, Mengele met newcomers debarking from trains at Auschwitz. With a jerk of his thumb, a flick of his swagger stick, a smile on his face, kind words on his lips, he passed sentences of immediate execution by gas upon from 200,000 to 400,000 people.

2

The Phantom

The bill of particulars against him lists shootings, clubbings, and chemical injections by his own hand, bringing death to nearly a dozen individuals. Some survived their encounters with him only at the cost of maimed bodies, indelibly branded memories of torture in the guise of medical experiments.

He was a man of some intellect and black-humored wit. "They come here as Jews," he said, "and leave as smoke up a chimney." "He was a pleasant fellow," insists a former associate at Auschwitz. "He was a man with a very wide horizon, a very interesting person." One inmate actually called him "a beautiful person." Another referred to him as "kindly." Some prisoners among the Gypsies would run to greet him, *"Vater," "Väterchen,"* and *"Onkel"* (Father, Daddy, Uncle). Immaculately uniformed in a pristine blue shirt, emitting the fragrance of perfumed soap, "gorgeous" Joseph Mengele inspected the lines of wretched, filthy, head-shaved starving prisoners, marking some for death. Even as he condemned her sisters in degradation, a young woman said, "If I could only spend the night with *Schöne* Joseph."

"I was surprised how really handsome and indeed attractive they were," says Dr. Olga Lengyel, an inmate-doctor recalling visits of Mengele and one of his entourage, Irma Grese, a warder for women and so sadistic that the British hanged her for her war crimes in 1945.

But Joseph Mengele was not a simple sadistic brute popularly associated with prison personnel. He was no underprivileged kid up from poverty by the bootstraps, bent on venting years of frustration upon the hapless. He was the favored eldest son of a wealthy, close-knit family. He earned a doctoral degree in philosophy as well as his medical certification. He loved music, came by the musical flourishes described by Grete Salus naturally. He was well read, a student of Dante. The intellectual curiosity that made him a genial conversationalist with his colleagues directed him into medical research. As much as his

3

power over life and death, the inmates feared his research at Auschwitz.

"His experimental clinic," says inmate-doctor Gisella Perl, "was just a torture clinic for living guinea pigs."

His work, says Dr. Robert Jay Lifton, professor of psychiatry at City University of New York, was "apparently following standard practices of the physical anthropology of his time."

"He was a man who believed in nothing but power, the ultimate cynic," says Dr. Ella Lingens, another inmate who dismisses Mengele's research.

"He conducted his experiments like a mad amateur," scoffs Dr. Olga Lengyel.

"He would spend hours bent over his microscopes while the air outside stank with the heavy odor of burning flesh from the chimney stacks of the crematoria," remembers Dr. Miklos Nyiszli, a Hungarian pathologist-prisoner and collaborator of Mengele.

Whatever the quality of his work, none who were incarcerated at Auschwitz can forget his enormous power over them. Says Gisella Perl, "Our whole being concentrated on Mengele's hands. Those hands had the power to condemn us to immediate execution or prolong our miserable life by a few days." Forty years later, Perl says that she still has nightmares and daydream anxieties that somehow Mengele will return and decide her fate.

An anonymous inmate left a poem:

> *Like an all powerful demon*
> *I surge from the depths of night.*
> *I am a skillful doctor*
> *And the deaths I cause have no*
>   *limit.*

Mengele showed a mercurial air that defied interpretation. Magda Bass, a seventeen-year-old Rumanian girl, tumbled off the train at Auschwitz on June 6, 1944, the day the Allies waded ashore on the beaches of Normandy. For all that meant, the troops could have been landing on the moon. As she and her mother tried to understand the harsh, guttural commands from bullhorns, "someone seized my arm. I could see he was an officer. In a gentle voice he asked, 'Are you sisters?'

" 'No,' my mother answered. 'I'm her mother.' " That brief encounter spared Magda Bass and her mother from the death column headed for gassing. Later she was to feel the sting of Mengele's experiments, and then came the moment when "I saw Mengele laugh. Groups of prisoners would be forced to kneel in ranks on the ground, holding their hands over their heads. It is very difficult to do that for any length of time. The guards would have these big German shepherd dogs. They were trained at the clap of the hands, the snap of fingers and the shout 'Jew!' to race through the rows of people. They would tear pieces of flesh from men and women, ripping them to pieces. Mengele would laugh.

"What I don't understand after all of these years is what could have been in Mengele's mind."

That is a question that for so long helped spur the hunt for Mengele, who disappeared from Auschwitz in January 1945. But it is only one of many questions. Legends tend to form around a figure central to catastrophe, the more so as other events, subterfuge, time, and the tricks of memory conspire to conceal the truth. So it has been with the concentration camps and the people who ran them. The culpable silenced most of the witnesses through mass murder and then destroyed their records. The life and times of Joseph Mengele thus amount to a stew of fact and fiction, flavored by errors of memory, hypes from headline-hunters, disinformation from interested parties, uncheckable tales from shadowy informants, secret ingredients added or removed by those who cook the recipes for affairs of state.

Until recently there has not even been agreement on his physical appearance. "A small, swarthy, dark-haired man with a slight squint in the left eye and a triangular cleft between his upper front teeth," said Wiesenthal, quoting a witness. "He was tall, blond and blue-eyed," insisted a graduate of Auschwitz forty years later. She was not alone in her misperception, but the record as well as photographs describe a man about five foot eight inches tall, weighing 140 pounds, with greenish brown eyes, dark brown hair, and a distinctive space between his upper incisors.

Many questions can now be asked about Mengele, questions whose answers add up to a portrait not only of a man but also an era. For example, was there any purpose to his actions at Auschwitz beyond murder? Was he as terrible as claimed, or, conceivably, have his transgressions been exaggerated? Was he alone in his endeavors? Did anyone resist? Are there any heroes even in that place of such abandoned hope?

As the embers of the Holocaust still flickered, Mengele slipped away. One persistent story says a Jewish mistress smuggled him through Red Army lines and hid him in the major cities of Europe until he could make a final dash that put him eleven thousand miles away from the scene of his crimes. Why has that story lived on? Could it contain any truth? Or was he the beneficiary of a conspiracy of silence by thousands of people who owed their allegiance to the local grand seigneur? Was he captured by the victorious armies only to escape through stupidity or a sinister indifference?

What drove this once apparently rational, educated man, this specialist by background in the healing arts? If a psychiatrist could have brought him to the confessional couch, what of his upbringing would have emerged, what kind of clinical diagnosis might follow? What about his sexuality? He married twice, but was there not a libidinous tinge to his work at Auschwitz, and did his sex drive affect his last years?

What about Mengele's apparent affinity for death, which like the reek of a decaying swamp clung to him during his wanderings? Was he indeed an abortionist, a participant in shootouts and murderous intrigues after he left Europe? Death supposedly claimed him at least five times before the waters at Bertioga Beach.

How was it possible for one man to evade the vengeance of the most powerful nation on earth, to escape the probing eyes of the most dedicated and cunning secret intelligence agencies? How could the U.S. Central Intelligence Agency and the highly regarded Israeli Mossad, for all of their professionalism, have been so wrong?

Who aided Joseph Mengele in hiding? Who protected him? Was he the beneficiary of a secret, highly skilled Nazi organization—the dreaded ODESSA, *die Spinne* or *Kameradenwerk* to name three obvious candidates? Was there a disinformation network that deliberately confused the professional and amateur Nazi hunters?

What do we know now of his beliefs? To paraphrase Dr. Samuel Johnson, "Nothing so educates a man as to be on the losing side," but did defeat soften or harden his convictions? Did guilt possibly gnaw at Joseph Mengele, or could he have faced accusers with equanimity? From his Brazilian retreat, what were his perceptions of the world, its leaders, its governments, its peoples?

And among those with whom he found refuge, did a man who condemned to death with the flick of a finger ever learn to relate to another human being? Who were these Hungarians and Austrians who provided sanctuary and companionship?

The first news of the remains at Embu elicited considerable skepticism. However, the report from an international panel of seventeen experts in forensic medicine, anthropology, radiology, dentistry and handwriting analysis declared, "It is . . . our opinion that this skeleton is that of Joseph Mengele within a reasonable scientific certainty." Later Dr. Lowell Levine, a forensic odontologist from Huntington Station, New York, added, "The odds are astronomical that another person would have all these characteristics [in common] and no differences."

Menachem Russek, the Israeli police officer charged with pursuit of war criminals, initially said it was a hoax. After traveling to São Paulo where the examination of the body was conducted, he slowly came around to believe that it was, indeed, Mengele. The Israeli government continued to reserve its conclusions. Elie Wiesel, an Auschwitz survivor, only two months before, in his appeal to President Ronald Reagan not to visit the Bitburg Cemetery containing the bodies of SS troops, had specifically cited Mengele. He also withheld his acceptance of Mengele's death, pending the decision by Israel. Simon Wiesenthal and the other most famous Nazi hunters, the husband-and-wife team of Serge and Beate Klarsfeld, went along with the scientists.

The doubters had reasons and motivations for their reluctance. He had, after all, "died" on five other occasions. There were so many reliable sightings in which Mengele was stashed away on some remote well-guarded estate in the protected outback of Paraguay. How could he have lived quietly in a small house in the São Paulo environs? Why would his family have concealed his demise for six long years in which they were constantly hectored by the press, the family business injured by its association with the doctor?

The media felt cheated by the anticlimax to this long-publicized thriller. More important, many of his victims felt swindled, denied their opportunities to work out their lifelong anguish. They wanted Mengele to stand trial, not only to face his accusers and suffer the consequences but also to preserve the memory of the Holocaust and refute the obscene revisionists who claimed it never happened.

The Phantom

There is a pervasive sense that Joseph Mengele was the last of the Nazis. A writer for the *Los Angeles Times,* William Montalbano, said in his account from São Paulo that perhaps World War II finally ended on the beach at Bertioga in 1979. Simon Wiesenthal once said that he hoped to complete his career of chasing war criminals with the capture of Mengele. As the evidence of the doctor's death accumulated, Serge Klarsfeld remarked, "If it is true, then it is almost all over," which to many meant that the hopes of keeping Holocaust memories alive and perpetuating the fight against the remnants of Nazism would be compromised.

While the media may turn away from memories of the Holocaust and its aftermath, and politicians find it convenient for purposes of statecraft to proceed as if Nazism died in 1979—or as President Reagan conveyed through his visit to Bitburg when he said that those who participated in the Nazi horror were at least almost all dead—the ability of Mengele to escape justice for thirty-four years raises questions about the death of Nazism. It is more than a matter of reunions of old SS units or even small, fitful efforts to revive the Nazi party. What needs to be addressed is whether the philosophy is now largely extinct, or whether it lives on, smoldering like some subterranean fire that could erupt under the right combination of circumstances. Can one see in Joseph Mengele's life, in his role in the Holocaust, and then as a man on the run, something that irresistibly points to the continuing reality of the movement that he so uniquely represented?

The Young Nazi

ABOUT EQUIDISTANT between the cities of Stuttgart and Munich lies the town of Günzburg. The district is known as Swabia, the southwest of Bavaria. At Günzburg the meandering Günz River flows into the larger Donau, which as it travels east widens into the proud Danube.

The countryside surrounds Günzburg with flat, fertile farmland, fields of rape plants, whose cabbage-like leaves feed livestock. Günzburg possesses a modest edifice listed as a castle, but the bucolic tranquility has never been seriously disturbed. No decisive battles mark the area; no concordats were struck here;

no princes of the Roman Catholic religion erected a magnificent church here in tribute. Guidebooks tend to ignore Günzburg.

There is no doubt as to the first family of Günzburg; it is Mengele. The family roots dig deep in Swabia. Joseph Mengele's seventeenth-century antecedents came from the villages of Hochstadt and Lutzingen, both short distances from Günzburg. Paternal grandfather Alois, a Litzenberger, married Theresia Mayr and manufactured bricks in Hochstadt. The business prospered enough for son Karl, born in 1884, to obtain a university degree. (Joseph Mengele gave this date; others say Karl was born in 1881.)

In 1907 Karl Mengele arranged to take over a small Günzburg machinery factory originally established in 1872. The firm employed seven people and produced threshing machines for local farmers. His first act as proprietor was to put up the Mengele name on the shed. In 1908 the young manufacturer claimed a bride, Walburga Hupfauer, four years his junior.

Ambitious and inventive, Karl Mengele spent little time on the shop floor. Instead he worked upstairs to design new devices that would chop fodder, shred beet root, cut chaff, and spread dung. He was so successful that within four years he was able to buy a Mercedes as the company's first car for salescalls.

Along with a new automobile, 1911 brought Karl Mengele his first son, Joseph. The boy was named for his maternal grandfather. His brothers, Karl, Jr., and Alois, were born in 1912 and 1914, respectively.

During World War I Karl Mengele served two years as an infantryman on the Western Front, and during her husband's absence Walburga Mengele, with three young children to raise, also managed the family business. One report says Karl Mengele finished the war as a finance minister for the Kaiser in Rumania, and after the Armistice in 1918 he returned to build his company into the largest employer in Günzburg.

Then, as now, Günzburg was divided by class. In the *Oberstadt* —upper-town—lived the professional people, doctors, officials, and entrepreneurs like the Mengele family. The blue-collar, low-income workers occupied the *Unterstadt*. But the Mengeles were always somewhat separate, aloof from everyone. As a clan they occupied a baroque-style house until as late as 1952.

As a boy, Joseph was less than robust, bedded by an almost endless series of colds and childhood diseases. Sickness shut him off from much of the companionship and pastimes of other youngsters. He never developed a talent or interest in team sports. Later, when he described himself for SS records, he listed as his sporting skills "mountaineering and driving a car." He once dismissed athletics as "superfluous." It is reasonable to speculate whether his isolation from other children, both on account of health and being the richest boy in town, the one whose father employed so many of his comrades, stunted Mengele's ability to relate to other people.

Compensation for his time cooped up at home came in the form of extra attention from his mother, Wally. Mengele confided in his later years that he "liked his mother very much." The word "love" apparently stuck in his throat as a sign of weakness. Wally Mengele, however, was not a soft woman. Mengele described her as "very strict; she treated us severely. She was a woman of strong character." The beloved mother was a disciplinarian, a parent who inculcated her firstborn with a strong respect for rules.

He offered only a grudging approval of his father; Mengele said he "admired him as a self-made man, one who created a business with his own hands and became wealthy through his own efforts." Karl Mengele was not, in fact, the sort to engender affection. He ran his business as an autocrat, dispensing favors as the patriarch of a 1,200-member family. Workers referred to themselves as "followers." When Karl Mengele neared the premises, employees warned one another of the approach of *der Alte* (the old man). "As soon as he entered the front door," remembers a foreman, "warning shouts could be heard at the other end."

Although the family was wealthy by Günzburg standards and could have afforded private institutions, the children attended local public schools. Joseph enrolled first in an elementary school and then the gymnasium designed for those with academic aspirations. Childhood acquaintances knew him as "Beppo," a common nickname for Bavarian Josephs and perhaps a reference to his dark Mediterranean looks. He performed well in the classroom. A contemporary, Julius Diesbach, remembers him as "an extraordinarily ambitious student. He always wanted to do something outstanding, to be a great scientist." Another schoolboy acquaintance recalls him as "aggressive and exceedingly patriotic."

The family's religion was Roman Catholic, in keeping with the dominant preference of Bavarians. Wally Mengele was very devout, but the men in the family were less so. According to Joseph, the sons attended church irregularly.

By the time he completed his courses at the gymnasium, Joseph, considered something of a loner, had acquired the superficial social graces . . . he had learned to be a skillful ballroom dancer, which along with his good looks attracted young women. With these attributes and his certificate from the gymnasium in 1930, Mengele enrolled at the University of Munich, driving there in his own white automobile. Whatever had been his social inhibitions in Günzburg, photographs of him in Munich show him enjoying beer, tobacco, and military finery.

The Munich that Joseph Mengele embraced was a center of political turmoil. Mengele was only twelve when Adolf Hitler led the ill-fated Munich *Putsch* in 1923, for which the future Führer earned a jail sentence, but put his mild conditions of incarceration to use, drafting *Mein Kampf.*

Hitler emerged from prison more determined than ever to capture power. The Weimar Republic futilely tried to govern Germany. Inflation and economic upheaval as well as growing resentment of the terms of the Treaty of Versailles—one of the few surrenders in history in which the losers still occupied hundreds of square miles of the victor's territory and their own borders remained inviolate—encouraged political anarchy. Support for radical forces swept through university students like Joseph Mengele. Adolf Hitler's National Socialist German Workers' Party, the NSDAP, or Nazi movement, attracted a strong following.

Hitler spoke often in Munich, the large numbers of students guaranteeing him a receptive audience. Joseph Mengele's first tangible support for the new German politics came through one of the groups falling under the rubric of the Free Corps.

By the terms of the Treaty of Versailles, Germany was restricted to an army of 100,000. As the Weimar Republic's control eroded, various factions shored up their own ideas of order with private paramilitary units. For the most part such organizations served right-wing political groups, operating behind legitimate business establishments, trucking, road construction, detective, and agricultural communes.

These freebooters included the *Sturmabteilung* or SA, created in 1921. Its storm troopers wore brown shirts and supplied bully-boy squads for Hitler. In their uniforms they cheered Nazi speakers, beat up hecklers and disrupted meetings of other parties. The Brownshirts provided the Nazi movement with the necessary muscle in the hurlyburly of the Germany of the period. They also embarrassed their more respectable sponsors with their unbridled brawling and rampant homosexuality.

During the mid 1920s Hitler sired another paramilitary organization, the *Schutztaffel*—not much more than a bodyguard for Hitler until 1929 when a former chicken farmer from the Munich area, Heinrich Himmler, assumed command. Himmler transformed the original 200 members into an organization that eventually dominated Germany, terrified and tormented much of Europe, and gave Joseph Mengele his power.

Older than either the SA or the SS was the Soldiers' League or *Stahlhelm* (Steel Helmets), formed in 1918. Egalitarian at first, the Steel Helmets even backed the democratic regime, but the organization, born out of the camaraderie of the trenches and subservient to the authoritarian nature of its military background, eventually lost faith in the Weimar government. "We hate the present form of the German State with all our hearts because it denies to us the hope of freeing our enslaved fatherland. It denies us any opportunity to cleanse the German people from the war-guilt lie and works against the grain of necessary living space in Eastern Europe." That 1928 resolution by the Stahlhelm encapsulates much of the rationale for all the anti-democratic movements, including the Nazis'. Hitler, too, repudiated the Versailles penalties and cried out for *Lebensraum,* more territory, more living space, for the German people.

The Steel Helmets split internally, with Prussians against Bavarians, Protestants against Catholics. But the one unifying issue was an as-yet unspoken policy of anti-Semitism.

By 1931, 300,000 marched under the banners of the Stahlhelm. In their field gray uniforms, mimicking the battle dress of 1914–1918, they paraded in support of their choices. The SA not only tramped through the streets but also put their jackboots to whomever they perceived as the enemy. In the campaign of 1933, for example, no fewer than fifty-one anti-Nazis were murdered; the Nazis claimed eighteen of their members were killed. A nice ratio in their favor.

16

Whatever their distaste at the time for the excesses of the SA, Hitler and his closest associates regarded it as critical for their success. The German Army, theoretically obedient to the existing government, may have been small in number but it was sufficiently strong to pull off a coup or arrest the Nazi leaders and destroy the Party. The SA provided a major force to confront such adventures generated by the army.

Still, while Joseph Mengele may have been mesmerized by the oratory of Hitler, the SA apparently was too tainted by vulgarity and sexual freakiness—high irony in the perspective of history —to enlist him. Instead the twenty-year-old student signed up on May 29, 1931, with the Steel Helmets.

Günzburg was relatively calm during this time when other German communities bubbled with political ferment. After the World War I Armistice the mayor summoned men and women from all strata to the town hall, where he praised the abolition of the emperor's authoritarian government, "to be replaced by a better people's government." A socialist named Otto Geiselhart asked for immediate formation of a "workers and soldiers council," though the sole change was abolition of the 70-mark poll tax.

Nazis did begin to make their appearance in Günzburg in 1922, a year before Hitler's abortive Munich *Putsch* by which he sought to seize power, and Karl Mengele, Joseph's father, is believed to have become active in the Bavarian wing of the Party during the 1920s. Joseph's mother, Wally, presumably also supported the movement since her relatives, the Hupfauers, were prominent enthusiasts. Fervent nationalist Wally was quoted later: "Thank God. I could hug the French. There is war."

The political campaigns of the 1930s stirred Günzburg. In 1930 the Communists accumulated a sizeable 315 votes at the ballot box. And not surprisingly, industrialists like Karl Mengele worked harder for the man who promised to destroy the Bolshevik threat. Stumping for public office, Hitler spoke twice in Günzburg. On the second occasion Karl Mengele hospitably provided the hall in his factory for the address, attended by some 8,000 hailing the speech.

In the last free election before the imposition of totalitarian government, 33 percent of the Günzburgers backed Hitler, which, with even greater support nationwide, was enough to make Adolf Hitler chancellor in January, 1933. Not surprisingly Karl Mengele soon occupied a chair in the district council, then held a number of local government posts structured by the Nazis. Old socialist Otto Geiselhart, a member of the Reichstag, "committed suicide" after the Gestapo arrested him in 1933.

It was January 3, 1934, before young Joseph Mengele mistakenly thought he read the future and quit the Stahlhelm in favor of membership in the SA. As a fellow student recalls, "He was not so much a courageous as a cautious man." He really was quite naive, for Hitler had already marked the SA for extinction. Even though two and one-half million people like Mengele wore the SA brown, its usefulness to Hitler had passed. The SS under Himmler had slipped from beneath the wing of the SA six months earlier. SA leader Ernst Röhm was the second most powerful man in the country, and Hitler and Himmler recognized the threat.

In the pre-dawn hours of June 30, 1934, a motor caravan led by the Führer drove thirty miles from Munich to the resort town of Wiessee. Röhm and several associates still lay abed after a night of carousing. Several of the SA hierarchy were dispatched instantly with bullets. On Hitler's order Röhm was executed after turning down an offer of a pistol and suicide. Some 150 other SA officials were shot down by firing squads organized by Himmler and Hermann Goering.

"Cautious" Joseph Mengele, even as an outsider, grasped the significance of what had happened. While the SA continued to exist, it soon degenerated into a ceremonial organization, and Mengele resigned in October 1934, citing "kidney trouble" as his excuse.

He then confronted a more troublesome matter of choice much closer to home. It was the dream of the father that the firstborn would join the family business, making the name "Karl Mengele und Sohn" a reality. Joseph would have none of it. He said he was not interested in machines, factories, or money for its own sake. He rejected the way taken by the "admired," "respected" father. There were rows over the decision, but Joseph held firm.

At least superficially, and not unreasonably, a Freudian might diagnose the strong feelings for mother Wally and the pulling back from father Karl as evidence of an unresolved Oedipal conflict—one in which the luckless Jews of Europe were to become surrogates, killed in place of the imperious, demanding and, of course, unassailable father.

Joseph Mengele now proceeded to plunge into his studies. From the University of Munich he secured a doctoral degree in philosophy. He also passed examinations for medical school, and for his medical education moved to the University of Frankfurt am Main. Except for a sojourn in Vienna, Frankfurt served as Mengele's training ground.

It was at Frankfurt that he came under the influence of Professor Otmar von Verschuer, a specialist in the popular new "science of race." Von Verschuer was an ardent Nazi, and in furtherance of racial science became fascinated by the phenomenon of twins. Mengele, under Von Verschuer, produced a paper on cleft palate in children that was published in a medical journal.

At age ten Joseph Mengele (second row, second from left) is shown with his classmates in Günzburg. The original source of the photo in West Germany blacked out the faces of all but Mengele.

In Munich, college student Mengele (third row, second from right) joined with his fellow students in a beer party.

At age nineteen Mengele dressed in a showy uniform as part of an amateur theatrical production.

As a student at the University of Munich, Mengele studied philosophy and earned a doctorate in that field before going on to medical school.

Just married in 1939, the former Irene Schoenbein and Mengele, now a doctor in Frankfurt am Mein, made a handsome couple.

Young doctor Mengele and his new wife Irene occupied this handsome house near the Main River in Frankfurt after their marriage.
Credit: Gerald Astor

Joseph Mengele, circa 1940. The cleft between his upper, front teeth was remarked on by many witnesses and forensic dentists who found evidence of the same gap in the skull dug up in 1985.
Credit: Sipa

In order to marry Irene Schoenbein in 1939, Mengele filled out this SS questionnaire. The details include his military service with the 137th Regiment, the cause of death of his grandparents, his religious preference (Roman Catholic) and that of his fiance (Lutheran).

In 1936, Mengele appeared before a board in Munich and convinced the members of his qualifications as a physician. He then served a term as an intern at the University Hospital in Leipzig before returning to do research under Von Verschuer at the Institut für Erbbiologie und Rassenhygiene (Institute for Heredity and Eugenics) at the University of Frankfurt.

The direction of racial science inevitably followed the strong current of German anti-Semitism. André François-Poncet, a French diplomat who served in the Berlin embassy, remarked in his memoirs: "Antisemitism has always been widespread in Germany. It has strong and ancient roots; it is a popular prejudice and passion. Already violent before 1914, it developed considerably as a result of the role played by Jews in the Weimar Republic and in leftwing parties. . . . Hitler did not diverge from the people; he drew them closer; he was their reflection; his drastic antisemitism did not impair his popularity; it was on the contrary one of its basic elements."

As far back as 1879 nineteenth-century German historian Heinrich von Treitschke had accused the Jews of being the cause of Germany's problems. "The Jews are our misfortune." His writings and the climate of the times were enough to produce a movement to ban Jews from public offices, and anti-Semitism became the sole plank in the platforms of several political parties.

The Protocols of the Elders of Zion, the fake documents claiming a conspiracy among Jews to control the world, first appeared in late-nineteenth century Russia, surfacing in Germany in 1919, just in time to ride the rising tide of frustration in that country.

German anti-Semitism had also infected its arts. Men like Richard Wagner, whose operas so entranced Mengele, openly proclaimed their disdain for Jews. As historian George L. Mosse notes, "German anti-Semitism is a part of German intellectual history. It does not stand outside it."

The press and politicians labeled Jews both as usurious financiers driving the country to ruin and as the vanguard of communism, seeking to overthrow private property, private ownership of factories such as Karl Mengele und Sohn and the banks. Never mind the unreason. Inbred prejudice was *über alles.*

Scientific underpinning for the debasement of Jews was supplied by the likes of Walter Darre, an agricultural expert, whose *Blood and Soil,* published by the Nazi Party, extrapolated barnyard eugenics to humans. Not surprisingly his ideas captivated the former chicken breeder, Heinrich Himmler, who chose Darre to operate the SS's Race and Settlement Office.

Race purity and the contaminant threat of Jews became gospel in lower and higher education. When Mengele began his college studies at the University of Munich, anti-Semitism had already sprouted in the sciences, along with the more standard atomic tables and Newton's laws of motion. The impressionable young man from the bucolic atmosphere of Günzburg soaked up writings like those of a German oriental scholar, Paul de Lagarde, who despised "those who out of humanity defend these Jews, or who are too cowardly to trample these usurious vermin to death. . . . With trichinae and bacilli one does not negotiate, nor are trichinae and bacilli to be educated. They are exterminated as quickly and thoroughly as possible." The metaphor of Jews as diseased organisms was of inestimable value for the purveyors of mass murder, particularly physicians intent upon justifying their actions to outsiders and to themselves.

Anti-Semitism also infected many other countries, including the United States, where polls between 1938 and 1942 indicated 10 to 15 percent of the people would support anti-Semitic statutes. But only in Germany did it rally significant political groups.

And in the United States, as well as elsewhere, many citizens also strongly resisted anti-Semitism. In Germany it passed largely unopposed. Some Protestant Church groups protested the persecution of converts from Judaism but showed little concern for the Jewish faithful. The Roman Catholic Church—Catholicism being the religion of Joseph Mengele—had made peace with the Nazis. In a 1933 concordat both parties agreed to respect the other's prerogatives. One architect of the pact, Bishop Alois Hudal (claimed by Bavaria and Austria as a native son), was an influential member of the Vatican Curia and later was to figure in the life of Joseph Mengele.

The Nazis and the Roman Catholic Church found common ground in their antagonism to communism, but the concordat was to serve overwhelmingly only one side—an estimated 4,000 clergy, both Catholic and Protestant, were killed by the Nazis.

Major stimulants for the virus of anti-Semitism, as it came to infect Joseph Mengele were Hitler and his associates Alfred Rosenberg and Julius Streicher. Rosenberg was a theorist of sorts. Streicher translated anti-Semitism into crude and vicious publications. But it was Hitler who set the tone:

"The Jewish doctrine of Marxism rejects the aristocratic principle of Nature and replaces the eternal privilege of power and strength by the mass of numbers and their dead weight. [As he spoke the Jews of Germany numbered one percent of the population.] Hence today I believe that I am acting in accordance with the will of the Almighty Creator. By defending myself against the Jew I am fighting for the work of the Lord. [Outwardly hostile to religion and an unearthly God, the Nazis and their Führer were quite capable of declaring themselves fighters on the Lord's side when it suited their purpose.] With satanic joy in his face, the black-haired Jewish youth lurks in wait for the unsuspecting girl, whom he defiles with his blood, thus stealing her from her people. With every means he tries to destroy the racial foundations of the people he has set out to subjugate. Just as he himself systematically ruins women and girls, he does not shrink back from pulling down the blood barriers for others, even on a large scale. It was and it is Jews who bring Negroes into the Rhineland always with the same secret thought and clear aim of ruining the hated white race . . ." Similar sexual rhetoric would characterize Mengele while he was at Auschwitz.

Closer at hand for Mengele was his mentor at the University of Frankfurt. In 1937, while Mengele was still in residence, Otmar von Verschuer published an article in which he said, "Hitler is the first statesman who has come to recognize hereditary biological and race hygiene and make it a leading principle of statesmanship." Two years later von Verschuer announced: "We specialists of race hygiene are happy to have witnessed that the work normally associated with the scientific laboratories or the academic study room has extended into the life of our people."

Mengele's former brief attachment to the SA apparently deterred him from further sudden political affiliations. It was not until three years later, in May 1937, that he applied for membership in the Nazi Party. And finding the atmosphere most congenial, he went a step further and in May of 1938 enlisted in the elite SS.

When Heinrich Himmler began to reconstitute the SS he envisioned it as a hothouse for the propagation of the Master Race. The ideal recruit would be blue-eyed, blond, marry a woman with the same characteristics and their offspring would multiply this Teutonic image. Himmler, himself a small, mousy specimen, and Hitler, too, for that matter, did not fit the mold, but after all, the hallmark of the fanatic dreamer is soaring beyond the limits of oneself. And nothing could be further removed from Himmler's and Hitler's selves than the Aryan fiction they propagated.

Still, the exacting standards set by Himmler soon proved too exclusive. Men were even rejected because of fillings in their teeth. By 1934 the SS chief realized manpower was rather more important than surface purity. The organization had begun to accept almost all the volunteers. Membership had become stylish, and the SS offered opportunists bright futures in the New Order. SS members were expected to give unquestioning loyalty and obedience to their masters, to be disciplined in their behavior, and to be above corruption.

Still, even with opening the ranks Himmler struggled to protect the SS from racial taint. Harkening back to his experiences with chickens, Himmler, who frequently discarded science in favor of folklore, made eugenics a cornerstone of membership. Every person in the SS filed a pedigree with the organization, tracing back lineage, maternal and paternal, a minimum of 150 years. Joseph Mengele was one who dutifully submitted an entry to the *Sippenbuch* (stud book, as it was known), the details in his case as in others coming from a family Bible and church registry. Applicants had somehow to demonstrate a pure Aryan strain, and Joseph Mengele complied. Where possible, cause of death of parents was listed; officially the SS would not tolerate genetic weaknesses, but exceptions were made—Reinhard Heydrich, Himmler's chief deputy, who was assassinated in Czechoslovakia; Field Marshal Erhard Milch of the Luftwaffe; and Hans Frank, *Gauleiter* of Poland, all had Jewish antecedents.

Not only were members of the SS required to demonstrate their purity but it was also demanded of their brides, which created a problem for Joseph Mengele, who had fallen in love with one Irene Schoenbein. Research into her family history revealed a maternal grandfather born out of wedlock. Great grandfather Harry Lyons Dumler, in fact, was an American. Born in Buffalo, N.Y., Dumler had served in the U.S. consulate at Nice. A public hearing at Darmstadt in 1896 generated a document in which Dumler "undertook to provide for the child born to Fraulein Anna Schoenbein in October 1883 until his 14th year of life," paying maintenance costs of twenty marks per month. The record further showed that "Herr Dumler agrees to this obligation solely under the condition that Fraulein Schoenbein will leave him totally in peace from now on, especially that no further accusations, defamations of any kind will be continued and that no further claims will be lodged against him . . . He also expressly protests against filing or having ever filed recognition that he be the father of this child."

The disclaimer clearly disturbed the examining SS officer, who noted: "Paternity of Harry Lyons Dumler has not been unobjectionably proven." Indeed, there was no way to detect her family history any further back on her maternal side since the Germans could not gain access to records on Dumler even if he admitted he was a branch of the family tree.

Long afterwards Mengele spoke of Irene as "the great love of my life." She was beautiful, intelligent, and more broadly educated than he, having attended schools in Italy and Switzerland, mastering four languages. She liked to travel and reading delighted her. However, Irene did not delight her in-laws. She did not fit the family notion of a wife as a *Hausfrau*. She was too independent. Furthermore, to Catholic Walburga Mengele's dismay, Irene was a Lutheran.

The delay in SS approval and the family's acceptance of his bride may have caused anxious moments, but Joseph Mengele, a physician and the son of an industrialist who had demonstrated strong, tangible support for the cause, was determined to marry Irene in spite of the SS officer and parental objections. The wedding was a Roman Catholic one, but to add further to the family's discomfort it was held outside of Günzburg. In a

1938 photograph the young couple make a splendid-looking pair; people who might have just stepped out of a Noel Coward play.

The rigamarole of SS approval that confronted Mengele and his wife was hardly unique. But the massive amount of paperwork involved in such exercises in genealogy, involving hundreds of thousands of people, typifies the awesome bureaucratic regimentation of Nazi Germany, and acceptance of this intrusion of the State into personal life by well-educated, affluent citizens bespeaks the lack of intellectual resistance to such excesses of SS ideology. The expenditure of time, money, and energy on such works also marks the bullheaded insistence of the Nazi regime on activities that lowered the efficiency of the State.

As part of his obligation to the SS Mengele had served in the army, training with a mountain regiment in the Tyrol for several months. But for most of the brief interval between his wedding and the start of World War II he worked as an assistant physician at the Institute for Heredity and Eugenics in Frankfurt. The couple lived in the Sachsenhausen section of the city on the southern side of the River Main. The address, ironically, was 30 Paul Erlichstrasse. For some reason the Nazis failed to extirpate the Jewish Nobel prize winner's name from the roster of city streets. Spacious and elegant, the house lay within walking distance of the institute. (Although many nearby buildings were destroyed by Allied bombing raids that battered Frankfurt, 30 Paul Erlichstrasse appears to have gone untouched, just as Mengele, its tenant, was to survive the war remarkably unscathed.) Then for a short interlude Mengele practiced medicine in Freiburg, an address that would be significant later.

German troops, following the Case White battle plan created in April 1939, now rolled across the Polish Border on September 1, 1939, to begin World War II. The blitzkrieg that crushed Poland did not require any contribution from Mengele, but with a two-front war a growing possibility—peace with the Soviets could not last—the specialist in race biology was among those mobilized. In the sparse records of Mengele's military exploits there is mention of service on the Western front, the conquest of France and the Low Countries, but no details are given. However, he is described as having been attached to the Waffen SS Viking Division, which fought on the Eastern front.

Ever mindful of the independence of the Werhmacht, the traditional German army, Himmler set about to create his own fighting force, the Waffen SS. Even Hitler pondered the dubious phenomenon of a separate armed force, and the original prospectus limited the Waffen SS to only four divisions. But Himmler prevailed and by 1945 the Waffen SS totaled thirty-five divisions. While tactical command of Waffen SS units lay with the high command, the administration and internal control was strictly a matter for the SS itself. If the army ever became so dissatisfied with the Nazi government that it would attempt a coup, the Waffen SS, armed with tanks, heavy artillery and highly trained infantrymen, could be deployed.

After the fall of France one of the new Waffen SS divisions was the Viking. It had recruited Dutch, Danish, Norwegian and Finnish Nazis; the remainder of the complement came from the former Fifth Panzer Division, which had great success in France and may have included Mengele.

By the summer of 1942 the Viking Division was sloughing through the Ukraine as part of the push to tie off the Soviet oilfields in the Caucasus. A key attack point was the City of Rostov on the Don River. Antitank obstacles and ditches with saturated mine fields slowed the Germans as they hammered into the strongly defended city. Facing the men of the Viking were not ordinary soldiers—these were NKVD troops, the Soviet version of the Waffen SS. Well-armed, fiercely resolved not to surrender, they engaged the invaders in hand-to-hand streetfighting. There was little room left for armor to maneuver. Red Army men ripped up paving blocks from the streets to erect barricades several feet thick. Steel girders stuck in the ground halted sudden advances. The Russians had also stockpiled thousands of Molotov cocktails laced with phosphorus and gasoline in their basement redoubts. Tanks became fiery tombs for Viking crews. The Germans advanced from house to house, meeting at almost every door booby traps, trip-wires, fire from covering pillboxes. It was an orgy of flamethrowers, grenades and machine guns, rifles and bayonets. The defenders seemed determined not to be taken alive. If bypassed or ignored because of their wounds, the Russians would resume firing behind the backs of the Germans. The Viking wounded had to be placed in armored troop-carriers and guarded or else the enemy infiltrators would beat or stab the helpless men.

The invaders, however, did manage to gain control of Rostov, and then the Viking Division struck off south in the direction of Tuapse. Thrusts were aimed at the Maykop oilfields. But by autumn of 1942 the offensive had stalled here, and further north German units attacking Stalingrad were in deep trouble. Even with the enlistment of disaffected Ukrainians and anti-Soviet Cossacks, the Nazi armies could go no further. During these adventures, Mengele himself was seriously wounded and sent back to Germany to recuperate. For his efforts during the campaign he was awarded an Iron Cross First Degree, Iron Cross Second Degree plus the standard decoration for service against the Red armies.

Both armies, and the Soviet civilian population, suffered staggering casualties. For a doctor, the sight of thousands of corpses, dismembered bodies, men beaten and stabbed to death, the human form maimed beyond imagination, could have had a profound effect. What sense of human life would he retain? How much would he have been hardened to human suffering? Others with similar experiences had the inner strength to overcome revulsion followed by indifference to the suffering of their fellow beings. Joseph Mengele surely did not.

When Mengele's wounds had healed he was declared unfit for a return to the combat zone. And so he volunteered for his new post, *Lagerarzt,* camp doctor, at an installation in the southwest of Poland—Auschwitz.

CHAPTER

Anus Mundi

DR. HANS HERMANN KREMER had achieved scientific distinction along with an education in the classics—a background similar to that of Joseph Mengele. Appointed to the post of professor of medicine at the University of Münster in 1929, Kremer joined the Nazi Party a year later. In 1941 he enlisted in the Waffen SS. During the summer of 1942, while the Viking Division with Joseph Mengele battled for Rostov, Kremer received a temporary assignment to Auschwitz as a replacement for another physician. And Kremer kept a diary, recording the sights and his reactions.

31

His entries began: "First time present at a *Sonderaktion* (special action) at 3 hours in the morning. Compared to this, the *Inferno* by Dante seems to me as a comedy. Auschwitz is not called for nothing the 'camp of extermination.' "

The *Sonderaktion* that momentarily shocked him was a great pyre of humans dumped on flaming, gasoline soaked wood. Frequently, people were still alive when the blazes were ignited. Kremer noted, "Men all want to take part in these actions because of the special rations they get then, consisting of a fifth of a litre of schnapps, 5 cigarettes, 100 grams of sausage and bread."

Other diary entries mix the gothic with the commonplace: "This morning I got the most pleasant news from my lawyer . . . that I got divorced from my wife the first of this month. (Note: I see colours again, a black curtain is drawn back from my life!) Later on, present as doctor at a corporal punishment of eight prisoners and an execution by shooting with small caliber rifles. Got soap flakes and two pieces of soap . . . In the evening present at a *Sonderaktion.*

"Listened to a concert of the prisoners' band this afternoon in bright sunshine. Bandmaster; conductor of the Warschauer Staatsoper. 80 musicians. For lunch we had port, for dinner, baked tench.

"Last night present at the sixth and seventh *Sonderaktion* . . . In the evening at 20.00 hours, dinner with Obergruppen führer Pohl . . . a real banquet. We had baked pike, as much as we wanted, good coffee, excellent ale and rolls.

"Today we fixed *living* [author's italics] material of human liver, spleen and pancreas.

"Present at the ninth *Sonderaktion* (foreigners and emaciated females).

"Present at an infliction of punishment and the execution of seven Polish civilians.

"Present at an infliction of punishment and eleven executions. Taken out living, fresh material of liver, spleen and pancreas after injection of pilocarpin [a poison].

"Innoculation against typhoid, after that in the evening, fever. In spite of that, present at *Sonderaktion* during the night. 1600 persons from the Netherlands. Terrible scene outside the last bunker.

"It was wet, cold weather present at the eleventh Sonderaktion (Netherlanders) on Sunday morning. Shocking scenes with three women who beseech us for bare life.

"We had a nice time in the leaders club, invited by Captain Wirths. We had Bulgarian red wine and Croatian plum-schnapps.

"Living, fresh material of liver, spleen and pancreas taken from a Jewish prisoner of 18 years of age who was very atrophic. First we took a photo of him."

Fittingly, a man who would be one of Mengele's colleagues at Auschwitz gave Kremer a suitable label for the camp. The visitor's diary contains an entry: "This afternoon present at a *Sonderaktion* from the female concentration camp. The most horrible of horrors. Captain Tilo, doctor of the troops, is right when he told me this morning that we are at *anus mundi.*"

The concentration camp (KZ in the vernacular) German style, first appeared in 1933 at Dachau, about thirty miles from Munich. Herding together alien peoples did not originate with Nazis. Ghettos were an ancient tradition in Europe. In the United States indigenous Indians were taken off to reservations and in the Soviet Union, dissidents and criminals were and still are dispatched to Gulags.

Dachau was started by the SA as a place to put kidnap victims, a convenient place to terrorize and kill opponents. Gustav von Kahr, head of the Bavarian state government which suppressed Hitler's 1923 *Putsch,* was hacked to death with pickaxes and his body discarded in a swamp near Dachau. The KZ seemed like such a good idea that once the Nazis took power fifty of them mushroomed around Germany. Initially, the camps were deemed a temporary measure. Hitler himself announced a Christmas Eve amnesty for 27,000 inmates in 1933, but Hermann Goering and Heinrich Himmler ignored the directive and freed only a few persons.

Following the murder of Röhm and the decline of the SA, Himmler and the SS received control of the camps. Smaller, inefficient operations closed down. The Nazis constructed Buchenwald near Weimar, Sachsenhausen near Berlin, while Ravensbrücke in the vicinity of Mecklenburg was reserved for women. Dachau expanded, and after the *Anschluss* absorbing Austria, the SS erected Mauthausen near Linz.

At first the camps held alleged political leftists, particularly communists, clergymen who voiced opposition, editors whose papers were perceived as anti-Nazi and a group lumped together as undesirables. These included homosexuals and some common criminals. In the beginning Jews as a group were not indiscriminately thrown into concentration camps.

An SS thug named Theodor Eicke was commissioned as the first inspector of the KZs. He instilled a twisted esprit de corps. Recruits to the staff underwent a series of humiliations and physical hazings. Eicke forced them to watch floggings and tortures of prisoners. Any sign of compassion or revulsion was considered a dereliction of duty. He created a new insignia, the *Totenkopfverbande,* the skull and crossed bones. KZ guardians proudly labeled themselves members of Death's Head units. Eicke and his cadre trained the men to accept merciless treatment of prisoners as evidence of high devotion to the cause. The guards, though, were also taught that however brutally they behaved their acts should bear a surface legality. Discipline and professionalism were to be hallmarks of KZ warders.

34

In perverse theory, the concentration camps were to rehabilitate inmates, show them the errors of their thinking, and convince them to support the regime. The "rehabilitation" employed primitive behavioralist training—negative reinforcement to the extreme. Eicke decreed hanging for anyone who "politicizes, holds inciting speeches and meetings, forms cliques, loiters around with others, who for the purpose of supplying the propaganda of the opposition with atrocity stories, collects *true* [author's italics] or false information about the concentration camp; receives such information, buries it, talks about it to others, smuggles it out of the camp into the hands of foreign visitors . . ."

He also announced execution on the spot for anyone attacking an SS representative, for refusing to obey or work, or for "bawling, shouting, inciting or holding speeches while marching or at work." Critical remarks in a letter home could be worth two weeks of solitary confinement and twenty-five lashes.

(Some similarities in approach show up in the camps created by the Vietnamese and the Cambodians for the "re-education" and indoctrination of those considered insufficiently supportive of the regimes of the 1970s.)

By the time World War II began, the concentration camps were a going series of operations. To be sure, the men entitled to sport the Death's Head insignia were not the elite of the SS. Many were drawn from a pool of SS rejects.

The conquest of Poland offered the Nazi hierarchy more than territory and economic gains. It could provide the opportunity to make Western Europe and particularly Germany, *Judenrein*—free of Jewish inhabitants. The subject peoples of Poland and the Soviet Union—for the Germans recognized that war with Stalin was inevitable—would serve as slave labor. The Polish real estate could house factories exploiting the local population and absorb the Jews shipped east.

But even before these ambitious plans could be implemented came the *Einsatzgruppen.* They followed on the heels of the Nazi armies sweeping through Poland. Himmler, with his chief deputy Rheinhard Heydrich, a virulent anti-Semite—tall, blond, and aristocratic, unlike his superior—formed the *Einsatzgruppen* from SS troops with a mission to weed out partisans, potential sources of opposition, and to round up Jews and force them into ghettos.

The *Einsatzgruppen* acted as mobile hit squads, massacring thousands of Jews and Poles, in some cases wiping out entire towns. Often they turned the job over to local fascists, murderous anti-Semitic Poles and Ukrainians. Hermann Graebe, a German civilian engineer stationed at a grain warehouse in the Ukraine, observed a unit in action:

"Armed Ukrainian militia were making people get out, under the surveillance of SS soldiers . . . The people in the trucks wore the regulation yellow pieces of cloth that identified them as Jews. I went straight toward the ditches without being stopped. When we neared the mound I heard a series of rifle shots close by. The people from the trucks—men, women and children—were forced to undress under the supervision of an SS soldier with a whip in his hand. They were obliged to put their effects in certain spots, shoes, clothing and underwear separately. I saw a pile of shoes about eight hundred to one thousand pairs, great heaps of underwear and clothing. Without weeping or crying out, these people undressed and stood together in family groups, embracing each other and saying goodbye while waiting for a sign from the SS soldier who stood on the edge of the ditch, a whip in his hand. During the fifteen minutes I sat there, I did not hear a single complaint or a plea for mercy. I watched a family of about eight, a man and a woman about fifty years old, surrounded by their children of about one, eight and ten, two big girls about twenty and twenty-four. An old lady, her hair

completely white, held the baby in her arms, rocking it, and
singing it a song. The infant was crying aloud with delight. The
parents watched the group with tears in their eyes. The father
held the ten-year-old boy by the hand, speaking softly to him;
the child struggled to hold back his tears. Then the father
pointed a finger to the sky and stroking the child's head seemed
to be explaining something. At this moment, the SS near the
ditch called something to his comrade. The latter counted off
some twenty people and ordered them behind the mound. The
family of which I have just spoken was in the group. I still
remember the young girl, slender and dark, who passing near
me, pointed at herself saying, 'twenty-three.' I walked around
the mound and faced a frightful common grave. Tightly packed
corpses were heaped so close together that only the heads
showed. Most were wounded in the head and the blood flowed
over their shoulders. Some still moved. Others raised their
hands and turned their heads to show they were still alive. The
ditch was two-thirds full. I estimated that it held a thousand
bodies. I turned my eyes towards the man who had carried out
the execution. He was an SS man. He was seated, legs swinging
on the narrow edge of the ditch, an automatic rifle rested on his
knees and he was smoking a cigarette. The people, completely
naked, climbed down a few steps cut into the clay wall and
stopped at the spot indicated by the SS man. Facing the dead
and wounded he spoke softly to them. Then I heard a series of
rifle shots. I looked in the ditch and saw their bodies contorting,
their heads already inert, sinking on the corpses beneath. The
blood flowed from the nape of their necks. I was astonished not
to be ordered away . . . A new batch of victims approached the
place. They climbed down into the ditch, lined up in front of the
previous victims, and were shot.

"The next morning, returning . . . I saw thirty naked bodies
laying thirty to fifty yards from the ditch. Some were still alive;

they stared into space with a set look, seeming not to feel the coolness of the morning air, nor to see the workers standing all around. A young girl of about twenty spoke to me, asking me to bring her clothes and help her escape. At that moment we heard the sound of a car approaching at top speed; I saw that it was an SS detachment. I went back to my work. Ten minutes later rifle shots sounded from the ditch. The Jews who were still alive had been ordered to throw the bodies in the ditch. Then they had to lie down themselves to receive a bullet in the back of the neck."

Otto Ohlendorf, for several years in the economics and intelligence branches of the SS, completed his role in World War II as a foreign trade expert. But for at least a year this professionally schooled man headed *Einsatzgruppe* D. During his interrogation by American prosecutors at Nuremberg in 1945, Ohlendorf matter-of-factly confessed, "When the German army invaded Russia . . . Action Group D in the Southern Sector . . . liquidated approximately 90,000 men, women and children. . . . The unit . . . would enter a village or city and order the prominent Jewish citizens to call together all Jews for the purpose of resettlement. They were requested to hand over their valuables . . . and shortly before execution to surrender their outer clothing. The men, women and children were led to a place of execution which in most cases was located next to a more deeply excavated anti-tank ditch. Then they were shot, kneeling, or standing and the corpses thrown into the ditch. . . . In the spring of 1942 we received gas vehicles from the Chief of Security Police and the SD (SS Secret Service) in Berlin . . . We had received orders to use the vans for the killing of women and children. Whenever a unit had collected a sufficient number of victims, a van was sent for their liquidation."

A few of the Wehrmacht leaders believed the massacres of civilians abhorrent. Commanders who protested were cashiered. Admiral Canaris, chief of the Intelligence Bureau for the

German High Command, remonstrated with Field Marshal Keitel, the head of the high command about the atrocities. Keitel curtly answered: "The Fuhrer has already decided on this matter." He added that if the army wanted to avoid its own participation in such actions it would have to accept the presence of SS and Gestapo units to execute the orders.

General Franz Halder, chief of the Army General Staff, noted in his diary: "Army insists that "housecleaning" be deferred until Army had withdrawn and the country been turned over to civil administration." The military appears to have been more worried about its image than with mass murders committed under aegis of the government which the army faithfully served.

Many ranking members of the military felt no qualms. Early in the war against Poland a Waffen SS artillery regiment, having dragooned some fifty Jews into repairing a bridge, then corraled them in a synagogue and killed the entire lot. Shocked local commanders convened a court martial to deal with such unmilitary behavior. However, even a lenient sentence of one year in prison was quashed by the army commander in chief as part of a general amnesty. The case received much publicity among the troops. The outcome signaled an end to fear of consequences when dealing with civilians.

The head of the Sixth Army, four months after the invasion of Russia, appealed this way to his troops: "In the regions of the East, the soldier is not only a combatant in conformity with the rules of the art of war but also the bearer of the intransigent populist idea and the avenger of all of the bestialities inflicted on the German popular entity or on a related species. That is why the soldier must have a full understanding of the necessity of a tough but just expiation inflicted on the Jewish subhumanity. Another goal is to nip in the bud revolts behind the back of the Wehrmacht which, as experience proves, are always fomented by Jews." The statement of course legitimized gunning down groups of civilians and assuaged possibly troubled consciences among common soldiers. SS men were already indoctrinated with the rightness of murdering Jews and other potential enemies. Himmler explicitly instructed his SS administrators to deal leniently "with offenses into which the perpetrator had allowed himself to be drawn by excessive zeal in the struggle for the National Socialist Ideal."

On another occasion, Himmler spoke of the SS man's burden. "Among ourselves it should be mentioned quite frankly—but we will never speak of it publicly—just as we did not hesitate on 30 June 1934 to do the duty we were told to do and stand comrades who had lapsed up against the wall and shoot them, so we have never spoken about it and will never speak of this . . . I mean cleaning out the Jews, the extermination of the Jewish race. It is one of those things it's easy to talk about— 'The Jewish race is being exterminated . . . it's our program and we're doing it' . . . Most of *you* must know what it means when a hundred corpses are lying side by side, or five hundred or a thousand. To have stuck it out and at the same time (apart from exceptions caused by human weakness) to have remained decent fellows, that is what has made us so hard. This is a page of glory in our history which has never been written and will never be written . . ."

In spite of all of the methods of training, there were members of the *Einsatagruppen* who succumbed to what Himmler called "human weakness." A German neuropsychiatrist with the Wehrmacht told noted American psychiatrist Robert Jay Lifton that twenty percent of the *Einsatzgruppen* suffered "significant psychological difficulties due to their participation."

For all of their valiant efforts, the *Einsatzgruppen* had their limitations. The policy towards the Jews was shifting. Shooting teams and even mobile gas vans could kill only thousands. There were, the Nazis calculated, eleven million Jews in Europe and resettlement in the East was no longer an answer to the problem of making Europe *Judenrein.*

Appearing before the Reichstag in January 1939, Hitler told his rubber stamp parliament, ". . . if financial international Judaism in Europe and beyond Europe were to succeed in pushing the peoples into a world war, then the result of it would not be the Bolshevization of the earth, thus the victory of Judaism, but the destruction of the Jewish race in Europe." Hitler used the world *"Vernichtung"* when he predicted the fate of the Jews in the event of a world war—it translates as either "destruction" or "annihilation."

In the summer of 1941, Reichsmarshall Hermann Goering issued an order to Reinhard Heydrich: ". . . make all necessary preparation as regards organizational, financial and material matters for a total solution *(Gesamtlosung)* of the Jewish question . . . submit to me as soon as possible a general plan showing measures for organizing and for action necessary to carry out the desired final solution *(Endlosung)* of the Jewish question." In his final sentence Goering employed what became the definitive phrase—"final solution."

Several months later, Heydrich held a small conference in Wansee, a town near Berlin. Here he outlined the plot to move all Jews to camps in the east. On hand was Adolf Eichmann, chief of research for Heydrich, his "traveling salesman" who dispensed Heydrich's policies over Nazi-controlled territory. During his Jerusalem trial (in 1961, Eichmann would claim to have had a letter signed by Himmler in which the SS leader said the Führer had ordered the final solution, and temporarily exempting "all Jewish men and women who were able to work." No proof of any such letter's existence was ever presented.)

Preparations for the final solution were already well underway with the establishment of a number of large camps in the Polish territory. In February 1940, SS Oberführer Richard Gluecks, chief of the Concentration Camp Inspectorate, discovered what he called a "suitable site for a new quarantine camp," thirty-eight miles west of Cracow. The closest town, Oswiecim, numbered about 12,000 Poles, but Auschwitz, as the Germans came to call it, lay in a sparsely inhabited, marshy area. Not only was the place a discreet distance from possible witnesses but it also lay along the rail line from Vienna to Warsaw, making it most convenient for shipment of inmates. When trains not bearing human cargo for Auschwitz rocketed through the center of the camp, all that was visible from the windows was a vast plain of huts.

In May 1940, Rudolph Hoess, a former guard at Dachau, trained by Theodor Eicke and subsequently promoted to chief of warders at Sachsenhausen, was given command of the new Auschwitz camp. Another Bavarian, son of a strict father who intended his son for the Roman Catholic priesthood, Hoess at age sixteen had wangled his way into the German army during World War I. He fought on the Eastern front and then returned to civilian life. No longer interested in a religious vocation, Hoess joined the fledgling Nazi Party and served an apprenticeship in political intimidation. For his part in a 1923 political murder he received a life sentence. But like Hitler, Hoess spent only five years in a cell. Back on the streets he was recruited by Himmler to become one of the first to wear the Death's Head insignia.

When Hoess arrived at Auschwitz only the semblence of a camp existed. The Polish Tobacco Administration had occupied the site and left a legacy of ramshackle huts, stables, and an abundant supply of vermin. Initially instructed to prepare for 10,000 prisoners, Hoess used 300 Jews supplied by the obliging mayor of Oswiecim and another 300 prisoners shipped from Sachsenhausen to construct quarters for the expected inmate population.

The plans for Auschwitz constantly expanded. To accomodate the larger size and to conceal activities, the Nazis deported 2,000 residents from the surrounding area, demolished 123 houses. By March of 1941, Auschwitz added even further to its capacity as war with the Soviet Union loomed closer. In addition to Auschwitz I, Auschwitz II and III were constructed. Auschwitz II, some two miles from the original camp, was named Birkenau because of a stand of birch trees. The third major installation was at Monowitz, sometimes known as Buna because of a plant that produced a substitute for rubber. The area housed a number of factories owned by I.G. Farben, Krupp, and Siemens— Germany's largest electrical manufacturer. Also at the site was Deutsche Augrustungwerke, German Defense Works, an SS operation designed to earn profits for itself.

The industrial complex at Monowitz indicates the awesome dimensions of Himmler's organization. The SS had acquired two important economic assets. First, it held the exclusive right to sell its slave labor to private industry. The companies paid the SS six marks a day for each worker (about the equivalent of $1.50 at the time). The cost of subsistence to the SS for its inmates ran as low as 30 *Pfennig*.

Theoretically, the SS prescribed a diet of about 1,500 calories a day for KZ residents. In practice, corruption, indifference, and a deliberate policy of slowly starving people to death reduced the actual nutrition to 350 to 500 calories daily. The menu consisted of a dirty bowl of carrot, cabbage, or turnip soup at lunch, a single ounce of moldy bread made from ersatz flour and sawdust for supper. The intensive physical labor required should have consumed 3,000 calories daily. Under these conditions, slave laborers quickly burned their body fat, then muscle tissue until they became too weak to work. On the average, a slave laborer lasted three months.

The second source of income for the SS lay in its right to

43

confiscate all personal assets of those consigned to concentration camps. Deportees to Auschwitz often lost most of their possessions to the SS, who rounded them up in ghettos and packed them aboard trains and trucks. But those who managed to hide clothes, furs, jewelry, precious heirlooms, diamonds, or even gold were stripped of these valuables on arrival. The SS even collected furniture, including several pianos, that somehow accompanied prisoners. Camp authorities stockpiled merchandise in a warehouse section known as Canada. On the other hand, a section of the camp called Mexico was the locale for executions.

Auschwitz was not a barren wasteland. Wildflowers sparkled in the high grass. Patches of shrubbery and trees, aside from a green belt planted to hide the gas chambers and crematoria, dappled the camp. The SS men lived comfortably outside the miles of electrified wire punctuated by watchtowers with machine guns. The Death's Head corps had its own bakery, slaughterhouse, and sausage factory. Dr. Kremer obviously enjoyed the cuisine. SS troops could also frolic in a swimming pool during the hot, muggy summers. Himmler agreed to a camp bordello for the men. The whores serviced the German soldiers and occasionally the non-Jewish kapos—criminals who helped run the place as trustees. Kapos and other prisoner support staff even earned small sums for their work in the camp.

Inside the electrified fence lay a forbidden zone. Any prisoner who stepped over the line could be instantly shot down, and guards who killed someone trespassing in the forbidden zone received rewards.

The barracks for the prisoners, designed for maybe 300, usually held 1,200 to 1,500. Instead of beds, inmates slept on *"Pritschen,"* wooden planks nailed together. *Pritschen* designed for five bodies held as many as fifteen. Neither blankets nor pillows were ordinarily issued.

Common criminals at Auschwitz wore a green triangle on their uniforms; political prisoners wore red. Jews were issued a yellow triangle with a red one superimposed to form a six pointed star. Homosexuals wore pink.

Because of its swampy terrain, Auschwitz was not suited for a septic system to dispose of waste. Fill-in latrines—holes in the ground where dirt would be dumped as the waste piled up—were the only toilet facilities for most prisoners. The water supply became polluted. Disease carrying insect life proliferated and periodic epidemics of dysentery, typhoid, and skin rashes plagued inmates and their guardians.

In the summer of 1941, Hoess received a summons to the offices of Himmler for secret orders. On this occasion, Hoess said he was told that the Führer had given orders for the "final solution" to the Jewish question, although whether Himmler actually used the phrase is unknown. In his memoirs, Hoess quoted Himmler: "We the SS must carry out this order. If it is not carried out now, then the Jew will later destroy the German people." Hoess was instructed to consult with Adolf Eichmann to learn the most efficient apparatus for the annihilation of the Jews.

Ambitious to make Auschwitz a model for other camps, Hoess personally researched the known ways of mass killing. He visited the Treblinka camp and observed a killing through the use of carbon monoxide piped into vans loaded with victims. He decided it was not very "efficient" and continued to look for another means.

Some experts suggested that a pesticide called Zyklon B produced hydrogen cyanide gas and could be used on humans. A ghastly kind of competition ensued. And caught in the middle was a strange figure, SS Obersturmführer Kurt Gerstein. Assigned to the SS Central Office of Administration, Gerstein held the post of chief disinfection officer. His enemy was supposed

45

to be lice, and his arsenal consisted of poisonous preparations like Zyklon B.

In June 1942, Gerstein was ordered to take 200 pounds of Zyklon B to the Belzec camp in Poland. The commandant was Captain Christian ("Wild Christian" was his nickname) Wirth, once a Hoess superior. Wirth proudly guided Gerstein through his death factory. The visitor noted a pestilential odor hung over the entire place. He saw a dressing hut with a window for checking valuables, signs reading "To the baths and inhalants" and a long bathhouse type of building garnished with concrete pots of geraniums. On the roof was a Star of David and a sign, "Heckenhold Foundation."

Gerstein watched a trainload of Jews arrive. Loudspeakers directed them to strip, to hand all money and valuables in at the appropriate windows. Women and young girls were sent to a line of barber chairs for haircuts. Everyone was then marched to the Heckenhold Foundation building. A voice instructed, "Nothing is going to hurt you. Just breathe deep and it will strengthen your lungs. It's a way to prevent contagious diseases. It's a good disinfectant."

Some of the stark-naked multitude seemed somewhat pacified by statements that the men would be assigned to work, the women given housework. But according to Gerstein, most of the condemned realized their fate because "the smell betrayed it." He recalled a woman of about forty who "with eyes like fire cursed the murderers" as she disappeared into the gas chambers after being struck several times by Captain Wirth's whip. Many prayed. When 700 or 800 persons had been jammed into the building and the doors shut, Gerstein suddenly realized the meaning of the name on the building. It was Unterscharführer Heckenhold who drove the diesel engine that generated the gas. On this particular occasion, the motor balked. Gerstein clocked the operation. His stop watch showed a delay of two hours and

46

49 minutes before Heckenhold could start the diesel. During that wait, Professor Pfannstiel, who occupied the chair of hygiene at the University of Marburg, kept his eyes glued to a porthole in the building, and reported the sound of weeping, "as though in a synagogue."

Most of the victims died twenty-five minutes after the engine began to run. All were dead after thirty-two minutes. When the doors opened, Gerstein observed the victims still standing because they had been packed in so tightly. "Like columns of stone," he wrote. "The bodies were tossed out, wet with sweat and urine, the legs smeared with excrement and menstrual blood. Two dozen workers (Jews who would soon be consigned to the same fate) were busy checking mouths "which they opened with iron hooks," seeking gold. Bridge and crowns were knocked out with hammers; the scavengers checked anuses and vaginas looking for money, diamonds or gold secreted on bodies.

The corpses were dumped in a huge ditch. After several days, the ground heaved and the rotting mass rose two or three yards because of gases. Later, diesel fuel was poured over the remains and set ablaze.

Wirth, greatly disturbed by the breakdown of his method, begged Gerstein not to report the misadventure. Gerstein went along and thereby evaded a test comparison on the effectiveness of Zyklon B vs carbon monoxide. He buried his 200 pounds of Zyklon B on the pretext of spoilage. As a consequence, the camps at Kulmhof, Belzec, Sobibor, Lublin and Treblinka continued to kill with CO.

Hoess, however, availed himself of an opportunity to see a test of Zyklon B on a group of Red Army political commisars taken prisoner. The SS crowded about 900 Russians into the mortuary of a former army camp. The gas was introduced through holes in the ceiling. Hoess recalled: "Then the powder was thrown in, there were cries of "Gas!" Then a great bellowing, and the trapped prisoners hurled themselves against both the doors. But the doors held . . . It made me feel uncomfortable and I shuddered, although I had imagined death by gassing would be worse than it was . . . The killing of these Russian prisoners-of-war did not cause me much concern at the time. The order had been given, and I had to carry it out. I must even admit that this gassing set my mind at rest, for the mass extermination of the Jews was to start soon . . . Now we had the gas, and we had established a procedure."

Hoess in fact showed considerable talent at establishing "a procedure." He began with a white farmhouse at Birkenau. Workmen altered the building, removing windows, knocking out interior walls, plugging any air leaks. The structure became the first of five gas chambers at the camp.

Hoess quickly understood that killing was only part of the job. Swift and effective disposal of corpses called for more than mass burials, as demonstrated by the incident Gerstein witnessed at Belzec. Hoess had his first crematorium erected next to the former farmhouse. He improved on efficiency with subsequent units. Designed by Heinz Kammler, who later drew up the plans for the V-rocket sites, the new installations linked an anteroom where the condemned undressed, the gas chamber, and the ovens. Elevators hauled the bodies from the gassing to the crematoria. The SS's own outfit, Deutsche Augrustungswerk, made the doors and windows. Topf and Sons in Erfurt supplied the ovens, as it did for Buchenwald.

In the new buildings, some of the interior support columns were perforated. Pellets of Zyklon B, dropped by an SS man wearing a gas mask through the roof vents, passed into these perforated columns. Mushroomlike caps were quickly placed over the vents to prevent gas leakage. Inside, the gas pellets dissolved on contact with the humidity in the air, enhanced by the sweat from the body heat of the people. Special window-ports enabled observers to watch and detect the onset of death, usually within twenty to twenty-five minutes. (Inhalation of cyanide gas destroys the mechanism by which red blood cells retain oxygen. The symptoms are loss of bowel control, hemorrhages, and finally paralysis of the respiratory system leading to asphyxiation.)

Exhaust vans vented the gas chamber once it was certain everyone was dead. Prisoners—*sonderkommandos*—hosed down the bodies washing away body wastes and then scavenged for gold teeth or hidden jewelry. They loaded the corpses on small trolleys, three children on a cart or two adults. The bodies were then fed to the crematoria, the ashes trucked a few miles to be dumped into the Sola River.

Rudolph Vrba, one of the first two inmates of Auschwitz to escape and who provided the first eyewitness accounts of the Holocaust, says, "On principle, only Jews were gassed. Aryans very seldom as they are usually given *Sonderbehandlung* (special treatment) by shooting. Before the crematoria were put into service, the shooting took place in Birkenau and the bodies were burned in the long trench. Later, however, the executions took place in the large hall of one of the crematoria which had been provided with a special installation for this purpose. Prominent guests from Berlin were present at the inauguration of the first crematorium in March 1943. The "program" consisted of the gassing and burning of eight thousand Cracow Jews. The guests, both officers and civilians, were extremely satisfied with the results and the special peephole fitted into the door of the gas chamber was in constant use. They were lavish in their praise of this newly erected installation."

A private firm, DEGESCH, an abbreviation for German Vermin Combating Corporation, manufactured the gas pellets. Since Zyklon B deteriorated in its containers, Auschwitz could not stockpile large amounts. Canisters of gas were produced, ordered, and delivered on a regular basis. Zyklon B had other uses; it exterminated rodents and insects in enclosed spaces and it fumigated buildings and ships, disinfected clothes, and deloused humans, if they wore gas masks. Since Jews frequently were described as parasites or insects that in the propaganda of the Third Reich "should be exterminated like vermin," the SS considered the use of Zyklon B as highly appropriate for the final solution.

The gas-induced destruction of huge numbers of people was not secret within the upper echelons of the Party. Nevertheless a polite fiction covered procurement. Shipments went directly to the so-called Auschwitz Extermination and Fumigation Division (very little was ever used for vermin control) and the trucks dispatched for the supplies were sent "to pick up materials for the Jewish resettlement."

Hoess and his colleagues learned how to move the assembly line of murder more smoothly. According to Filip Müller, one of the first of the *Sonderkommandos* and who miraculously survived four years at Auschwitz, chaos marked the first gassing. The victims, still dressed, sensed doom approaching when they were shoved and beaten toward the farmhouse. Guards shot several who resisted. Because no one thought of stripping them of their clothes, the corpses were a tangle of bodies, garments, feces, urine and menstrual blood. The *Sonderkommandos* could salvage very little.

Hoess promptly switched tactics. When people destined for gassing disembarked from the trains, he or one of his cohorts often delivered a brief speech. "It was most important," he explained in his memoirs, "that the whole business of arriving and undressing should take place in an atmosphere of greatest possible calm." Prisoners were questioned if they had a trade. "Tailor" would shout some unknowing soul. "Excellent" smoothly answered an SS officer. "Nurse," would cry a woman. "Yes, we need trained nurses."

Sometimes as they were unloaded from the trains they saw the inmate orchestra, led by violinist Alma Rose. The musicians wore white blouses, dark blue skirts and played cheerful tunes from the *Merry Widow*, or the "Barcarole."

In the rooms where they undressed, the victims noticed numbered hooks. They were told to remember their numbers in order to reclaim their clothing after the disinfectant shower. The hallways bore signs with arrows pointing to *Wäsche und Disinfeksraum*. Posters advised "One louse may kill you," and "Cleanliness brings freedom."

Some victims became apprehensive as the guards hit them, used whips and clubs to force laggards into the showers. A flash of reality came when those in a position to see discovered the shower heads were fake. But it was too late even for a show of resistance. The steel doors were securely locked. SS troopers, masked, were already dropping the fatal pellets through the rooftop slots following the signal of Sergeant Möll who gleefully shouted, *"Na, gib ihnen schön zu fressen"* (All right, give them something nice to chew on).

A camp doctor patiently sat at one of the thick glass portholes. He could see the naked throngs standing there, waiting for the flow of water when suddenly they became aware of gas. The victims would stampede for the exits, massive metal doors. They trampled on children, women, and the old and feeble. Some tried to climb above the gas, scrambling over the bodies of the fallen. The agony lasted only four or five minutes. The shrieks and prayers ceased.

Within a few minutes the first tongues of fire from the ovens leaped into the sky. The flames and smoke spewed from the chimneys night and day. A thick pall of smoke with a sickening stench hung over the camp twenty-four hours during the busiest period, when 12,000 or more died in a single day. During the peak of destruction the furnaces became so overloaded that Hoess improvised outdoor cremation pits to handle more bodies. A confident Auschwitz official remarked, "Our system is so terrible that no man in the world will believe it to be possible, even should a Jew escape from Auschwitz and tell the world all he saw, the world would brand him as a fantastic liar and nobody would believe him."

Later, a Wehrmacht colonel who saw Auschwitz offered another view of how the world would react. "After all that happened at Auschwitz it will devolve upon the SS to win the war as quickly as possible. For if Germany were to lose the war then let us be assured that after all that happened at Auschwitz certainly no German will be left alive." His error was to think that the victors' passion for justice against the perpetrators would last much longer than the embers of the last crematoria victim.

It was in September, 1942 that Dr. Kremer described Auschwitz as *"anus mundi."* Some months later, as Dr. Joseph Mengele drove through the gate with the sign, *Arbeit macht Frei* (Work brings Freedom) Auschwitz was beginning an even more terrible era, one in which Mengele would play a leading role.

The Selector

WHEN CAPTAIN JOSEPH MENGELE took up his duties as one of the twenty-two camp doctors at Auschwitz, the annihilation process organized by Rudolph Hoess was fully operational. SS troopers unlocked the cattle-car-like tumbrels shouting, *"Raus, raus!"* (Out, out). Penned in the boxcars for days and nights, often while the train sat for many hours on the siding at Auschwitz while earlier arrivals were processed, the deportees from Holland, Belgium, France, Italy, Germany, Yugoslavia, Greece, Rumania, Czechoslovakia, and Hungary blinked in the sunlight after their prolonged stay in darkness.

Tired, scared, filthy, sick, hungry, thirsty, men, women, and children clutched one another while the guards yanked away valises and other luggage. Still on the train lay a number of corpses, those too old, too young or too sick to have lived through an extended trip without food or enough water. Others too feeble to take a few tottering steps to climb down also remained aboard.

"It was more like a slow motion stampede," remembers one inmate. "There was complete bedlam, guards yelling and cursing, the dogs snapping and growling, a mob of people who could not understand what was happening." They may have been lulled somewhat by the sight of the orchestra or the first soothing speech about jobs, but the fires leaping into the sky and the terrible stink quickly frightened them all. And then there were those strange men in ragged, black-and-white striped clothes, prisoners obviously, who moved among them, piling up their baggage.

The officer on the bullhorn explained that men and women would be separated. Those qualified for work would form one column. A second column would include the old, the young, women with small children and anyone considered too weak to labor for the Third Reich. The second column would go immediately to the villages where inmates lived and set up housekeeping.

It was all part of the elaborate fiction maintained in the KZs. Those who were judged unfit for work went directly to the gas chambers, pausing only to disrobe. They were never even registered as having come to Auschwitz; camp officials did not know their names or places of origin.

The system, of course, required a doctor to judge who was qualified to perform slave labor and who was to be sent directly to his or her death. Dr. Joseph Mengele commenced fulfilling this role in May 1943, almost immediately upon his arrival.

Witnesses have since testified to having seen him performing this function a total of seventy-four times. Quite possibly he was at the railroad siding on many more occasions but those who saw him there have perished.

Nevertheless several survivors offer vivid memories of Mengele as the selector for arrivals. On the day Hungarian pathologist Miklos Nyiszli first saw the light of Auschwitz he noticed "a young SS officer, impeccable in his uniform, a gold rosette gracing his lapel, his boots smartly polished." When that dandy called for volunteers with medical experience in autopsies, Nyiszli stepped forward. He was allowed to live.

When Nathan Shapell stumbled from the train in 1943 he saw "hundreds of SS and Gestapo men waiting. We were welcomed by the man I soon came to know as Doctor Mengele, the Butcher. As the column approached the officers it funneled down to a single line past this inhuman monster, who stood with a few others on a small platform above us, raising his hand with the thumb extended and moving it back and forth. They herded us past him, beating us to make us move faster and faster. We did not at that moment know what the movement of his finger meant, but it soon became apparent. One line to the left was young men and girls, eighteen to thirty-five. The middle aged, the old, the very young went to the right . . .

"Franja [a friend] and her sister had started towards the left but when they saw their mother going the other way, they went back and spoke to Doctor Mengele, asking if they could stay with her. He smiled and said, 'Yes, of course.' They went to the other side."

Gisella Perl, a physician from Hungary, was able to avoid transport to the concentration camp until the ruler of her country, Admiral Horthy, seeing his German ally edging towards defeat, sought a separate peace. The Nazis and local fascists immediately snatched control of Hungary. Full-scale shipments of Jews to Poland and its KZs began. When Perl reached the selection point she was tempted to take the trucks proffered for the weak but her daughter argued her into walking. "An SS officer asked me how old I was and I took a few years off. He said, 'You can walk.' In this way I was sent into life. The officer was Mengele." But she saw her father, tightly gripping his prayer book, being led away after he reached Mengele. She never saw her father again.

"They unloaded us," says Elizabeth Mermelstein, an inmate from Viskovo, Czechoslovakia, "and there was the famous Doctor Mengele saying, 'Left, right, left, right.' There were lots of Jewish people advising what to do. But we were totally bewildered. Mothers ran after children. Children ran after parents. I was running after my parents, and Mengele said in German, 'You there, fatty—you can go to work. You're young enough.' I'll never forget that. Three times I ran to be with my parents and three times he threw me back. My sister was with me. They took her children."

David Mark from Czechoslovakia was directed by Mengele to one line; his father to another. The elder Mark took advantage of the confusion to reach out and drag his son to his side, thereby saving him from gassing.

Gizelle Hersh came in a shipment of Hungarians that included her brother, three sisters and her parents. They were appalled by the sight of "strange people in gray striped clothes. I don't know if they are men or women. They have no hair," she reported to the others. Having deposited their packages, pocketbooks, suitcases, and knapsacks, the family tried to keep their coats. A soldier pointed a rifle and ordered them to leave the garments. "Don't worry," he reassured, "everything will be returned to you in the barracks."

A puzzled Mother Hersh asked how it was possible they could sort out the piles of belongings to ensure that the owners received their possessions.

56

The Selector

Gizelle Hersh's impressions are recorded in her book, *Gizelle, Save the Children:* "Suddenly, incredibly we heard music. A Strauss waltz! The sounds lilted through the dark gray air of the early morning. Soothing. Reassuring . . . The gay melody spoke to us of the life we had known. And it promised a future. A tall handsome SS officer strode by us, walking back and forth, inspecting." It was Mengele, in search of an interpreter. He discovered Gizelle Hersh spoke German as well as her native tongue. He commandeered her skills and instructed her: "Ask one question of every adult. 'How old are you?' Ask in Hungarian and tell me in German."

A bearded old man stood at the head of the line. He gave his age as seventy-two, which Gizelle Hersh repeated to Mengele in German. "The doctor flicked his finger. A brown-shirted officer standing nearby shoved the old man off in the direction in which the doctor had pointed." Then a mother appeared with a babe in arms. Her age was twenty-two and Mengele pointed his finger to the right, the same pathway taken by the old man. Next came a child of three, somehow kept neat by her mother. She wore slacks, black patent leather shoes. Hersh recognized her as Sophie. The child chattered about eating a nice big breakfast. Mengele demanded her age. Her mother, sickly, fatigued, appeared next; her age was twenty-three. Mengele dispatched Sophie and her mother to the right. The child dropped her stuffed dog and went to retrieve it. A soldier prodded the youngster with a gun, then kicked the stuffed animal away. Sophie's father, next in line, spoke up. "It's all right. I'll bring her the dog."

Mengele demanded silence. He obtained the man's age, twenty-nine, and shunted him to the fit-for-work column. The man protested he wanted to be with his family. A soldier said he would see them later. The men would breakfast in separate barracks. The father objected and the soldier raised his weapon. Still ignorant of the meaning of selection, the father took his place in the left line.

Throughout the morning Gizelle Hersh put her single question to each person. A fifteen-year-old assigned to the work column asked if she could be with her parents on the right. Mengele shrugged and let her go to her quick death.

As her own family approached the head of the inspection line, Hersh tried to decipher the meaning of the two columns. She had noticed that all of those as young as her twelve-year-old sister Katya were sent to the right, "toward the factory with its thick gray smoke belching continually into the gray sky. The old people went there too. That would mean, of course, that the people sent to the right were those who need not work." That made sense to her, as it fit with Eichmann's promise to the departing Hungarian contingents. But Hersh was puzzled by the disposition of women over thirty-five. Many were fit to work but still sent to the right. And Hersh's own mother was thirty-five.

When her sisters appeared, she signaled them not to show they knew her. She added a couple of years to the age of each, making certain even the youngest was listed as fifteen. All of the girls and her brother were directed to the left.

Her parents then stood before her. Gizelle Hersh chopped a year off her mother's age, making her thirty-four, took five from her father to announce him as forty-nine. Her mother addressed her: "Gizeka, Papa and I go together."

"The woman wants to go with her husband," Hersh told Mengele. The finger motioned sharply. Her mother and father, holding hands, walked off in the direction of the line destined for "the factory." She never saw them again.

By October of 1943, the armies of Benito Mussolini had surrendered and the dictator himself had fled to the safety of the north. SS soldiers and remnants of the fascist police ruled Rome. On a Sabbath of that month, a roundup of Jews dispatched 1,000 to Auschwitz. Even Commandant Hoess was at the siding to greet the Italian contingent. The Romans were rumored to be people of great wealth, garbed in furs and jewelry, the women dressed in the height of fashion.

Arminio Wachsberger, a worker in a photo optical shop and born in the Austrian city of Fiume before it was ceded to Italy as part of the World War I peace, was among the Roman Jews who clambered down from the train after an anxious night of waiting on the siding. Mengele was in charge, although at the moment Wachsberger did not know his identity.

Curiosity over these exotics satisfied, the Nazis attended to business, bawling orders to the newcomers. When it was obvious they did not understand the instructions, Mengele asked if someone could serve as an interpreter. As Robert Katz reports in his book *Black Sabbath,* Wachsberger volunteered.

"He told me to say that the older women and those women with children would be put into trucks to travel to the camp, which was ten kilometers away. The younger people were to remain behind and do the journey on foot. If anyone of those feels tired and doesn't want to walk the distance" Wachsberger remembers there were about 450 young and able-bodied persons in the contingent "they can also travel in the trucks. About 300 of them chose to board the lorries." And died for it.

Throughout the selection, Wachsberger observed Mengele's demeanor. "He had a gentle manner and a quiet poise that almost always lay between the edges of smugness and the height of charm. He whistled a Wagnerian aria as he signaled right or left for prisoners.

"I wanted to go in the trucks also because my wife and child were among the passengers but as I got in, Mengele came and pulled me out saying, 'You'll stay with us because we need you as an interpreter. You'll find your family when you get to the camp.' After only ten minutes of walking, however, we arrived at the camp. It wasn't ten kilometers." The discovery alarmed Wachsberger.

Skulls shaven, numbers tattooed on their arms, doused with a cold shower and a stinging spray of disinfectant, Wachsberger and his fellow Romans saw quick violent death their very first day at Auschwitz. They saw a prisoner shot for failing to move swiftly enough, a man who fell to the ground in exhaustion beaten to death where he lay. Another in despair had thrown himself on the electrified wire.

"The older Jewish prisoners said, 'Your families are in those places where there is smoke coming out.' We didn't want to believe them. Other prisoners said that our families had only gone to a disinfection area and then been transferred to family camps. We wanted to believe that they had gone to family camps.

"The next day Mengele came to our hut and interrogated us. He asked us news of Italy and requested me to go to his hut that evening. He wanted me to recount in every detail what had happened in Italy starting with July 25, 1943 [the date of the coup which deposed Mussolini], and tell him about the sentiments of the population with respect to Fascism and Nazism. Just before I was to leave he handed me a gift of some morsels of bread, a bit of margarine or blood sausage."

Mengele summoned Wachsberger for an evening chat several more times. "He wanted to know what had happened in Italy after the fall of Fascism. He was most anxious and curious and I told him everything I knew. The more I told him, the more he asked for details. He drank a great deal of vodka and was often quite drunk. One evening when he was particularly inebriated, I asked him where my family was.

" 'What do you mean you don't know,' he said. I told him that there was a group of prisoners who had told us of a family camp.

" 'Look, *Dolmetscher*' " (translator) Wachsberger remembers the doctor's reply. " 'This is a labor camp. We need people who can work. The others—' His hands suggested there were not others."

Wachsberger persisted. He himself had interpreted Mengele's words promising that workers would see their families. *"Deine Familie existiert nich mehr,"* said the doctor in his soft voice. Had not Wachsberger seen the chimneys spewing black smoke? Mengele could not believe that no one had told the Italians about the crematoria.

Wachsberger argued, mostly to himself, that in a camp of this size there was sickness, old people died and their bodies had to be disposed of. And he so clung to his belief that his wife and child lived.

Mengele then pulled from a file cabinet the registration papers for the inmates of Auschwitz. He showed Wachsberger a list of prisoners' names. "I saw my name but none of my family's names. I asked him 'What happened?'

" 'We need workers,' Mengele replied.

"My wife was young and strong. She could have worked," said Wachsberger.

" 'But her child had been killed,' said Mengele, 'and mothers won't work well if they know their children are dead.' "

Wachsberger questioned Mengele about the 300 young, able-bodied people whom he had encouraged to go the way of the gas chambers.

" 'Dolmetschu, anyone who can't walk ten kilometers after spending five days on a train is not capable of the work we have to do here.' "

Wachsberger concludes that Mengele acted at least partly on his own in overstepping the bounds set by Himmler, who wanted an abundant supply of slave labor. Ordinarily, the quota for survival leaving the train was between 20 and 25 percent of the passengers. But in some cases as many as 80 to 90 percent went directly to their deaths.

The trains with their human cargo arrived three or four times a day and during the nights. Theoretically, ramp selection should have been equally divided among the camp physicians.

But Mengele performed the function far more than his share, probably with the blessings of other doctors less comfortable than he with the assignment. "Indefatigable" is the word Nyiszli uses to describe Mengele's devotion to ramp selection. *Sonderkommando* Arie Fuks, whose job was to relieve newcomers of their baggage, insists that in his opinion, Mengele engaged in selection of arrivals "always, night and day."

Incidents of outright resistance at the ramp were very few. The Jews who disembarked from the trains, although they had already seen incidents of barbarism and even killings by Nazis and local sympathizers in their homelands, could not believe that a civilized nation—yes, many still thought of Germany this way, as a land of scientists and musicians and poets—would ship carloads of human beings thousands of miles only to murder them.

Rumors of death camps circulated through Europe, but Hoess had arranged for inmates of the camp to sign prettified postcards stamped "Waldsee." The cards bore the printed message: "We are doing very well here. We have work and we are well treated. We await your arrival." And as Gizelle Hersh remembers, the *Judenrat,* the councils of elders who governed the ghettos for the Nazis, were assured by Adolf Eichmann that there would be work for the young and strong and a family camp for others . . .

A transport from Bergen–Belsen brought several thousand inmates with no illusions of their future. The rods and whips cowed most, but several hundred still refused to leave the dressing room. A handful of SS men entered to drive them out and a battle began. The prisoners beat the guards and tore down the lights. Wild shooting started as the inmates took up the weapons from the SS troopers. Hoess hurried to the scene. The revolt petered out when the prisoners ran out of ammunition, and the men were led out one by one and shot in an adjoining room.

Mengele himself turned violent when the selection process

broke down. Zahawa Morgen observed an elderly man, directed by the doctor to the line of the dead, start toward the other group where his son, who qualified as a laborer, stood. Furious, Mengele snatched up a thick rod and smashed it down against the old man's skull. The offender, who did not even realize his own feeble effort to evade gassing, fell dead.

Responsibility for determining the capability of new arrivals for work fell upon the camp physicians, necessitating their presence at the ramp. But in practice the system was ludicrous. Anyone unable to rise to his feet and leave the train was considered by the SS doctor to be "officially dead." These often included babies whose mothers had succumbed or who were too weak to carry the child. Many of the victims unable to crawl from the boxcars went directly to the crematoria, even though they were still alive. Newborn infants might be thrown into the laundry furnace as a matter of convenience.

As for those able to pass before Mengele he often decided on the basis of age; on other occasions simply by a cursory glance at the person. Such decisions could have been made by any of the SS minions and involved no medical skill. Dr. Mengele obviously enjoyed the work.

Camp rules also insisted that a physician certify the achievements of the gassing. Filip Müller, as a *Sonderkommando,* watched Mengele on the scene. "As we stepped out of the lift [where bodies were loaded for the crematorium] Lagerführer Schwarzhuber and Doctor Mengele were standing outside the door to the gas chamber. The doctor was just switching on the light. Then he bent forward and peered through a peephole in the door to ascertain whether there were still any signs of life inside. After a while, he ordered the kommandoführer to switch on the fans which were to disperse the gas." Muller notes that when the doors of the gas chamber opened on this occasion, the top layers of corpses spilled out into the yard.

The quick destruction of a high proportion of new arrivals helped keep the camp population within tolerable limits. But each shipment also brought new, healthier and stronger slave laborers. To make room for them, selections for death were held frequently within the camp. These were also handled by physicians.

At rollcall—*Zaehlappel*—the head count was often marked by selections. The most obvious candidates were the Mussulmen, men and women who developed a zombie-like stare. Emaciated, dirty beyond description, they no longer seemed to care about their fate. The term came into use because to the Germans, these individuals, from a distance, resembled Moslems at their prayers.

The causes of the deadly depression were the deaths of loved ones, the clubbings and the starvation diet. Some persons before falling to the level of the Mussulman summoned up enough resolve to throw themselves on the electrified fence; others deliberately ventured across the dead-line.

But there were never enough Mussulmen to feed the appetites of the gas chambers and crematoria. Charlotte Delbo, who fought with the French Resistance, was captured in 1942 and then shipped to Auschwitz. Her husband was executed. In her book, *None of Us Will Return* she remembers roll call: "An SS appears at the end of the *Lagerstrasse* (camp street) comes towards us, stops in front of our ranks. By the caduceus on his cap he must be the doctor. He looks us over. Slowly. He speaks. He does not scream. A question. No one answers. He calls: 'Interpreter.' Marie-Claude steps forward. The SS repeats his question and Marie-Claude translates. 'He is asking if there are any among us who cannot endure the rollcall.' The SS watches us. Magda, our *Blokova,* watches us and moving a bit to the side blinks slightly.

"Who in fact can endure the rollcall? Who can stand for

hours? In the middle of the night. In the snow without having eaten, without having slept. Who can stand this cold for hours? Some raise their hands. The SS has them step out of ranks. Counts them. Too few. Softly he utters another sentence and Marie-Claude translates again. 'He is asking whether there aren't any others, elderly or sick who find the rollcall too hard in the morning.'" It is one more effort to make the victims accomplices in their own murders, to select themselves. "Other hands go up. Then Magda quickly nudges Marie-Claude and Marie-Claude, without changing her tone, says, 'But it is better not to say so.' The hands that have been raised are lowered. All but one. A little old woman, quite tiny, who raises herself up on tiptoe, stretching and waving her arm as high as she can, afraid they will not see her. The SS moves on. The old woman speaks up: 'Sir, I am sixty-seven years old.' Her neighbors shush her. She gets angry. Why should they stop her if there is a less harsh routine for the sick, the aged. Why should they stop her from taking advantage of this? In despair at having been forgotten, she cries out. In a shrill voice as aged as herself. 'Me, Sir. I am sixty-seven years old.' The SS hears, turns around.

" '*Komm,*' and she joins the group now formed which the SS doctor escorts to Block 25." As the *Blokova* knew, this was a selection for gassing, and Block 25 was the holding pen for the condemned. Delbo then watched the trucks bearing those selected. They now knew their fate. "The screams remain inscribed in the blue of the sky. For eternity, shaven heads squeezed together and bursting with cries. Mouths twisted with cries that are not heard, hands waving in a mute way."

"*Zaehlappel,*" says Gisella Perl, "was a time of life and death. There would be no light in the sky. It would be three a.m., four a.m., five a.m. or maybe early in the evening, any time of day when we would be rousted for rollcall. Standing in a row, we were cold, hungry, in rags. It could last one, two or three hours;

however long, it seemed years. And there was Mengele, elegantly dressed, a beautiful blue shirt, so elegant, so handsome, smiling, smelling of a fine soap or eau de cologne."

At a rollcall Perl made an attempt to break through to the doctor in Mengele. On her own she had tried to use her professional skills for the benefit of sister prisoners. She had been delayed in taking her place at rollcall because of administering first aid to an injured woman. "I felt, he's a doctor. He will understand. I began to explain why I was late." Mengele lashed out with his booted foot, striking her in the side. For two months, Perl passed blood in her urine.

Ruth Eliaz was pregnant in December 1943 when the authorities sent her in a cattle car to Auschwitz. She survived ramp selection; the child was not due for many months. In May 1944 she heard that the young, strong inmates were to be sent to Germany to clean up the rubble from Allied bombings. It was an opportunity to leave the death camp but there was also the risk of her condition being discovered.

"I am in the seventh month. I am told that pregnant women are sent to the gas chamber! I am only twenty years old! I want to live! Friends succeed in placing my number on the Transport to Germany list. We young strong workers are brought to the women's camp. Now there is further selection. This time, Doctor Mengele will personally make the selection. We are naked, and must march like geese past Doctor Mengele. A few young women have decided to place me in their midst and thus try to direct the attention of Mengele to themselves. We never get near to him. Is it possible? Doctor Mengele doesn't notice me! I may live? And the new life stirs within me."

Ruth Eliaz did go off to Hamburg, thinking she had escaped Mengele, but she would face him at another selection and the consequences would be all but unbearable.

Gisella Perl had a friend named Ibi who escaped the sentence of selection half a dozen times, leaping off the trucks carrying her toward the gas chambers. When Mengele discovered her in a hospital bed he selected Ibi again. As the SS marched a column of naked women off toward the gas chambers, Ibi broke and ran. This time, Mengele himself chased her. He caught up with her, then hit her on the head with a club. He hit her over and over, pounding the woman to her knees. When she could no longer struggle, she was forced back into the death-bound column.

As the women moved towards the trucks, Mengele shouted, "You want to escape, don't you. You can't escape. You are going to burn like the others. You are going to croak, you dirty Jew." Perl's last sight of her friend was her naked, forlorn figure, her head a bloody ball from Mengele's attack. Shortly after, she saw him in the hospital, whistling as he washed his blood-soiled hands with perfumed soap.

Mengele's assault on Ibi not only demonstrated his quick temper but also his dedication to his role as selector. Anyone who challenged his rights risked his fury. He relished the job with its power to bestow life and sentence to death. Numerous incidents so demonstrate:

In October 1943, on Yom Kippur, the holiest of Jewish holidays, Mengele on his motorcycle rode up to a soccer field now holding 2,000 boys. "Suddenly, a visible spasm passed through us all," remembers Joseph Kleinman, fourteen years old at the time. Mengele climbed onto a platform and looked down on his congregation. He asked a fourteen-year-old his age. Well versed in the ways of the camp, the slightly built youngster answered that he was eighteen.

Enraged, Mengele shouted, "I'll show you." He ordered one of the guards to fetch a hammer, nails and a piece of wood. He instructed the soldier to nail the wood to a certain height on one of the goal posts. "Pass beneath that," Mengele commanded the children. The boys understood instantly. Anyone whose head did not reach the level of the marker would be selected.

Kleinman frantically stuffed stones in his shoes to add height. Other frightened boys milled about while Mengele bawled orders at them. Kleinman managed to hide himself among some taller youths and so escaped selection. However, about 1,000 failed to measure up to Mengele's standard. A wild scramble followed as SS troopers with dogs rounded up the petrified smaller boys. Mengele, who had been joined by his close friend, Dr. Viktor Capesius, observed the commotion with laughter. His hilarity seemed to increase with the cries of the boys for their mothers. On that Yom Kippur massacre all 1,000 were selected and gassed.

Mengele's Yom Kippur selection was not capricious. He was familiar with the religion of his captives. He knew that on the Day of Atonement, Jews recite a prayer that tells of the flock passing beneath the rod of the shepherd—the Lord—who decides which will live. Yom Kippur was an occasion for Mengele to demonstrate to the inmates of Auschwitz that he was their shepherd, their Lord, in control of the rod.

He often improvised during his selections, looking for different ways to display his power. Kitty Hart was among a group of women forced to parade naked outdoors before the doctor and his staff. Mengele then ordered the scabby scarecrows to run. Anyone who could not summon enough energy to break into a trot went to the death column. Hart pushed herself until she jogged the required distance. Mengele was only partially satisfied. He stared thoughtfully at the lice-and-diet-induced pimples, boils, and abcesses scarring her body before finally pointing her to the life line.

The dramas of selections were heightened by the physician's deliberate obscurantism. The right column did not always mean death nor the left always mean survival. When her mother headed off to the gas chambers her last words to Gizelle Hersh were, "Save the children." Separated from her brother, who was to die in another camp, and haunted by the admonition, Hersh saw selections as the chief threat to fulfilling her obligation.

On a bright sunny morning after a routine rollcall the women of her barracks, instead of returning to their quarters for a cup of watery tea and a chance to use the toilet, were marched off in another direction. Hersh realized it meant a selection but she was unprepared for the sight of a large field, "dense with naked women. They stood in lines which stretched up the field and doubled back down, and up again; thousands of pale-bodied women and girls, wearing only wooden clogs, carrying their striped dresses."

Her sisters balked at undressing but their resistance melted after sharp instructions from the kapo. "Strip. Shoes stay on. Hold your dress. Stand in line. And quiet. Not a sound from any of you. Or you will be shot."

The naked lines of women, heads shaved, shuffled forward. Hersh suddenly recognized the officer in charge: "So handsome, slender, straight, Doctor Mengele." He no longer required her services, and without her red polkadot dress and shorn of her long black hair he did not remember her.

Women moved to the right and left, in accord with the doctor's shifting motions. Hersh became confused. She could not detect whether it was preferable to be on one side or the other. Both columns contained women fit for work. A woman separated from her sister protested. An SS man grabbed her, knocked her to the earth where her skull slammed against a rock. Two kapos dragged her away. If she were not already dead she soon would be.

Hersh agonized over a way to save her sisters and herself. Finally she decided—guessed was more like it—that the right side was earmarked for death. And when her first sister came abreast of Mengele, he pointed to the right. A second sister, "skinny with shoulder blades that stuck out like wings," also went to the right. The third sister was waved to the left and so was Gizelle Hersh. To the astonishment of Mengele and his entourage, she spoke up in German. "Please, sir. We are four sisters. I would ask you, please. Do not separate us. We would like to remain together."

Mengele appeared nonplussed.

"We are all strong and healthy. We are all good workers. We can work fifteen to twenty hours a day without getting tired. Please, sir. Let us prove this to you. Allow us to remain together." Mengele and an SS woman strolled off a few paces to discuss the situation. They walked back and the SS woman nodded to Hersh, who thanked God that her prayers had been answered. Mengele inquired which were Hersh's sisters. When they were identified he grouped them all on the right.

Right! To die, thought Hersh.

She heard Mengele say, *"Vier Schwestern,"* (four sisters) and then laugh. But on this occasion, right did not mean death.

Whim appears to have guided many of Mengele's actions, but he seemed never to have been troubled by the consequences. The Austrian-born prisoner-physician Ella Lingens remembers the demeanor of Mengele at selections, "the way he stood there with his thumbs in his pistol belt. I remember Doctor Koenig and to his credit I must say he always got very drunk beforehand, as did Doctor Rohde. Mengele didn't. He didn't have to. He did it sober."

Selection surely meant death for most, but for some it meant life. Zvi Goldberg was close to Mussulman status. He had learned that his mother and sister had been killed. "The news crushed me completely. I did not want to live any longer." It was a Saturday morning, Shabat, a favorite occasion for choosing fodder for the death machinery. Goldberg was sitting on the ground with some companions draining the remains of watery soup. A band of drunken SS soldiers surrounded the group and hustled them off. "My knees buckled as I realized we were being driven to the gas chambers . . . This was the first time I had stood near the iron doors behind which a hideous death awaited us all . . . We stood petrified, refusing to move. Our captors went into a rage and began to force us into the gas chamber. We responded with hair-raising cries. The delay and tumult helped save some of us. Doctor Mengele heard the noise and came out to see what was happening." Mengele rebuked the soldiers who had usurped the role of selector. However, rather than disgrace the SS troopers he decided to go ahead with selections on the spot. Mengele seemed in an expansive mood. He asked Goldberg's age. The youth responded in fluent German, adding that he was fit to do all kinds of hard labor. Mengele praised his command of German, and after hearing that the boy had studied at German schools in Danzig returned him to the living. He was one of only fifty-two of the original three hundred rounded up by the soldiers that were saved.

"As I returned to the camp," says Goldberg, "it looked to me like a veritable Garden of Eden." But he owed his survival not to Mengele's compassion but to his sense of himself as the only true selector. Strangely yet perhaps understandably, given the circumstances, Goldberg, along with others who were granted life in the face of death by Mengele, could never quite resolve a sense of ambivalence toward the Angel of Death.

The Healer

EXCEPT FOR A BRIEF STINT at a Leipzig hospital, where he interned, and his tour with the Viking Division, Joseph Mengele practiced very little doctoring of the sick and injured before he came to Auschwitz. The evidence indicates that he added nothing to his clinical experience there.

If Mengele had been interested in treating diseases he might have found Auschwitz an arena of opportunity. Frank Stiffel, a Polish Jew and a medical student transferred from Treblinka to the camp, described the sanitary conditions in *The Tale of the Ring:* "... lice by the thousands, fleas by the millions; contagious diarrhea, which made people run to the bathroom almost incessantly; and the king of them all, the ever-present companion of all big wars, His Majesty the Typhus . . . They were all terrible, all very intimate, and all very constant. You slipped your hand into your sock and brought out a fist full of fleas. You scratched your shirt and found lice under all your fingernails. You felt a pain in your belly, and a minute later your pants were full of a foul, semi-liquid, bad-smelling mass. You got a fever and you knew it was probably typhus. And the most important vital decision you often had to make was this: how do I prefer to die? By beating, by shooting, by gassing, or by God-sent natural blessings such as diarrhea or typhus?"

For a prisoner, illness involved great risk. Anyone with a serious ailment or disabling injury chanced immediate selection for Zyklon B therapy. On the other hand collapse from sickness while on a labor detail invited a bullet in the head. Or a person who fell might lie there for the day, dying from exposure to the sun or sub-zero temperatures. Work parties usually toted home five or six corpses daily.

For admission to the hospital, an inmate first sought permission from his block senior. If the trustee was agreeable the prisoner could present himself before a camp doctor and an SS physician. The infirmary itself offered little in the way of cures. Mainly, it was an opportunity to enjoy a more comfortable place to sleep. Medical supplies were not issued. The camp actually contained a generous stock of pharmaceuticals and medical equipment. Many patients transported to Auschwitz brought their medicines with them, but these were confiscated on arrival. Doctors brought the tools of their craft. These too went into the storehouse at Canada. The prisoners who staffed the hospitals bartered for drugs and equipment with valuables that patients and contributors managed to hide from the SS. Additional help came from a few humane guards and in particular from Dr. Hans

Münch, an SS physician who at some risk to himself tried to practice his profession for the benefit of prisoner-patients.

The medical facilities treated inmates only to ensure the supply of trained slave labor. Furthermore, men and women were hospitalized to reduce contagion from the likes of what Stiffel called, "His Majesty the Typhus."

Fear of an epidemic that might envelop the entire camp led Mengele to draconian measures when confronted by one of the periodic outbreaks of typhus. Early in the summer of 1943 the doctor himself came down either with typhoid or typhus and spent nearly a month recuperating. When he returned he was determined to attack the sources of infection with his usual vindictive rage. He arranged for the entire population of a women's barracks, between 750 and 1,500 people, to be immediately gassed, regardless of their individual health. They and their lice were thus simultaneously exterminated.

With that barracks emptied it was sealed and fumigated, with Zyklon B, of course. The occupants of a second hut were then disinfected, while all of their belongings, their ragged garments, their coverings for their beds, were distroyed. The sanitized group was issued new, disinfected uniforms and what passed for bedding and moved into the now sterilized first unit. Then their original abode was deloused and the women of a third barracks given the disinfection treatment. The process was repeated until the sources of typhus in that section of the camp were eradicated. Mengele's method cost 750 to 1,500 lives. Obviously the same result would have occurred without a single death simply by erecting one new sterile hut and then thoroughly disinfecting the inmates as each building was fumigated.

Mengele continued to have an almost phobic reaction to symptoms that hinted at typhus. Polish inmate-doctor Janina Kosciuszkowa saw panic in his eyes when patients exhibited typhus-like skin eruptions. To keep him from experimenting on children under her care, she and associates applied a harmless plaster to the skins of the youngsters. Ugly rashes broke out causing Mengele to shy away from the children.

Nothing in the record suggests that Mengele possessed any notable skills as a clinical physician. Occasionally, he demonstrated a dangerous ability to diagnose certain diseases. Gisella Perl was horrified to see him point to a prisoner during one rollcall and diagnose her as suffering from scarlet fever. Mengele was correct, but confirmation meant not only the death sentence for her but anyone with whom she had associated. And so it became a contest to hide the true nature of many illnesses from Mengele. Whenever Ella Lingens had a patient she suspected of being infected with typhus, she wrote pneumonia on the chart.

Mengele would demand blood samples from any patients exhibiting signs of a highly contagious disease. Perl and the other inmate-doctors conspired in an attempt to fool him. If they believed one of their charges might have an illness that meant death by gas they would use their own blood for specimens and submit it for the inspection of the German doctors.

Often inmates pleaded with Perl to cooperate and let them spend a night or two in the hospital where they could rest. Aware that the sickbay provided Mengele with one of his favorite sites for selection, Perl more often than not refused. "I would say, 'You don't want to sleep in the *Revier* [infirmary]. It is infected.' "

Mengele ordered Lingens to draft meticulous lists on patients with a diagnosis and a date for recovery. A prognosis of a long hospital sojourn to recover from a serious illness was tantamount to writing a prescription for execution. Minimizing a person's condition and predicting an early discharge also invited disaster. Mengele would make his rounds and after reading the chart would say mockingly, "What, you say you're a doctor and you mean to send this half-dead wretched creature out of the hospital in less than four weeks?"

Quick release from the hospital might bring death in the Auschwitz yard. When the victim faltered there was almost always a guard prepared to snuff out the flicker of life. And if not a bullet, there was the risk of death from exposure or selection at rollcalls. Mengele was not to be denied often by subterfuges, since in many cases he kept his own record of who was to be discharged by a certain date.

Both Perl and Lingens observe that Mengele persisted in the fiction that genuine medicine was practiced at Auschwitz. "Characteristically," remembers Lingens, "Doctor Mengele addressed a gathering of all the prisoner-doctors in May 1944, when the worst of it was over for the time being. 'Ladies, now we've created conditions in our hospital compound which might be called relatively bearable,' he said referring to the use of windowless stables now set aside as wards for TB victims."

In further irony, notes Lingens, "Scarcely fifteen minutes later the chimneys began to belch thick clouds of a black sweetish smelling smoke which bellied across the camp. A bright sharp flame shot up six feet. Soon the stench of burned fat and hair became unbearable."

Finicky about his own clothing and always well scrubbed, Mengele imposed this obsession on the staff charged with maintaining the pitiful shacks designated as hospitals. He forced Perl and her associates to keep the walls clean, the floors swept even as soap was denied for personal use by prisoners or patients. With no drugs to treat incontinent patients there was precious little that could be accomplished in the way of institutional sanitation.

Men and women did recover from infections when allowed in the hospital, but it was a dodgy affair. Nathan Shappell was injured while working in the mines operated by the SS at Auschwitz. In the hospital he developed an infection. Every Tuesday Mengele inspected the men in that unit and anyone still invalid after two Tuesdays was taken away by van for gassing. The fourteen-day limit had perhaps less to do with Mengele's impatience with recovery than with the economics of slave labor. After all, I.G. Farben paid the SS for only two weeks of sick leave for an individual.

Fortunately for Shappell, his abnormally high fever piqued Mengele's interest, particularly since the attending Czech inmate-doctor could not explain the cause. Mengele chose seven or eight fellow patients for transport by the vans on the second Tuesday, but allowed Shappell to remain. The Czech immersed Shappell in icy sheets three times a day in an effort to lower his temperature. Mengele appeared for a third time. He wiped out every other person in the small hospital, but gave Shappell one more week's grace. On the occasion of Mengele's fourth visit, as soon as the physicians had left his bedside, Shappell took the thermometer from under his left armpit and placed it on top of his chest, exposing it to the cold air. When he heard the footsteps of the returning group of medicos, Shappell quickly replaced the instrument under his left arm. The reading showed a distinct improvement over previous ones. Mengele seemed satisfied that the treatment was effective and departed. Sensing that his luck had run out, Shappell discharged himself before the next visit even though he still was sick.

As a doctor, Mengele could have been expected to view naked bodies with clinical detachment. But in his case there are signs of a prurient interest in his captives. He had a penchant for performing selections with the female candidates stripped of their clothes. The practice was also popular with other physicians, and it served the further purpose of humiliating prisoners, robbing them of their personal dignity. Mengele, however, added his own specialty to the practice. In his appearances at hospitals he began by ordering all of the patients to remove the rags that passed for clothing. Then, according to Ella Lingens, he questioned them about intimate details of their sexual lives. The interrogations seemed rooted in sexual perversity. Mengele constantly referred to the Jewish women as "dirty whores." Gisella Perl believes that his abhorrence of—attraction to?—Jews was so strong that if confronted with an opportunity to have sexual intercourse with a Jew he would be incapable of an erection. Guilt is also a companion of detumescence.

Perl, of course, had physically felt the sting of his anger. Many SS men at the KZs, in spite of Himmler's strictures against relations with Jews, used their positions sexually to exploit prisoners. Fania Fenelon, the singer who wrote *Playing for Time,* telling of the experiences of the Auschwitz orchestra, occasionally obeyed a request to sing for Mengele in his quarters. Shortly before Fenelon died she spoke of her encounters with the doctor, and the interviewer drew the distinct impression that she was talking of a former "lover."

Rumors of Mengele's involvement with women in the camp circulated constantly. One prime candidate was the twenty-one-year-old female guard Irma Grese, who formed part of his retinue. Blue-eyed, blonde, described by many as "beautiful," Grese trained as a nurse under Dr. Karl Gebhardt, Himmler's personal physician and an orthopedic surgeon. Grese gave up nursing for a job in a dairy, but then enlisted in the SS. Himmler from the chickens, Grese from the cows—a natural selection.

Grese sufficiently impressed her superiors to be placed in charge of 30,000 women. Like Mengele, she took enormous pride in her appearance, primping for hours before showing herself in the best of confiscated clothes. On other occasions she delighted in strutting about the yard in her jackboots, a pistol on her hip, a whip in hand. She seemed to enjoy lashing women on the breasts, exhibiting a sadistic streak with sexual origins.

Perl believes Grese was a lesbian, but at one point she commanded Olga Lengyel to perform a a gynecological examination for the purpose of determining whether she was pregnant. The results were negative, and Lengyel received a small cache of food as a reward. There are also reports that a woman prisoner performed an abortion on Grese.

Grese was awarded a medal for her efforts at Auschwitz and then transferred to Bergen–Belsen, where she continued to whip and kill prisoners. Captured by the British when they liberated the camp, Grese was convicted of war crimes and hung in 1945. There is no evidence that Mengele ever remonstrated with Grese for what she inflicted on women at Auschwitz, though he seemed righteously upset by lesbianism. On one occasion, for example, he startled Ella Lingens with an angry accusation of rampant lesbianism among the women. She held her tongue, knowing that an explanation justifying such behavior would only inflame his weirdly priggish sensibilities in this area.

Internal sexual conflict, hatred of Jews (not unrelated), and obsession with controlling the inmate population combined in Mengele to assign especially harsh treatment for women unlucky enough to become pregnant. During a rollcall, according to Judith Sternberg Newman, a nurse imprisoned in the camp, Mengele invited pregnant women to step forward for lighter duty. As they did they self-selected for their final truck ride. At another rollcall he instructed guards to draw red crosses on the stomachs of women showing signs of pregnancy. They too died. Perl adopted a routine: "I report to you with humility there are no pregnancies in the camp."

As inmates became aware of Mengele's attitude they began to conceal their pregnancies. Mengele approached Gisella Perl and told her to report to him the names of women who were with child. He explained they would be transferred to another camp with better food. Hearing the good news, some misguided souls actually volunteered directly to Mengele that they were pregnant. Again they self-selected for death. "If someone came to me and said she was pregnant," Perl says, "I worried she might be a spy for Mengele, testing me." Mengele would switch his tactics. He instructed Perl that mothers-to-be would be allowed to carry to full-term and deliver their children. While he promised not to destroy the mothers, he did not guarantee the lives of the infants.

Perl realized the doctor only wanted the newborns for his experiments, that a baby meant death for *both* mother and infant. "Two lives would be thrown into the crematorium," says Perl. "I decided that never again would there be a pregnant woman in Auschwitz." She practiced the role of midnight abortionist, "in the night, on a dirty floor, using only my dirty hands."

Unfortunately in many cases the pregnancy was too far advanced for abortion. "In the dark of night, when everyone else was sleeping in the dark corners of the camp, in the toilet, on the floor, without a drop of water I delivered their babies. I took the ninth month pregnancies and accelerated the birth by rupture of the membrane. Usually within one or two days came spontaneous birth requiring no further intervention. Or I produced a dilatation with my fingers, inverting the infant and thus brought it to life. In the dark, always hurried, in the midst of filth and dust with just my five fingers, no drugs, no instruments. After delivery of the child I quickly bandaged the mother and sent her back to her hut, ready to work. If she needed to rest in the hospital I admitted her as having pneumonia. No one will ever know what it meant when I had to destroy those babies. I loved those newborns, not just as a doctor but also as a mother who had given up her own daughter. I gave my child to a family that was not Jewish when I was arrested. Again and again I felt like I was killing my own child to save the mother's life. I prayed to God to help me save the mother. And if I hadn't done it, both mother and child would have been murdered."

Mengele confirmed Perl's apprehensions. In several cases he arranged for total care for a pregnant woman, including aseptic conditions at birth. He severed the umbilicus with great care. Perhaps thirty minutes later, mother and neonate went to the gas chamber.

A Parisian named Jeanette approached her time of delivery during this period. It had been a difficult pregnancy and Gisella Perl discovered that Jeanette carried twins. She felt she had better advise Mengele. He came immediately after labor began. "Twins! Twins! he shouted. "At last, twins will be born here." In apparent gratitude to the mother, he arranged for a basket for the babies, some tiny shirts and real blankets, undoubtedly from the plunder at Canada. Jeanette herself received an unheard of luxury—a white sheet.

A day after the births, a pair of SS troopers entered the hospital demanding, "Where are the twins?" They then scooped the infants up and left, leaving the mother raving with fear. Perl and her associates comforted Jeanette with lies about routine examinations. Each evening the babies returned, looking a little the worse for their day with Mengele. After two weeks one died; its brother followed shortly after. And then Jeanette herself was selected.

Ruth Eliaz, in her seventh month, escaped a Mengele selection by placing herself in the midst of other naked young women destined to work at Hamburg cleaning up bomb rubble. But when she arrived at Hamburg the authorities shipped her back to Auschwitz. Back in the camp, Mengele could not understand how he had overlooked her pregnancy during his selection of those eligible to work away from Auschwitz. He sent her to the hospital to complete her pregnancy.

When the baby was born, Mengele extracted his revenge for

having been fooled: he bound the mother's breasts to keep her from nursing. Ruth Eliaz remembers her torment. "My child is crying from hunger. She wants to be fed. I chew a tiny piece of bread and place it in my child's mouth. My breasts are full of milk. I am swollen from it up to my neck. Every day, Doctor Mengele comes to enjoy himself by looking at this spectacle. After eight days he orders me, 'Be ready tomorrow morning with your child. I shall come to get you.'" The mother understands he intends to send her and the infant for gassing.

A prisoner on the hospital staff came to Eliaz's bed that night and counseled her. "Don't despair. I will help you." After lights out, the samaritan returns with a syringe. "Give this to your child. It is a strong dose of morphine and the child will die." Eliaz protests that she could not murder her own newborn.

"You must do it! I am a doctor. Your child cannot survive. It is half-starved. It has hunger edema." It took two hours of debate and maddening self-doubt, but Eliaz finally plunged in the fatal needle.

"I am hysterical. The doctor talks to me. My child dies slowly, very close to me. I can still hear her last breath, her last groan."

Early in the morning attendants gathered up the corpses from the night and carried them off to the pile by the crematoria. Eliaz's infant was among those taken. When Mengele came he asked Eliaz, "Where is your child?" She responded that it died. "I want to see the corpse." She answered, "Died during the night."

Mengele showed no reaction except to say, "Then you are lucky once again. You leave for work with the next transport."

Mengele's behavior in this case was not only a desire to punish Eliaz, but also one of his more cruel experiments aimed at data on newborn starvation.

Sarah Nomberg-Przytyk worked at one of the women's hospitals. A female inmate-doctor initiated Nomberg-Przytyk in the intrigue surrounding a delivery. In her book, *Auschwitz,* she says: "The birth had to take place in secrecy. Nobody is supposed to know about it. In the hospital block it is impossible to conceal the birth of a child from the Germans. Our procedure now is to kill the baby after birth in such a way that the mother doesn't know about it." In spite of all of the evidence, some women stubbornly clung to the belief that they and their infant would be spared by the Nazis. "We give the baby an injection. After that the baby dies. The mother is told the baby was born dead. After dark, the baby is thrown on a pile of corpses and in that manner we save the mother."

Nomberg-Przytyk also observed a clandestine birth. Her role was to bring a bucket of cold water. "The birth started. The woman bit her lips in pain until she drew blood. But she did not utter a sound. She held my hands so tightly that afterwards I had black and blue marks. Finally the baby was born. Mancy [the physician] put her hand over his mouth so he would not cry, and then she put his head in the bucket of cold water. She was drowning him like a blind kitten. I felt faint."

" 'The baby was born dead,' " Mancy announced to the mother. Later the dead baby, wrapped in an old shirt, was placed among a stack of corpses in the yard.

Mengele justified the murders of mothers and newborns with a remarkable piece of sophistry:

"When a Jewish child is born, or when a woman comes to the camp with a child already, I don't know what to do with the child. I can't set the child free because there are no longer any Jews who live in freedom. I can't let the child stay in the camp because there are no facilities in the camp that would enable the child to develop normally. It would not be humanitarian to send a child to the ovens without permitting the mother to be there to witness the child's death. That is why I send the mother and child to the gas ovens together."

84

The Healer

With few exceptions, other SS physicians behaved much as Mengele did. Dr. Edmund Koenig, says Lingens, repeatedly complained how he agonized over ramp duty, and swallowed large amounts of liquor in order to endure his ordeal. But Koenig also killed without signs of remorse. He became fascinated with a case of noma, a gangrenous facial ulcer that proliferated at Auschwitz. Koenig applied sulfa drugs and dosed the patient with vitamins. This was benign and unusual treatment for a prisoner. On her recovery from the noma, Koenig sent the patient to her death.

Dr. Fritz Klein, a middle-aged SS doctor, occasionally evinced compassion. Offended by some inmate behavior, Irma Grese once locked 350 women in a washroom for three days without food or water. Olga Lengyel prevailed on Klein to release the captives. As an officer and physician, Klein's authority superseded Grese's. (When Grese heard that Lengyel had appealed to Klein successfully she angrily banged the butt of her pistol against Lengyel's head.)

But Klein's momentary compassion had no effect on his settled convictions. In an effort to challenge his values, Ella Lingens questioned him, not on the desirability of assimilation or even whether Jews might live separately among Germans but whether as a doctor he could claim he respected human life. Underscoring, she pointed toward the smoking chimneys. His answer: "Out of respect for human life I would remove a purulent appendix from a diseased body. The Jews are the purulent appendix in the body of Europe."

One doctor clearly distinguished himself from his colleagues —Wilhelm Hans Münch. Originally classified as unfit for military service, bacteriologist Münch was subsequently drafted into the Waffen SS. The Hygienic Institute of the SS assigned him to Auschwitz in the spring of 1943, about the same time Mengele arrived.

At the lab in Auschwitz Münch's superior revealed the true nature of Auschwitz. "That is all new to you, but it's not half so bad. We have nothing to do with people being killed here. That is none of our business. If after two weeks you don't want to stay here, you can leave." Münch says he made up his mind to quit the place as soon as possible.

His reluctance to remain grew when after his first few days in camp, Dr. Edward Wirths, the chief medical officer, ordered Münch to the ramp for selection duty. Münch refused. Wirths backed off slightly, explaining that he would not receive ramp duty often. Münch immediately went to Berlin and conferred with the head of the Hygienic Institute. Fortunately for Münch his superior sympathized with his views and telegraphed Auschwitz to excuse Münch from selections.

"One could react like a normal human being in Auschwitz only for the first few hours," says Münch years later. "Once one had spent some time there, it was impossible to react normally. In that setup everyone was sullied. You were caught and had to go along." But contrary to his own assertion, Münch did not go along. He broke rules, obtained medicines and supplies, secretly treated prisoners at great risk to himself.

Shortly after the end of World War II Münch's name appeared on the circulars naming war criminals. He was extradited from Bavaria to Poland and tried with forty others. So many camp inmates came forward to testify on Münch's behalf that the jury acquitted him.

Dr. Franz Lucas presented a murkier case. A recruit to the roughhouse SA in 1933, Lucas quit a year later "because the attitude of the members was anything but ideal." Still, he enrolled in the Nazi Party in 1937 and the SS accepted him the same year. Lucas was in the dock with twenty other officials from Auschwitz during the 1963–64 Frankfurt trials (authorities had hoped to include Mengele but he remained a fugitive).

86

The Healer

Dr. Tadeusz Szymanski of Cracow, an inmate-doctor, testified: "Through him [Lucas] we regained a belief in Germans. He procured drugs for the sick and threw away denunciatory reports. We were surprised that he subjected himself to dangers."

Another witness described Lucas as "the only doctor who treated us like human beings." And perhaps most favorable was the attitude of his fellow SS members. The court heard that on the transfer of Lucas from Auschwitz, his colleagues at the camp scorned him as "a bum and a traitor who failed to carry out his duty to the fatherland."

On the other hand, former inmates also testified Lucas appeared at the ramp and made selections. He steadfastly denied this role. A woman recounted an incident in which she was carrying her baby brother. Lucas, she says, pulled the child from her and tossed it to her mother, already burdened with another youngster. The witness said she was placed in the labor column while her mother and the two children went to their deaths.

An interested spectator to the trial was Emmi Bonhoeffer, sister-in-law of Dietrich Bonhoeffer, who along with her husband Klaus were executed for their opposition to Hitler. Emmi Bonhoeffer had formed a committee to assist those who came to Frankfurt to testify. She listened to the accusations and defenses involving Lucas and in a series of letters wrote: "I am haunted by the question, Did that doctor commit murder or did he save her [the young woman from whom he snatched the child] from death? The order to send those 750 people into the gas had not been his, as best he could he tried to avoid the murder duty. Or was it that he saved 250 he found fit to work.

"One cannot in fairness ask this question since aid or rescue had no part in it. I have described this scene to you nevertheless because it shows very clearly the dilemma in which some SS men could find themselves once they yielded just one little finger to the devil." She had made Münch's point.

The Frankfurt verdict held Lucas guilty for participation in a minimum of four selections with at least 1,000 deaths. He received a three-year sentence. However, a higher court freed him on the grounds that he failed to refuse ramp duty because he sincerely believed to do so meant dire consequences for him.

Some prisoners voluntarily aided their captors in hopes of extra food rations, an easier job, or just saving their lives. Inmate-doctors and nurses wrestled with their consciences and their sense of their calling when pressured by the SS. Some offered very little resistance to the authorities. Dr. Wladislaw Dehring, a Pole, put his skills at the disposal of the SS. But he sympathized with Nazi aims. Frank Stiffel as a hospital orderly assisted Dehring. "A Bolshevik from Lvov," snarled Dehring at his new aide. "We'll cut your testicles off." When another inmate defended Stiffel, Dehring said, "There goes Kurylowicz, defending a Jew again. When will you learn that all the Jews are Bolsheviks."

Later, after Dehring left the scene, Kurylowicz cautioned Stiffel: "Be careful, colleague. Never talk to Doctor Dehring. Who knows how many people have finished in the gas chamber because of him? You've got to make yourself invisible, as he doesn't seem to have much sympathy for you."

The SS rewarded Dehring for his collaboration. He was one of the few prisoners at Auschwitz ever released. Dehring participated in the sterilization program at the camp and reference to his activities in Leon Uris's novel *QB VII* as well as a TV show focusing on his role led to a celebrated libel suit in Great Britain.

Plaintiff Dehring argued that he performed for the SS under duress, that if he failed to cooperate he would be killed. The defense brought forward Dr. Adelaide Heutval, a French physician who adamantly refused to assist Mengele in any of his experiments. The SS did not punish her.

Dehring claimed he balked at administering fatal injections of phenol to experimental subjects. For his humane act he said the SS restricted him to quarters. A jury actually found in his favor that he had been libeled, though it awarded him only a single dollar in damages. Interesting justice.

Collaboration also did not ensure survival. An elderly Jewish physician named Samuel received his own laboratory, extra food rations, and the right to correspond with a daughter in Switzerland. One day both Dr. Samuel and his scientific research disappeared.

Few SS doctors came to places like Auschwitz ignorant of its purpose or in doubt of their own mission. When the chief of medicine for all the camps, Colonel Enno Lolling, interviewed one candidate, the naive physician promised he would make it his responsibility to minimize the number of deaths. Lolling instantly disqualified him for KZ assignment.

"To a doctor like myself," reminisces Gisella Perl, "a hospital is the most sacred place, a sanctuary set aside to provide relief from pain and suffering. Mengele made a sadistic joke out of the hospital. I studied medicine in Germany, and I know that all of the medical students there were instructed on the Hippocratic oath. I was amazed at how seriously it seemed to be taken. It was like a piece of the Bible, that document. And Mengele, he made a dirty piece of paper of it."

Mengele in a profile photograph taken around 1940.
Credit: Sipa

Carts on tracks carried the bodies of gassing victims into the batteries of ovens in the crematoria.
Credit: Wide World Photos

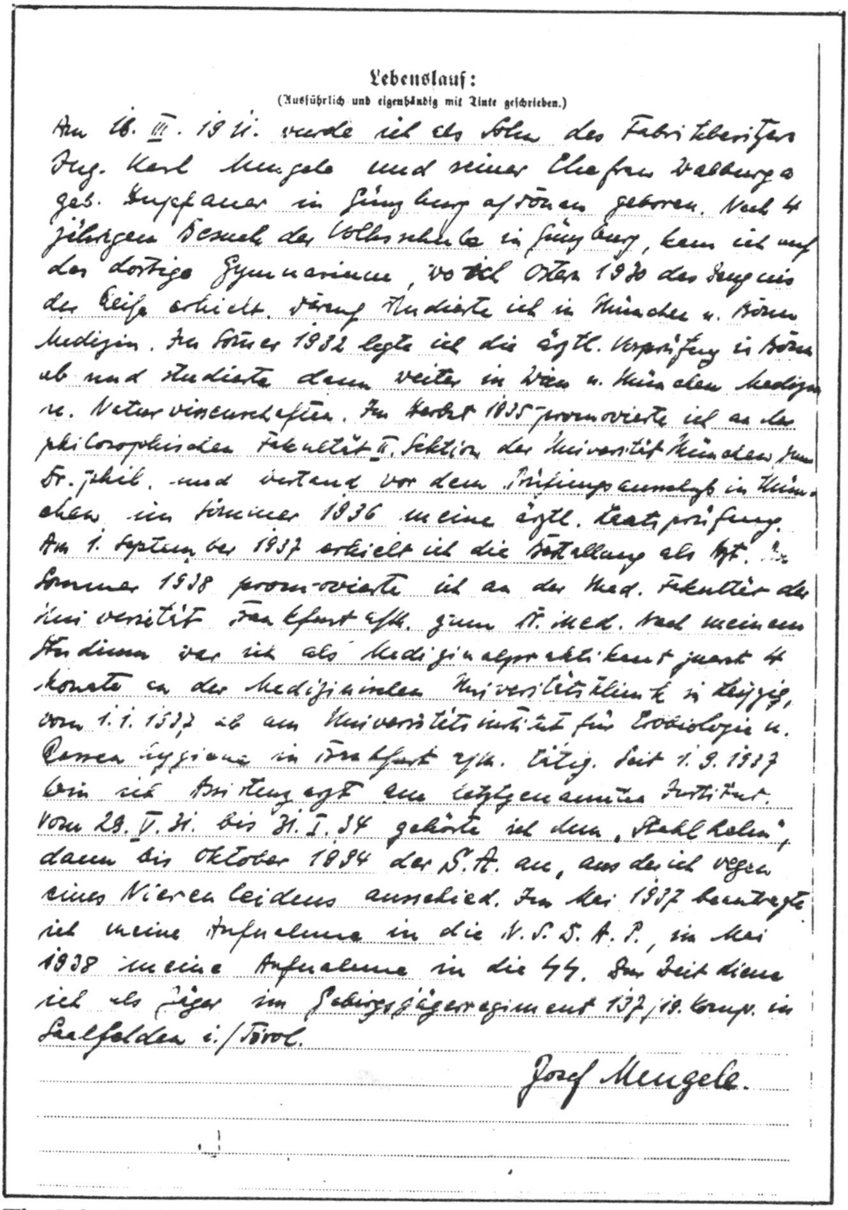

Lebenslauf:

(Ausführlich und eigenhändig mit Tinte geschrieben.)

Am 16. III. 1911 wurde ich als Sohn des Fabrikbesitzers Ing. Karl Mengele und seiner Ehefrau Walburga geb. Hupfauer in Günzburg a/Donau geboren. Nach 4 jährigem Besuch der Volksschule in Günzburg, kam ich auf das dortige Gymnasium, wo ich Ostern 1930 das Zeugnis der Reife erhielt. Darauf studierte ich in München u. Bonn Medizin. Im Sommer 1932 legte ich die ärztl. Vorprüfung in Bonn ab und studierte dann weiter in Wien u. München Medizin u. Naturwissenschaften. Im Herbst 1935 promovierte ich an der philosophischen Fakultät II. Sektion der Universität München zum Dr. phil. und bestand vor dem Prüfungsausschuß in München im Sommer 1936 meine ärztl. Staatsprüfung. Am 1. September 1937 erhielt ich die Bestallung als Arzt. Im Sommer 1938 promovierte ich an der Med. Fakultät der Universität Frankfurt a/M. zum Dr. med. Nach meinem Studium war ich als Medizinalpraktikant je 4 Monate an der Medizinischen Universitätsklinik in Leipzig, vom 1. 1. 1937 ab am Universitätsinstitut für Erbbiologie u. Rassenhygiene in Frankfurt a/M. tätig. Seit 1. 9. 1937 bin ich Assistenzarzt am letztgenannten Institut. Vom 23. V. 31. bis 31. I. 34 gehörte ich dem „Stahlhelm", dann bis Oktober 1934 der S.A. an, aus der ich wegen eines Nierenleidens ausschied. Im Mai 1937 beantragte ich meine Aufnahme in die N.S.D.A.P., im Mai 1938 meine Aufnahme in die SS. Zur Zeit diene ich als Jäger im Gebirgsjägerregiment 137/10. Komp. in Saalfelden i/Tirol.

Josef Mengele.

The *Lebenslauf*, or autobiography, was submitted to the SS by Mengele in his own handwriting. When the experts analyzed the letters and notebooks found in São Paulo in 1985, they compared them with the *Lebenslauf* and concluded that the materials found in Brazil were written by the same person.

At the Auschwitz arrival ramp SS troops, supervised by a camp physician like Mengele, separated men and women. From 10-30% would be classified as fit for slave labor. The remainder were immediately marched or driven to the gas chamber.
Credit: Lili Meier, Peter Hellman, Beate Klarsfeld Foundation

Women and children unknowingly spend the last few moments of life in a Birkenau thicket before being gassed.
Credit: Lili Meier, Peter Hellman, Beate Klarsfeld Foundation

Hyg.-bakt. Unters.-Stelle
der Waffen-SS, Südost

25. JUN. 1944

Auschwitz OS., am 29. Juni 1944.

WL 274/VII/50

Anliegend wird übersandt: .... (12-jähriges Kind)

Material: Kopf einer Leiche entnommen am ....

zu untersuchen auf Histologische Schnitte

Name, Vorname:

Dienstgrad, Einheit: siehe Anlage

Klinische Diagnose:

Anschrift der einsendenden Dienststelle: H.-Krankenbau
Zigeunerlager Auschwitz II, B II e

Bemerkungen   Der l. Lagerarzt
                                      K.L. Auschwitz II

                                      SS-Hauptsturmführer.
                                      (Stempel, Unterschrift)

Mengele signed this document which accompanied the head of a twelve-year-old boy shipped to a laboratory for further examination.

This photo taken between 1945 and 1949 suggests that the moustache was, perhaps, part of an attempt by Mengele to disguise himself.
Credit: Sipa

CHAPTER

The Scientist

MENGELE WAS DRAWN TO AUSCHWITZ by the camp's potential for research, a laboratory chock full of human guinea pigs. While getting over his wounds he had contacted his former teacher, Otmar von Verschuer. In 1942 von Verschuer had become director of the Kaiser Wilhelm Institute of Human Genetics and Eugenics in Dahlem, a suburb of Berlin.

Von Verschuer had continued to tubthump for Nazi racism, declaring in 1942, "We have laws to protect German blood and German hereditary health but not only these special laws but the entire leadership and the achievement of the present state are

91

fully conscious of the value of the concepts of heredity and race. This concept of race has now become the underlying principle of the solution of the Jewish problem."

Taking his cue from von Verschuer, Mengele had developed a strong interest in twins as a key to the secrets of heredity and race. Von Verschuer and Dr. Ferdinand Sauerbruch, the country's foremost surgeon (later to turn anti-Nazi), arranged for financing to cover Mengele's planned investigations at Auschwitz.

The choice of Auschwitz as the venue was made with good reason. SS Colonel Lolling, medical commander for the chain of KZs, told an audience in April 1943 that Auschwitz would establish "an experimental physiological, pathological station," connected to the great centers of German medicine at Heidelberg, Munich, Berlin and Königsberg. Even inmate-doctors at Auschwitz were impressed by this proposed dedication to science.

Twins research attracted Mengele. Children born from a single egg as identical twins, and to a lesser extent fraternal twins coming from two separate eggs fertilized at the same moment, offer prime opportunities to compare the effects of nature and nurture, genetic input vs experience and environment. Through twin-studies Mengele could hope to establish the supremacy of "blood" as the determinant of desirable characteristics in a human. Legitimate twins research has continued to lie at the center of much of the current controversies over intelligence, compensatory learning programs, and social betterment projects.

But Miklos Nyiszli attributed Mengele's fascination with twins to another purpose—"increased reproduction of the German race . . . pure Germans in numbers sufficient to replace the Jews, Czechs, Hungarians, Poles, all of whom were condemned to be destroyed but who for the moment lived on territories declared vital to the Third Reich." The conclusion put doubt on either Nyiszli's or Mengele's understanding of reproduction by humans; for such a purpose, a far more fruitful area of study would have been the mothers who generated the kind of eggs involved in multiple births.

In any event Mengele prowled the railroad siding during initial selection seeking his twins, and his obsession with his research may at least partly explain the excessive time he spent meeting transports. Members of the *Sonderkommando,* picking up luggage and removing corpses from the trains, aware of the doctor's passion, whispered to newcomers on the desirability of twinship. Parents hastily assembled children roughly the same age and appearance and coached them with a few answers. The children then announced themselves, *"Wir sind Zwillinge!* [We are twins]" The passwords conferred life, but an unexpectedly painful one.

Early in 1944 Marc Berkowitz, his twin sister Francesca, two other sisters and his mother, Jews from Carpathia, rode two bone-rattling nights and three long days jammed in a cattle car before the train halted. They waited in the locked car, waited nearly half a day and well into the night before the SS slid open the door.

"Nobody knew where we were," says Berkowitz. "Someone asked an SS man who answered, 'Auschwitz.' We had never heard of it but we knew there were terrible places to which they sent Jews. Actually we were on the ramp at Birkenau but no one would have recognized that name either.

"We became aware of an SS doctor. Our first impression was that he was most gentle, well meaning. I was eleven years old and pulled to the men's side, but none of us knew what the lines meant. When I looked around and saw the ambulances [used to ferry Zyklon B to the gas chambers] I became suspicious. I ran to my mother and said 'Something doesn't look kosher.' She reprimanded me for running back and forth. Then I saw a lot of well-dressed people up front and I argued that we should ask questions."

Her son's importuning shattered the mother's control. She burst out screaming: "You've taken my family, destroyed my life. [Her husband and one son had been mowed down by an Einsatzgruppen unit before the family was rounded up.] Don't separate my children. Don't kill my twins."

Two SS troopers heard the magic word, *"Zwillinge,"* and immediately shunted Berkowitz's mother and the boy to one side. "Don't move," they warned. "We're going to get the doctor."

The physician was hailed, and introduced himself: "My name is Doctor Joseph Mengele and I want to say how sorry I am about the commotion here. There is so much that has to be done. Please forgive me. May I ask your name?"

"Frau Adler," she replied. (Marc Berkowitz surrendered the Adler name after he was liberated from Auschwitz and entered the United States).

"Frau Adler," said Mengele. "You have beautiful children. Particularly your son seems so courageous. I have one question. Are they really twins?" Marc Berkowitz was blond; his sister's hair was black.

"I had only one bellyache," answered the mother.

"We were taken to one of the family camps," says Marc Berkowitz. "There were two of these. One was for Gypsies and the other for people used by the doctors in experiments. It was now two or three in the morning and we were exhausted. They placed us in an empty room. The SS men gave us some rags shaped like blankets. They smelled of urine. I could see dried human manure on them. We slept on the floor."

In the morning the family experienced its first rollcall and then breakfasted on a watery soup. No duties were required of them and for a few days they lived by themselves, eating the meager meals and showing themselves for the head count. Mengele visited several times, chatted inconsequentially for a few moments. One day he mentioned that he would like to register one of the twins. "If I ask for a volunteer, I know who it will be." He smiled. "We'll start with you." He nodded at the boy.

"My mother started to cry but Mengele assured her she had nothing to fear. An SS woman with him calmed my mother. He washed his hands with alcohol and sat on a chair. Using a battery-operated device he slowly started to put on my number. He was patient, meticulous. 'You're a little boy. You'll grow and someday you can say you were personally given your number by Doctor Joseph Mengele. You'll be famous. Just don't scratch it.' "

Apparently Mengele believed his twin research would result in a great breakthrough in genetic science, and then even those humble guinea pigs would bask in the limelight shed by the doctor.

In any case the next day Mengele inspected his handiwork and praised the boy for adhering to his instruction. "Your arm is just a little swollen. I can see the dried blood. You haven't touched it and that's fine. I like you already. I feel I can trust you."

To the family Mengele continued to display a benign countenance. They were not perturbed when he proposed to perform a few tests on the twins.

"We thought it would be some kind of study of our behavior," says Berkowitz. Brother and sister found themselves lying on adjoining tables in the laboratory. "I felt a needle digging into my back. My entire body was burning and the next thing I knew I was fighting from fainting." He also heard his sister whimpering.

"I'm sorry we have to do this," said a solicitous Mengele. "The pain will go away." Some forty years later Berkowitz still suffered from pains due to these injections. He received an endless number of probes, infusions of substances that filled his body with agony. Mengele drew a variety of fluids from him, stood him on his head for hours, dunked him in a steel vat filled with cold water. Suspension of the children upside down enabled Mengele to calculate the speed with which blood drained from the children's stomachs. The cold water tests supplied data on temperature levels as consciousness faded.

Others involved in the experiments speak of Mengele's gentle savagery. "When he took our blood, he was much gentler than all the nurses," says Hava Blau, then an eleven-year-old Czech.

Moshe Offer and his twin brother Tibi also participated in the tests. "They took X rays of us," says Moshe Offer. "Then Doctor Mengele came in. And he gave us sweets. He wore a white gown but beneath it you could see the SS trousers. He gave us candy and then gave us some horribly painful injections."

Mengele picked Tibi for special investigations. "On Tibi," says his brother," they decided to do surgery . . . frequently. After one on his spine he was paralyzed. They removed his sexual organs. After a fourth operation I did not see my brother any more."

Moshe Offer was lucky to survive his brother's death. As a rule, death of one twin called for the demise of the other. Mengele could not resist the opportunity of such a phenomenon. Explains pathologist Nyiszli, "Where under normal circumstances can one find twin brothers who die at the same place and at the same time? Twins, like everyone else, are separated by life's varying circumstances. They live far from each other and almost never die simultaneously. One may die at the age of ten, the other at fifty. Under such conditions, comparative dissection is impossible."

Nyiszli learned that at Auschwitz Mengele eliminated "life's varying circumstances." One day he was handed files on a pair of twin boys. A female *Sonderkommando* crew delivered a single casket containing a set of two-year-old twin boys. Nyiszli pored over the X rays, the detailed clinical reports on the children. It all seemed very thorough. He began his autopsies, beginning with the tiny hearts. He removed one, inspected it thoroughly. He discovered a tiny puncture made with a hypodermic needle. Further investigation revealed the odor of chloroform around a mass of coagulated blood. Nyiszli realized an injection of chloroform directly into the heart had killed the child. The cause of death in the twin was the same. The pair had been killed solely for the anatomical data available on simultaneous death.

Only then did the pathologist understand why the dossiers accompanying the pathetic victims bore no mention of the causes of death. Later Mengele instructed his subordinate to fill in the cause according to his own judgment and discretion. Nyiszli knew better than to certify the children had been murdered.

Where a death certificate was deemed appropriate at Auschwitz, KZ doctors usually inscribed "sudden onset of respiratory disease," or the less specific "heart failure." Those gassed on arrival did not require a fictitious report. They officially ceased to have existed the moment the Nazis boarded them on transports bound for Auschwitz.

On the day Nyiszli dissected the murdered two-year-olds he received three more sets deceased at the same time, and he discovered the basic reason these particular sets of twins were killed was on account of their eyes. In six of the eight children one eye was brown, the other blue. Heterochromes are an unremarkable oddity among non-twins, but the condition rarely occurs among twins.

The heterochromes were of special interest to Mengele's *éminece grise,* Otmar von Verschuer at the Kaiser Wilhelm Institute. Pathologist Nyiszli routinely saved organs of possible scientific value for examination by Mengele. "Those which might interest the Institute at Berlin–Dahlem were preserved in alcohol. These

97

parts were specially packed to be sent through the mails. Stamped, 'War Material—Urgent,' they received top priority in transit." (How an embattled Wehrmacht commander fighting for his life outside Stalingrad might have reacted to the designation needs little speculation.)

Nyiszli dispatched a stream of parcels, and the Kaiser Wilhelm Institute responded with precise reports on findings from its laboratories. Returns from the institute included instructions which mostly consisted of requisitions for more specimens. In addition to various organs and other tissue, Mengele arranged for a stream of blood samples to be sent to his mentor von Verschuer. A subordinate of von Verschuer's, a Dr. Karin Magnussen, was assigned to study the anomaly of heterochromes in twins, and her work became part of a joint investigation at Auschwitz and the institute into eye pigmentation. And all in the service of the higher calling of helping the Third Reich to populate the world with blond, blue-eyed Aryans.

A similar motive applied to other features. Mengele turned his hand to hair color, annointing scalps of his subjects with different substances, and mostly producing pain rather than any insight into the mechanism that actually determines hair color and shade. It seems likely that his absorption with physical coloration was also due to his own Beppo appearance.

The eye studies, apart from the terrible anguish created, produced some of the more gruesome visible consequences. Vera Kriegel, another twin, describes how she was taken into a laboratory where across an entire wall she saw scores of human eyes "pinned like butterflies." Inmate-doctor Jancu Vexler came on a similar scene: "In June 1943 I arrived at the Gypsy camp— Birkenau. I saw a wooden table. It was full of eyes. Each one had been marked with a number and a letter. The color of the eyes ranged from blue-yellow to a brilliant blue to violet, green and gray."

The Scientist

American psychiatrist Robert Jay Lifton, who is researching the role of doctors during the Third Reich, is less inclined to believe Mengele seriously thought he could change genetic patterns through chemical intervention. Instead, Lifton feels Mengele concentrated on the more prosaic line of compiling measurements of human anatomy, basically standard anthropological science. "His method was descriptive, the amassing of data, and I know no evidence that he had any significantly original scientific ideas." That does not confront or explain the painful chemical substances employed on the human guinea pigs. *That* was pure Mengele.

The collection of pieces of anatomy was standard practice in Auschwitz. *Sonderkommando* Filip Müller watched doctors in the camp scavenge like "cattle dealers" among the remains of the dead. Erne Spiegel, at twenty-nine the oldest twin to serve as a subject for the doctor, saw a bathtub filled with an unknown fluid. Into it Mengele put bodies of Jewish dwarfs, mongoloids and twins "so that their flesh would fall off and he could view their skeletons."

Physical exotics especially titillated the intrepid genetic researcher intent on proving the superiority of one race over another. And so Mengele focused on dwarfs and other genetic anomalies. Such focus led to an especially gruesome experience for Miklos Nyiszli. Mengele met a transport from the Polish Lodz ghetto one day in 1944. Created in 1939, it was the last ghetto to be liquidated. After five years of oppression and deprivation, those who arrived at Auschwitz were already at or nearing the Mussulman condition. Nyiszli estimates that as many as 95 percent went immediately for gassing.

But as Mengele was performing his selection this day he came on a father and son—the parent, about fifty, seemed hunchbacked; the fifteen-year-old offspring appeared to have a deformed right foot. Mengele plucked them from the line, and SS men guided them to Nyiszli. The pathologist was instructed to do a complete examination. He learned that the father, a wholesaler of cloth, had traveled widely, taking his son along to see specialists for treatment of the deformed leg. Skillful surgery and a special shoe now enabled the boy to walk without a limp. The father's bent back was not a congenital defect but a result of a rickettsial infection.

Nyiszli fed them, knowing they were doomed. Indeed, an SS sergeant named Mussfeld relieved Nyiszli of their custody following the examination and marched them off to a furnace room, from which Nyiszli heard two pistol shots. Summoned, he found the bodies on the cement floor, blood dripping from their neck wounds.

The pathologist was then forced to perform his autopsy on the still warm corpses. "The dissection revealed nothing more than I had previously ascertained," he said, but Mengele wanted the bodies as further evidence of physical degeneracy among the Jews—even though the deformities had no genetic roots whatsoever. In his haste to send the specimens to Berlin–Dahlem, Mengele rejected the usual means of preparing skeletons and instructed Nyiszli to use the quickest method—boiling the bodies in water until the flesh could be easily stripped away.

Sergeant Mussfeld produced large vats and under Nyiszli's direction placed the bodies in the casks and lit a fire underneath. After about five hours the fires were extinguished and the remains allowed to cool. Nyiszli was about other business when an associate rushed to him. "Doctor, hurry, the Poles are eating the meat in the vats."

A group of Polish masons working in the yard had finished their assignment. Scrounging for food, they had come on the simmering casks and assumed a *Sonderkommando* unit had gotten some precious meat for them. When Nyiszli told them the truth of the matter, the Poles were "sick, horrified, paralyzed."

The Scientist

One of the few existing documents that cover Mengele's time at Auschwitz is a paper he signed to accompany the head of a twelve-year-old Gypsy boy. On several occasions the head of a patient with noma was removed and sent to the Kaiser Wilhelm Institute.

The Gypsy camp furnished Mengele not only with his hetero-chromes but also with another favorite item—dwarfs. He was ecstatic when he discovered a family of ten that included seven dwarfs. "Now I have twenty years of material to study," is his often quoted exclamation.

Sarah Nomberg-Przytyk was in the infirmary when Mengele came for a closer look at the tiny people, who had managed to bring along their own small chairs and table. The women had powdered themselves in honor of his visit. Nomberg-Przytyk remembers them effusively praising the man they believed their benefactor. "How beautiful he is, how kind. How fortunate that he became our protector. How good of him to see if we have everything."

All stood at attention as the SS entourage led by Mengele entered. One of the dwarfs stepped forward and knelt to hug the doctor's shiny boots. "You are so kind, so gorgeous. God should reward you."

Mengele shook his boot, flinging her to the floor, then addressed the mother of several dwarfs, herself normal size. "Tell me how you lived with your midget." The old woman flushed, but when commanded to speak talked only of her husband's career in the circus.

"Don't tell me about that, only about how you slept with him." Nomberg-Przytyk describes Mengele as "salivating."

Mengele left this scene in an ill humor after being denied the intimate details. A few days later he took the three-year-old son of one of the tiny women to his examining room. By nightfall the child was dead. One of the dwarf men was tricked by guards into slipping between the wires separating compounds. An SS trooper shot him dead. The doctor was not to be denied; one way or another he got satisfaction.

The surviving dwarfs underwent the pain and humiliations of Mengele's tests. Dentists pulled healthy teeth, attendants siphoned blood weekly. The wombs of the women were invaded with drugs, and their bodies exposed to repeated X rays. As a final insult and exercise in degradation they were forced to perform nude before an audience of SS personnel.

Olga Lengyel summarizes Mengele as scientist: "His experiments were carried out in abnormal fashion. When he made blood transfusions he purposely used incorrect blood types. He did whatever pleased him and conducted his experiments like a rank amateur. He would inject substances and then ignore the results. He was not a savant. His was the mania of a collector." A traditional Germanic trait gone wild.

Layman Berkowitz echoes her appraisal: "Mengele had a zoo, a private zoo. Fifty percent of it was for real study, physical properties of humans, genetics, the effects of chemicals, pharmaceuticals, surgical procedures, ways to deal with people under certain conditions. But the other fifty percent was to supply victims for murder."

To his subordinate Nyiszli, Mengele seemed devoted to his "work," although Nyiszli also referred to it as "pseudo science." He recalled how the SS doctor scolded him for staining the cover of a report. "How can you be so careless with these files which I have compiled with so much love?"

Nyiszli further describes Mengele as "obsessed with the belief that he had been chosen to discover the cause of multiple births, here, within these bloodstained walls, where he sat hunched for hours at a time over his microscopes."

It is a picture to conjure with.

Caduceus
and Swastika

WITH THE BACKING of such luminaries of German science as Otmar von Verschuer and Ferdinand Sauerbruch, the Auschwitz Angel of Death could not be excused or written off as some Dr. Frankenstein functioning on his own in a distant corner of the Third Reich. Indeed, far from being a loose cannon, Mengele was considered a respectable member of a system altogether acceptable to the communities of German science and medicine.

The first and most persuasive precedent for his actions was the euthanasia campaign of 1939–40, and much of the impetus for the program came from educators, economists and, above all, physicians.

Robert Jay Lifton cites a 1920 German book, *The Release of (Permission For) the Destruction of Life Unworthy of Life.* The authors were distinguished in their fields—Karl Binding was a jurist and Alfred Hoche an esteemed psychiatrist. The malignant theme was in the title—"Life unworthy of life." At a 1931 convention Bavarian psychiatrists casually discussed sterilization and euthanasia as acceptable ways to deal with chronic mental illness, and films of the period favorably portrayed "mercy killing." The practice of euthanasia was mentioned in an official German medical journal, as pointed out by Dr. Leo Alexander, a consultant to the Chief Counsel for War Crimes, Nuremberg, in the U.S.-occupied zone of Germany.

The young were subtly indoctrinated by high school mathematics tests that presented as practical problems for students comparisons of the costs for care and rehabilitation of the perenially sick and handicapped with the number of housing units that could be built, the amount of marriage loans that might be available for the same money. Education was also twisted to encourage the military spirit. A typical problem: calculate how many gas bombs are required to poison a city of 50,000 people who live in an area of four square kilometers.

Euthanasia had strong support from economists who detailed the high cost of maintaining deaf mutes, the crippled, the mentally ill, or mentally defective. The coming of the war added to euthanasia's appeal. Apart from the economic drain, authorities now predicted an acute shortage of medical personnel and hospital beds to care for the expected casualties among troops and civilians. The director of the Egglfing-Haar Asylum near Munich put it this way: "These days, when our worthy men must make the hard sacrifice of blood and life, teach us impressively that it is not possible on economic grounds to continue operating the installations of living corpses. The conception is unbearable for me that, while the best young blood lose their lives at the front, the tainted asocial and unquestionably antisocial in the institutions have a guaranteed existence."

Backed, indeed underwritten, by certain respectables of economics and psychology, Hitler had a solid, even *respectable* base early on for the extermination of a large class of people—*not* Jews, but German citizens. To carry out the program, he wrote: "Reichsleiter Bouhler [director of his personal chancellery] and Dr. Brandt [director of health and sanitation for the Third Reich] are charged with the responsibility of expanding the authority of certain officially appointed doctors, so that after a critical diagnosis incurable persons may be granted a mercy death."

Of course the machinery for the murder of those considered incorrigibly damaged, was swathed in euphemism. A "Realms Work Committee of Institutions for Cure and Care" gathered questionnaires directed to state institutions about their patients. A "Realms Committee for Scientific Approach to Severe Illness Due to Heredity and Constitution" decided which died. The "Charitable Transport Company for the Sick" carted off the hapless to their deaths at designated sites. An institution at Grafeneck, near Württemberg, became the choice site for the designated killings. First the resident, physically handicapped children were disposed of through drugs in their food and injections. Doctors at other sanitoria then submitted questionnaires about their charges to the committee led by Brandt and Bouhler. Those judged "incurables" were shipped to Grafeneck and eventually several other places. Operations were secret; the selection committee did not inform hospitals who transferred patients what had happened to their patients. If pressed the committee explained that it hoped to employ radical new treatments. By 1940 the euthanasia program had been expanded to cover adults. Doctors, nurses, and hospital administrators began to grasp the nature of the "new treatments." But instead of protesting, many seized the opportunity to rid themselves of most troublesome patients.

Eventually overdoses of drugs and poisonous injections failed to accommodate the numbers consigned to death at the killing center, and so the Wurttemberg criminal police commissioner, Christian Wirth (who would go on to head the Belzec Concentration Camp) built a shed with fake shower heads. Coal gas or carbon monoxide fumes piped into the building suffocated the victims locked inside. A crematorium consumed the bodies. The procedures of Mengele's Auschwitz carried on the tradition.

At first the families of the murdered did not know what was happening. Next of kin in each case received an official notice stating that their son, daughter, husband, father, mother or wife had died of some acute disease, even though in numerous instances he or she had seemed in good health on the last visit. Bureaucratic bungles, in their time-dishonored fashion, eventually helped enlighten. In one instance a family was informed that their relative had died of acute appendicitis—his appendix had been removed ten years earlier. Another family received two separate certificates attesting that their loved one had died in two different places of two different diseases.

Bishop Wurm, head of the Lutheran Church for the area, becoming aware of what went on at Grafeneck, wrote a letter of protest to Wilhelm Frick, minister of the interior. "What conclusions will the younger generation draw when it realizes that human life is no longer sacred to the state? Cannot every outrage be excused on the grounds that the elimination of another was of advantage to the person concerned? There can be no stopping once one starts down this decline. God does not permit people to mock Him. Either the National Socialist State must recognize the limits which God has laid down, or it will favor a moral decline and carry the state down with it." Frick ignored the prophetic letter.

The mass murders did accomplish their purpose; they depleted the institutions housing the mentally and physically handicapped. Even veterans of World War I lost their lives for the New Order. Other bishops, including Count von Galen of Münster, voiced objections: "Citizens of Münster. Wounded soldiers are being killed recklessly since they are of no more productive use to the state. Mother, your boy will be killed too if he comes back home from the front, crippled."

At the time even Himmler retreated in the face of the mounting criticism: ". . . there is great unrest in the Wurttemberg mountains on account of the Grafeneck Institution. The people know the gray SS bus and think they know what happens in the crematory with its ever smoking chimney. What does happen there is a secret and yet it is a secret no longer. The public temper is ugly and in my opinion there is nothing to do but stop using this particular institution."

Stop using the institution, but not a word about stopping what went on there.

Eventually the opposition did force cancellation of the programs—after some 100,000 people had been destroyed. In the process, however, the Nazis had developed a system and an awareness of the logistics required for extermination projects directed against large numbers of people. The medical profession had shown the Nazis a willingness to cooperate. Wirth and others had pioneered in the technology of speedy mass extermination, and the Nazis had learned the need for secrecy and the danger of offending over-sensitive Christian clergymen. The lesson of Grafeneck was well learned: most of the mass murder camps that followed, including Auschwitz, were located in Poland, well removed from German territory.

The euthanasia project also linked up with medical research.

A neuropathologist named Hallervorden approached the managers of the euthanasia operations in this fashion: "If you are going to kill all these people, at least take the brains out so that the material can be utilized." In his deposition before a war crimes interrogator, Hallervorden added, "They asked me, 'How many can you examine?' And so I told them an unlimited number—the more the better!" The authorities supplied him 500 brains from the killing centers. The Charitable Transport Company for the Sick delivered the organs in batches of 150 to 250. Said Hallervorden, "There was wonderful material among those brains, beautiful mental defectives, malformations and early infantile diseases. I accepted those brains of course. Where they came from and how they came to me was really none of my business." His defense was typical of that offered by German doctors and scientists after the war, and echoed that of the major Nazi criminals as well, including Adolf Eichmann. Soldiers of the state all, not responsible for their actions.

The Nazi program in no sense equated with so-called mercy-killing, the purpose of which is to end the misery for the patient; the German politicians and doctors only desired to rid the New Order of those known as "useless eaters." The Third Reich also exported euthanasia to its conquered lands, regardless of whether their people and governments thought differently about "useless eaters."

The special significance of all this, of course, is that the extermination of the Jews was actually, to the Germans, a logical extension of the scientifically and economically accredited euthanasia creed. Women, children, old people, the sick and feeble, those unable to serve at least as slave labor were "useless eaters," an intolerable drain on the resources of the Third Reich.

From economics to national health—the rhetoric of the Third Reich hammered away at the Jews as "vermin," "pestilence," "insects"—all enemies of good health. As Ella Lingens noted, SS physician Fritz Klein used a medical simile to justify murder of Jews.

Hitler insisted the medical community underpin his plans for uplifting the race. In *Mein Kampf* he wrote, "The right of personal freedom recedes before the right to preserve the race. There must be no half measures. It is a half measure to let incurably sick people steadily contaminate the remaining healthy ones. This is in keeping with the humanitarianism which, to avoid hurting one individual, lets a hundred others perish. If necessary, the incurably sick will be pitilessly segregated—a barbaric measure for the unfortunate who is struck by it, but a blessing for his fellow men and posterity." And so Hitler stigmatized the chronically or seriously ill as Typhoid Marys, carriers of contagion, of defective genes.

The *Mein Kampf* message became deed with a 1933 decree: "Anyone who is suffering from a hereditary disease can be sterilized by a surgical operation." In theory, court procedures provided an appeal by a victim but due process was seldom invoked, and the good physicians of the Reich went along with the statute.

In 1937, after the occupation of the Rhineland, Hitler ordered the secret sterilization of what were known as Rhineland bastards, children sired by French and Belgian troops. Doctors, nurses, and hospitals complied without protest.

Medicine under the Third Reich was skewed by the primitive attitudes of the government chiefs, who placed credence in folk medicine and unscientific chimeras.

Karl Gebhardt, clinical chief of the SS, who knew well the attitudes of his Nazi superiors, told an investigator before his trial as a war criminal: "These people had little regard for scientific medicine, and they were all attracted by natural medicine. They had a childish enthusiasm. All sorts of popular drugs which were not approved by the medical profession, allegedly because we did not understand them or were too conceited or were financially interested in the suppression of them, were used experimentally in concentration camps. The sources of these experiments was Himmler's conception of medicine as pure mysticism." Notably, the Führer himself relied on the quack Theodor Morell as his personal doctor. Morell dosed him with nostrums that weakened him and probably contributed to his emotional instability toward the end of his life.

The regime also endowed several professorial chairs at universities for specialists in herb cures. A medical officer who treated tuberculosis with pendulums was protected after an attempt to discharge him. Chicken farmer Himmler proposed that frostbite cases be cured with rubbings of dog fat. Morell offered the sweat of horses as sure protection against typhus.

At Mecklenburg the Nazis established the Führer's School for German Physicians. Here Nazi racial theory was integrated into the normal medical training. (Mengele and many of his contemporaries had already joined the medical community by the time the Mecklenburg institution had become operational.) Himmler created the Institute for Research and Study of Heredity as well as an Ancestral Heritage Institute with jurisdiction over medical experiments.

The use of humans as guinea pigs for medical experimentation dated well back in history. For terrible example, in 1559 King Henry II of England, on a Paris sojourn, was amusing himself in martial sports. A lance accidentally pierced his visor and one of his eyes. His physicians, desperate to treat him, cut the heads off four healthy criminals and investigated the anatomy that surrounded the eye. The experiments failed; the king died. More recently the U.S. Army, at the turn of the twentieth century, employed volunteers, including doctors, to test the notion that yellow fever was spread by mosquitos. But at least the subjects offered themselves voluntarily.

The darker side to investigations using humans has been when the test subjects were unaware of their role.

For the most part, however, modern medicine has depended upon lower forms of life for research. But the Nazis had managed to separate groups of humans, designating Jews, Gypsies and Slavs as lower forms of existence. And Hitler had given his approval for medical experiments: "The criminals also are here to serve their Fatherland."

The Germans began programs testing humans in 1939–40 with observations of the effects of phosgene and mustard gas on 220 prisoners, tests conducted by a Dr. August Hirt under the auspices of Himmler's Institute for Research and Heredity. A witness to the research said, "The subjects suffered such appalling pain, one could hardly bear to be near them." One of the earliest to capitalize on the availability of concentration camp inmates was a Luftwaffe doctor, Sigmund Rascher, also a friend of Himmler. Rascher wrote to the SS chief about the lack of knowledge about the effect of high-altitude flights. He noted that experiments in this field were so dangerous that none of the Luftwaffe pilots appeared willing to volunteer. "Can you make available two or three professional criminals for these experiments?" asked Rascher, adding that he might be willing to accept as substitutes some of the feebleminded, who would then be eliminated through the euthanasia program.

Himmler enthusiastically endorsed Rascher's proposal. The SS leader had a childlike delight in "innovative" projects, and at Dachau opened the First Experimental Station of the Luftwaffe. Rascher was given a free hand. For the high-altitude experiments he placed men inside a pressure chamber from which pumps removed increasing amounts of oxygen. In some tests lungs ruptured. An inmate-assistant said, "Some experiments gave men such pressure in their heads that they would go mad and pull out their hair in an effort to relieve the pressure. They would tear their heads and faces with their fingers and nails in an attempt to maim themselves in their madness." Such "research" resulted in, among other things, making the air-pressure chamber a vehicle for executions.

Rascher also expanded his research to the effects of exposure to extreme cold, applicable to fliers downed in the sea. The First Experimental Station of the Luftwaffe outfitted prisoners in flying garb, summer and winter style, complete with lifejacket, and immersed them in tanks of ice-chilled water. During the winter at Dachau the involuntary participants spent nights outdoors in sub-zero temperatures. Rascher, taking the hands-on approach, ordered some specimens sprayed with water that then froze. In one of his more bizarre adventures, he investigated the revival of "severely chilled persons" through "animal warmth." After an unconscious man had been pulled from the icy water (body temperature of 25 or 26 Centigrade; 77 to 80 degrees Fahrenheit) he was placed between the bodies of two prostitutes confined at Dachau. Himmler personally approved of the study, at least suggesting the sexual problems of the SS chief. Altogether, Rascher employed about 300 prisoners for his studies—only two surviving the experiments, and they were diagnosed as "mental cases" and promptly put to death.

So impressed was Himmler by Rascher's work that he sought to transfer him from the Luftwaffe to the SS. In a letter to the Air Force Field Marshal Erhard Milch, Himmler said: "This research which deals with the reaction of the human organism at great heights, as well as with manifestations caused by prolonged chilling of the human body in cold water, and similar problems which are of vital importance to the Air Force, in particular can be performed by us with particular efficiency because I personally assumed the responsibility for supplying asocial individuals and criminals who only deserve to die, from concentration camps for these experiments . . . In the Christian medical circles the standpoint is being taken that it goes without saying that a young German aviator should be allowed to risk his life but that the life of a criminal is too sacred for this purpose, and one should not stain oneself with this guilt. I have personally inspected the experiments and have—I can say this without exaggeration—participated in every phase of this scientific work in a helpful and inspiring manner . . . It will take at least another ten years until we can get such narrowmindedness out of our people. But this should not affect the research work." Himmler's concern with "narrowmindedness" and conflicts with Christian doctors seems to have been misplaced, since hundreds of physicians, including Mengele with his Catholic background, never flinched from the "research work."

Chief SS clinician Gebhardt, an orthopedic surgeon whose father had been Himmler's personal doctor, dismissed Rascher's work as "useless" and "completely unscientific." But while he denigrated the Luftwaffe doctor's work, Gebhardt showed no hesitation about the use of human guinea pigs. In 1943 he announced that he assumed "full human, surgical and political responsibility for the experiments" being conducted at KZs. At his hospital in Hohenlychen, Gebhardt, with associates Dr. Fritz Fisher and Dr. Ludwig Stumpfegger, grafted shoulders, arms and legs amputated from live, healthy female prisoners at Ravensbruck onto other human guinea pigs. Such heteroplastic transplantation some forty years later would still be futile, but even in the 1940s enough was known of the neurological connection problems and the rejection of foreign tissue to have dissuaded even the most audacious among responsible scientists.

Undaunted by failures, Rascher proceeded to interest himself in treatment of battlefield wounds. To test various compounds prisoners were shot, limbs amputated, and other combat injuries replicated. Rascher also held what he called "leather inspections" in which he would examine naked candidates for experiments. If he grabbed one by the buttocks or thighs and adjudged him "good," it meant that after the man died the corpse was to be skinned. For along with his laboratory Rascher operated a kind of tannery where human skins were chemically treated, dried and then manufactured into gloves, saddles, riding clothes, slippers, and handbags. Tattooed pelts were especially prized. When the leather workers mentioned a shortage of raw materials, Rascher would respond, "All right, you will get bodies," and twenty or thirty new corpses would be produced. Bullets or blows to the head avoided skin blemishes.

Rascher did eventually fall out of favor, but not because other doctors or officials faulted him for his use of humans as test specimens or for his sadistic obsessions. He and his wife tried to fool Himmler into believing that they had discovered a technique whereby even women of advanced age could conceive. (They secretly adopted three babies taken from Poland and claimed they were the biological parents). When Himmler learned of this deceit he had the Raschers arrested and subsequently executed.

Rascher was only one of many German physicians who engaged in experiments on camp inmates. Dr. Claus Schilling, an aged specialist in tropical medicine, emerged from retirement under orders from Himmler to investigate malaria at Dachau. Bites from bacteria-bearing mosquitos and direct injection of the organisms infected subjects, after which Schilling studied the effectiveness of various antimalarial preparations. From thirty to forty of the 1,200 he infected died of malaria. Many others became so weak that they succumbed to other diseases common to the KZ population.

Inmates also supplied fodder for testing potential weapons. Dr. Ding Schuler, medical chief at Buchenwald found not even to have a medical degree, and critic Gebhardt observed the results of poison bullets: ". . . aconite nitrate bullets were used on five persons who had been sentenced to death . . . each subject . . . received one shot in the upper part of the left thigh while in a horizontal position. In the case of two persons the bullets passed clean through the upper part of the thigh. Even later no effect from the poison could be seen. These two subjects were therefore rejected. The symptoms shown were surprisingly the same. After 20 to 25 minutes, a disturbance of the motor nerves and a light flow of saliva began . . . after 40 to 44 minutes a strong flow of saliva appeared. The poisoned persons swallowed frequently; later flow of saliva is so strong that it can no longer be controlled by swallowing. Foamy saliva flows from the mouth. Then a sensation of choking and vomiting starts . . . One of the poisoned persons tried in vain to vomit . . . Later the disturbances of the motor nerves increased so much that the persons threw themselves up and down, rolled their eyes and made aimless movements with their hands and arms. At last the disturbance subsided, the pupils were enlarged to the maximum, the condemned lay still. Rectal cramps and loss of urine was observed in one of them. Death occurred in 121, 123 and 129 minutes after they were shot."

Other experiments directly related to the military were carried out elsewhere. Karl Gebhardt, so scornful of Rascher's science, exhibited no signs of softness in his own experiments. Although the sulfa drugs actually had been discovered in Germany, the Nazis, unlike the Allies, had failed to make them part of the medical armamentarium. So while enemy troops carried sulfa packets to ward off infection, the German troops remained vulnerable to infection and gangrene.

Ordered to determine the effectiveness of sulfa preparations, Gebhardt began to experiment at Ravensbruck. Combat wounds were simulated in healthy young female inmates. The doctors working with Gebhardt sliced open legs, inserted foreign objects such as wood shavings, dirt, glass and bacterial

115

organisms—streptococci, staphylococci. Some of the festering injuries were then treated with various drugs, including sulfa, as a control some injuries were permitted to degenerate into fatal gangrene. The project was stimulated after Reinhard Heydrich, the Gestapo chief, succumbed to the wounds received during an assassination attempt at Lidice, Czechoslovakia. Unfortunately for German soldiers, it was too late in the game to create a mass production system for sulfa.

Another series of investigations was aimed at preventing German soldiers from malingering—"goldbricking," as the American GI's called it. A significant number of the troops on the Eastern front had removed themselves from combat with surreptitious injections of benzine and other nonlethal chemicals. In Block 28 at Auschwitz, Dr. Fritz Klein, assisted by inmate-doctors, assembled thirty healthy Jewish boys. Dr. Geza Mansfeld, a prisoner and professor of pharmacology and experimental pathology from the University of Pecs in Hungary, wangled his way into the room and witnessed subcutaneous injections of benzine and naphtha into the boys. Mansfeld advised an inmate-doctor involved in the project that not only were the effects of the chemicals on humans known but that such experiments could be performed on animals. Klein went ahead with introducing the substances deep in both of each subject's legs. Predictably, within a week large abcesses formed, pus was extracted and shipped to the Institute for Histology at Breslau, clearly indicating once again the widespread involvement of German mainstream medicine in the concentration camp experiments. The research produced no solution to the problem, but did serve to reduce the prisoner population—all the victims went to the gas chamber.

Among the more atrocious chapters in the annals of concentration camp medicine was the research on race and heredity. Under the auspices of the Ancestral Heritage Society headed by

116

Himmler aide Wolfram Sievers, Professor August Hirt at the University of Strasbourg organized a collection of skulls and skeletons. Hirt then compiled scientific measurements of the remains of "79 Jews, 30 Jewesses, 4 Asiatics and 2 Poles." Ironically, Mengele's presumed death was based heavily on skull measurements. Hirt requisitioned specimens from a Himmler assistant, making very specific his needs: "Of the Jewish race, however, only a very few specimens of skulls are available. The war in the East now presents us with the opportunity to overcome this deficiency. By procuring the skulls of the Jewish–Bolshevik commisars, who represent the prototype of the repulsive but characteristic subhuman, we have the chance now to obtain scientific material." To ensure the integrity of his studies, Hirt insisted on having the heads of the specimens measured while they were still alive. "Following the subsequently induced deaths of the Jews," said Hirt, "whose heads should not be damaged, the physician will sever the head from the body and will forward it . . . in a hermetically sealed tin can."

Hirt also interested himself in intravital microscopy, the study of living cells in organs—which, stripped of the fancy language and euphemisms, meant in his case, removing vital organs from *living* humans.

Others also capitalized on the new opportunities for "research." The young SS Untersturmführer Dr. Edmund Koenig, for example, was moved to satisfy his curiosity about the effects of electric shock on the brains of young Jews at Auschwitz. Ernest Michel, a prisoner in the camp in the spring of 1943, had been injured while working at the I.G. Farben complex. As a calligraphy student, Michel had been reassigned to the duties of clerk. One day he and a male nurse reported for special assignment, guiding some young women from trucks to the hospital barracks. Six to eight prisoners, confused, agitated, and fearful of the immediate future, had arrived only a day before from

Hungary. Michel spoke with one, a beautiful teenager who seemed in control in spite of her anxiety. Michel and his companion brought the young women to a room in the hospital complex. Along with Koenig, Mengele was on hand. An hour later Michel returned to retrieve the patients. "In the room where the 'medical services' were performed, one woman was still connected to an electrical machine, presumably for electroshock experimentation. We had already been instructed to have a stretcher ready to carry the women out. We found two of them dead, one the Hungarian girl. Two obviously were in a coma. The others were breathing hard and irregularly. None was conscious. I noticed that the teeth of those still alive were clenched and that wads of paper had been placed in their mouths."

Koenig also amputated hands and legs where simple medical therapy would have cured the problem. Drs. Tilo and Fischer performed appendectomies, hernia, and gynecological operations even where no symptoms appeared. SS Hauptsturmführer Entress strove to perfect his technique in stomach surgery by doing major operations ordinarily prescribed for stomach cancer on patients who were not sick. His subjects died from the operations or survived to be sent to the gas chambers.

To cleanse the world of Jews and control population growth among non-Aryans the theoreticians and scientists of the Third Reich united in an effort to discover a fast, inexpensive way to sterilize people. Primary targets were the *"Mischlinge,"* individuals with a Jew as one parent, and the slave labor population.

Dr. Horst Schumann, a principal figure in the euthanasia program, proposed to bombard male Jews and others with high doses of X rays that would destroy their ability to manufacture live sperm. Viktor Brack, chief administrator of Hitler's chancellery, was Schumann's sponsor. Brack advised Himmler that a single X-ray installation could sterilize 150 to 300 a day. With twenty such machines in place, an assembly line could eliminate the reproductive powers of three or four thousand men daily. The devices were to be concealed, so that the X-rays silently assaulted the man while he sat at a desk filling out some papers. In practice the machines mostly produced horrible burns. Inmate-doctors who covered the wards treating the test specimens saw victims with grotesque discolorations of their genitalia. Joseph Mengele participated in these X-ray trials, but for his experiments he focused on the effects on women, using a group of Polish nuns.

Another approach to sterilization was surgical castration. The premium put on speed made operations to remove testicles into actually timed contests. The Nazis found several inmate-doctors willing to cooperate. Wladislaw Dehring, the Pole who worked under the direction of Horst Schumann, wielded a scalpel on behalf of his captors. Indeed, Dehring took great pride in his speedy technique, demonstrating that castration could be accomplished within ten minutes while using a local anesthetic. He also saved time by not sterilizing his instruments or washing his hands after each operation.

At first the men brought to the operating room did not realize what they were in for. Later, when word spread, many threw themselves on the electrified fence rather than submit to the operations.

A Soviet prisoner who escaped from one group scheduled for castration told Sim Kessel, a French Jew, of being taken with ten or twelve others to "the experimental biology section" run by Joseph Mengele. The Russian heard agonized screams of pain and jumped out of a window to escape . . . his companions had been desexed without an anesthetic.

The SS also irradiated women, making them barren. Olga Lengyel cared for young women with grotesque burns in the genital area. Dehring also helped out the SS by removing damaged ovaries for microscopic inspection.

Civilian Dr. Karl Clauberg, a professor of gynecology in East Prussia and an author of a number of scientific books and treatises, furnished not only a laboratory for research but a profit center as well. He struck a deal with I.G. Farbenindustrie to test their pharmaceuticals on inmates of Auschwitz, in exchange for which the company agreed to pay him goodly sums of money for each project. Clauberg theorized that a substance called caladium sequinum could sterilize both sexes and contracted to buy 150 women from the SS. The Nazis delivered a group of Jewish women from Holland. They were led off a few minutes after debarking from the train, surrounded by whip-wielding guards and snapping dogs. Some were pregnant, some young, some beyond the age of childbirth. Before the amused SS troopers, the candidates were forcibly undressed, their heads were shaven, their pubic hair removed. "A greasy delousing cream was spread over their bodies," said Dr. Karel Sperber, an inmate-doctor, while the onlockers joked as ointment was smeared over the genitalia. Clauberg then proceeded to inject caladium sequinum into various parts of the bodies, producing excruciating pains. Some Poles who were included in Clauberg's research cried out (according to the translation of their words) "The obese butcher is coming! The revolting rooster is here."

Clauberg's team plucked out ovaries, artificially inseminated women and then removed reproductive organs, even transplanted cancer cells into wombs before cutting them out a month later to determine the results. Indulging their prurient appetites as well, Clauberg and an associate, Dr. Kauffman, locked a naked, castrated man in a room with an equally undressed woman. The scientists then peeped through a glass in the cause of science and knowledge.

Mengele made himself a member of the group searching for a simple, chemical means of mass sterilization, and among those on whom he practiced was Magda Bass: "I was chosen along with other women to receive injections in our mouths and lips.

Mengele was there, watching us. A few days later, the heads of most who got shots swelled up. They disappeared. I was lucky. My head did not puff up. A short while later I was taken to the same place with more women. This time we received shots under our arms. Mengele again observed us. About ninety percent of those injected had their legs and feet swell. They too vanished. Later, when I finally came to the United States, I wanted to conceive a child but could not. Doctors at the Mayo Clinic have told me that I may have become sterile because of what I was given."

Sonderkommando Filip Müller had the job of disposing of the remains from the research of Mengele and his colleagues: "Some of the corpses were horrible to look at. Often they had been dismembered or dissected. Many were bodies of young men and women who bore strange burns and festering wounds on their testicles or lower parts of the body or abscesses on their bellies and thighs. Yet others had taken on a pinky-bluish hue or they had purple faces and clenched jaws."

The use of human guinea pigs for such experiments was justified in the name of improved therapy, or to purify the race. New means to treat stomach cancers, cures for ailments of the reproductive organs and drugs to control contagious diseases were promised. And the SS physicians were not shy about informing their colleagues. According to Leo Alexander, from 1942 on "such experiments carried out in concentration camps were openly presented at medical meetings. Sigmund Rascher even used the phrase "terminal human experiments." There was no audible outcry from the assembled medical scientists on hearing self-confessed corruption of the Hippocratic oath. In May of 1943 Dr. Ferdinand Sauerbruch, Mengele's sponsor, sat through a lecture at the Berlin Military Medical Academy in which Karl Gebhardt and his deputy, Dr. Fritz Fischer, lectured on their gas-gangrene experiments on prisoners.

At a libel trial in London in which Wladislaw Dehring was

trying to clear his name as a collaborator, Lord Gardiner, speaking for the defendant accused of libeling Dehring, referred to events before 1946: "And if anybody had asked, 'Do you think it possible that within relatively few years one of these countries [from Western Europe], the Christian flowering of civilization and culture, will drive millions of old people and children, literally naked, into gas chambers?' everybody would have said absolutely impossible . . . for two reasons. First, one cannot conceive of any reason why anybody should do this. They would bring on themselves the loathing of the world for a generation. If they did it in a peacetime situation they would soon be at war because everybody would stop them. If they did it in a wartime situation, what could they possibly have to gain to justify conduct of that kind and the opprobrium it would bring . . . and secondly we would have said, 'You'll never get the people to do it.' After all, a conscript army is made up of people from homes and factories who have women and children of their own. Can you imagine that you would ever get men with children of their own to drive children in tens of thousands into gas chambers? If it had been said or suggested that . . . human beings would have been used as guinea pigs and have their sexual organs removed literally in front of their eyes while they were conscious, as experiments . . . we would have said it is impossible and apart from that, a thing like that could only have been done by doctors, and where would you find doctors to do it? Well, we'd have been wrong. There was a doctor who did it. Antisemitism was one reason . . ." Gardiner, of course, was addressing himself to the case of Dehring, but his remarks applied to hundreds if not thousands of members of the German medical community.

When the shooting between the combatant armies ended in May, 1945—gassings had halted as early as November 1944, under orders from Himmler but selections and other killings continued to destroy inmates of the KZs—the Allied investigators reported a total of 350 German physicians who had participated in concentration camp activities. (The figure does not include prisoner doctors.) That is 3.5 percent of the 10,000 registered physicians in Germany at the start of World War II, a figure that should be adjusted downward by the number of Jewish doctors. To the 350, one must add on the support given by men like Otmar von Verschuer, himself a doctor, but not actually at a concentration camp. Many of the research activities involved scientists at universities who sought to profit by the activities at the KZs. Furthermore, there was constant traffic of doctors temporarily installed at camps, like Kremer, or civilians who visited them for the purposes of their own studies. Under such circumstances the awareness of the German medical community had to have been widespread.

H. Desoille and M. M. Lafitte, in *Psychologie Criminelle des Hitleri-ans,* offer a fitting epitaph: "The Nazis, including the Nazi physicians, pursued but one aim, extermination. The whole medical apparatus was nothing but a decor, nothing but a lie intended to disguise a massacre."

Jekyll
and Hyde

IN AUGUST 1944, an SS captain evaluated Mengele's performance: "Dr. Mengele has an open, honest, strong character. He
is absolutely dependable, straight forward and correct. His appearance reveals no weakness of character, no inclination or
addictions. His intellectual and physical predisposition can be
designated as excellent. He has applied his knowledge during
his activity in Concentration Camp Auschwitz practically and
theoretically in his function as a camp physician and in the fight
against grave epidemics.

"He has filled all of the tasks assigned to him with circumspection, perseverance, and energy to the complete satisfaction of his superiors and proven himself in command of every situation. More than that, he has as an anthropologist used the little free time at his disposal in order to extend his studies and has made a valuable contribution in the field of anthropology, using the scientific materials at his disposal. [A remarkable characterization of the nature of the experiments] In the manner of his appearance his official achievement and his attitude, Dr. Mengele shows absolute ideological firmness and maturity. He is Catholic. His speech in uninhibited, convincing and vivid . . ."

The report card went on to list Mengele's service with the Waffen SS and his medals. It suggested that he be considered for a promotion and new post. But he remained at Auschwitz, possibly frustrated by his failure to advance. And in the months that followed, the benign Dr. Jekyll would further metamorphose into the abominable Hyde.

For a time Marc Berkowitz actually regarded Mengele as a benevolent man forced to commit unpleasant acts. But as days passed, the boy saw other children used in experiments disappear. He learned the meaning of the great pall of smoke and its awful odor. And then came the moment when the entire barracks in which his mother lived received its notice of execution.

"Mengele had said to me when he separated our family, 'I'll arrange something for your mother to do. You'll see her from time to time.' But he already knew when she would die," says Berkowitz. On the day of her death Mengele invented an errand for his young messenger so that the son could walk a few steps with his mother before she climbed onto a truck. Shortly afterward the messenger returned to his post. Holding back his tears, he dusted the desk. Mengele questioned him. "Do you still believe in Herr Gott?"

Forty years later the memory of the German honorific preceding the deity's name turns Berkowitz's stomach. But in the

Auschwitz office he cautiously replied, "When it comes to defending God I do not know what it means. What it would mean to defend my mother, that I would understand. I started to say 'everything was taken from me' but that would have implied I had nothing to live for. Instead I said, 'Almost everything I had was taken away,' I wanted to hold onto something. *Mein Glauben, mein Leben für Gott."* (My faith, my life for God.)

The SS officer, a doctor who always wore a sidearm, ostentatiously unsnapped the top button of his holster and put his fingers on the butt of the pistol as if to draw it. Berkowitz heard very clearly the click of the fastener as it opened. "He looked at me, his hand on the gun and said, 'You're still a Jew?'

" 'I've almost lost everything but I have not lost God,' I said. 'You can take everything from me but you cannot take my God.' "

"That's the right answer," said Mengele, restored to good humor. He gestured toward his boots. "I want a good shine today." Later, when Berkowitz emerged from the office he noticed the billowing black smoke in the sky. He thought, I had better say Kaddish [the mourner's prayer] for my mother. Tomorrow, I may not be alive to say it.

Mengele continued to prick at the mind of the boy. "How do you like this place?" he asked genially one day.

"It seems to be good enough for you," sparred Berkowitz.

"Where are you!" Mengele came back. "Are you not talking to me in this place?" The question flustered Berkowitz. "Good," or "bad" might be a fatally wrong answer. He managed to avoid being pinned down. "Mengele wanted to hear the Jewish mind at work," thinks Berkowitz. "He was like a horse wearing blinkers. Nazi ideology was his jockey. There was no direction or goal. He just galloped away."

He pushed at Berkowitz about his religion. He invited him to attend the church services available to the captors and a few privileged prisoners. Mengele knew full well that among very religious Jews a church was such an anathema that they would cross the street rather than walk in front. It was not only a matter of religious conviction but of personal safety as well. Local zealots fired up by a sermon on the alleged perfidy of Jews sometimes emerged from church looking for vengeance on the nearest Jews. To attend a mass was unthinkable to many Jews. But Berkowitz had been raised in a community where he played with non-Jews, and so was able to indulge Mengele's curiosity by boldly going to a mass.

The doctor also liked to test his physical courage. "He kept suggesting to me that I could cool off in the summer by a swim in the pool they built for the SS troops. I went to the pool, and it was like getting into the water with the sharks. They held my head under the water, maybe teasing, maybe not."

Mengele, Berkowitz believes, at least seemed at times to admire his spunk. "He did not like tears or crying. I always acted as if I were unafraid. When I went to the gate on an errand for him I never mumbled. I would shout my name and number to the guard. Other messengers would fill their pants, knowing the guards were prepared to shoot. And there were those dogs on chains. It was barely possible to squeeze by them without having a piece torn out of your leg."

In his incongruously benign moments Mengele shared his passion for music, inviting the child to his quarters, teaching him songs, allowing the boy to crank the phonograph and listen to the tinny reproductions of arias. Mengele the anomaly, Germany the anomaly. Blood and iron, arias and verse.

"He was never a truly military man," says Berkowitz. "He wore the soft hat with the Death's Head insignia instead of the formal, stiff cap. Around his neck he had a cross, and the motto on his belt read, "With God's Speed." Together, translatable as "death with God's speed.""

Jekyll and Hyde

The cat-and-mouse game with Berkowitz reached its ultimate at selections. "He would say there is going to be a selection, at rollcall, to someone on the telephone. He knew I was listening. He would give a time for it and say there will be questions to the inmates like who wants to work and who wants to stay in the block. Not going to work could mean gassing but volunteering also might mean winding up on a truck bound for death . . . I would overhear him mention a rollcall for selection that could involve my sister. Then he would send me on an errand and insist I be back in a very short time. I knew short cuts in the camp where I could save three minutes, enough time to run and warn my sister to protect herself.

Concludes Berkowitz on the anomaly of Mengele: "A doctor of philosophy, a medical doctor, a man who enjoyed music and poetry, and his greatest weapon was his manner. He could get people to do everything by appearing to be decent. He would totally disarm someone. You could not believe he was lying, yet he lied all the time. He acted on the basis that if you tell a Jew good morning that proves you are a nice person."

In the context and environment of the daily violence meted out by kapos and the guards who saw no purpose in masking their personalities, the Mengele approach was understandably effective. "When you would see a person with an ugly face, beady little eyes, a hard stare, you would try to escape to the barracks. Mengele by contrast looked so handsome that if we saw him we almost had an urge to run to the gate and greet him." No question, for one fortunate enough not to have endured the hell of Auschwitz, it is difficult to conceive of such a reaction to the likes of Mengele. You had to have been there. And it is necessary to believe the testimony of witnesses such as Berkowitz. Confounding as it may be, it is also the source material for making some sense out of what seems beyond all understanding.

Gisella Perl agrees that Mengele coldly calculated the effects of his manner. "It was all part of his diabolical method of making us suffer, whether he had the orchestra playing for us, whether he smiled. He didn't just kill. He tortured us. I was a musician, my husband was one, and our son gave his first concert at age ten. To me music was something special, almost holy. Mengele would have us stand there for selection while the orchestra played a gay Viennese waltz.

"He delighted in coming before us, smelling of perfumed soap, so elegant, so handsome, his shirt that beautiful blue color. There were girls who would say to me, 'Gissy, I would love to spend a night with Mengele.' It was another way to drive us insane. You had to be insane to smell the crematorium and see him as an attractive man, one to spend the night with. He knew the attitudes of the women. He would call us 'dirty whores.' We smelled of urine, feces, and hunger, and he enjoyed humiliating us, reducing us to the lowest of animals, beneath whores."

The viciousness under the affable exterior exploded at the barest of transgressions. Berkowitz once wandered into an area reserved for piles of coal. There he saw Mengele pull his pistol and shoot a seventeen-year-old first in one knee, then the other. As the adolescent screamed in pain, Mengele grabbed him by the hair and fired a bullet into his brain. He turned to the horrified witness. "You know he had no business here. [The victim had been scrounging for a lump of coal for a fire.] You must respect the laws of this place."

Magda Bass remembers that even other SS men feared Mengele. Marc Berkowitz describes how Dr. Heinz Tilo behaved under the mere threat of Mengele: "Tilo tried to copy Mengele. He created an entourage for himself and he tried to develop research projects like Mengele. He was very jealous of him. One day Mengele left the camp for several days and he instructed me that nothing was to be disturbed in his zoo while he was gone.

Jekyll and Hyde

Tilo tried to make a selection among us, he was going to include me. One of the dwarfs said it was time to pray. I found my voice and said to Tilo that I had been told I was to take care of the records for Doctor Mengele while he was away. When Tilo heard the name he dropped the selection. Mengele's name was a password for us."

SS guards often amused themselves with what they called "sport." They forced prisoners to exercise in the snow or mud, goaded them to run until they dropped, compelled them to crawl through muck. Mengele diverted himself with more sophisticated entertainment: A consignment from Hungary emptied its passengers at the ramp. The doctor observed that among the newcomers was a group of about one hundred rabbis, mostly elderly men with flowing beards. He separated them from the others and moved them into an empty space pockmarked with mud holes and discarded desks, wire, and garbage. He ordered them to form a large circle, then commanded them to dance. Several versions of this incident exist. In one the rabbis removed their clothes and cavorted while holding up sacred books, Torahs, that they had painstakingly carried from home to Auschwitz. In another memory the men retained their clothes, and when Mengele shouted for them to sing they chanted the Kol Nidrei prayer, the text that precedes services at Yom Kippur. Whichever, there is no question that the divertissement ended with total selection of the rabbis.

From the evidence of Marc Berkowitz, Gisella Perl and others, the potion of anti-Semitism galvanized the Mr. Hyde side of Mengele. Confronted by Judaism as on the Yom Kippur when he selected the one thousand smaller boys, or with the spectacle of one hundred rabbis, his venom overflowed.

Ella Lingens was not Jewish, and as an inmate-doctor she saw Mengele two or three times a week when he inspected her hospital barracks and checked her files. He never showed his Hyde side to her. The Gestapo had imprisoned Lingens for her efforts to assist Jews in Vienna trying to escape the Nazis. When Mengele first met her he asked why she was in Auschwitz. Hearing her answer he said, without scorn or fury, "How could you believe you would succeed?" His tone was almost mild, almost friendly.

"Why not?" replied Lingens. "There were cases where Jews succeeded by bribing the Gestapo."

Her answer did not disturb him. On the contrary, he remarked, "Of course we sell Jews for money in some instances. We would be stupid not to do so. But why did you get mixed up in this business? What did you have to gain? Now you are a prisoner here in Auschwitz." Lingens now thinks that her attempt to help Jews offended him only because it was amateurish and brought no gain to her. She is convinced that he had decided to focus only on what profited him.

Marc Berkowitz relates an incident attesting to such venality. One day Mengele told his messenger to recruit four or five of the "strongest boys available." With an SS soldier as escort, the young prisoners went to a designated area where they found several rubber-wheeled hand trucks. Close by lay four crates, all tightly secured with black metal bands—"sharp as razor blades," Berkowitz remembers. The boys dollied the boxes to the railroad siding and loaded them aboard a freight car bound for Germany. Much of the space was filled with loose clothing and shoes, but Berkowitz noticed that the addresses on his four crates were for Günzburg. "I'm sure it was mostly gold bullion from teeth [Gisella Perl also claims Mengele stole] plus pens, lighters, watches, cigarette holders, and jewelry."

Conversations with Mengele also led Lingens to believe that Mengele was not a raving fanatic who always accepted whole the Nazi racist theories, though he surely acted as though he did—

perhaps because it suited his purpose? "The Germans and the Jews are the only intelligent nations in the world," he told her. "And it is now a question of which of the two will govern the earth." A strikingly different line from the one he usually prattled. Was this mostly for her benefit? Was he mostly testing again, looking for reactions? Did he believe it? Most likely a little of each.

Actually, Lingens concluded that even the most "rational" of the SS were united in their irrational defense of Hitler even as the fortunes of the Third Reich declined, and in their clinging to anti-Semitism. As one commented to her, although many "wonderful" things wrought by Hitler would be lost, "at least we are ridding the world of Jews." He was, in her view, deadly serious.

Hans Münch, whose behavior at Auschwitz differed so considerably from that of Mengele, continues to regard his colleague, forty years later, as "a man with a very wide horizon. He was open to general subjects, not only medical ones. Compared with other SS camp doctors—they were a special category—Mengele was very unusual. He was not only intelligent but generally and scientifically a very interesting person. In a friendly personal exchange of views I could express different opinions which he tolerated. Asked if he regarded Mengele as a "pleasant fellow," Münch laughs. "Absolutely. In contrast to others, a dozen of them, he was the easiest to get on with because he did not adopt a fixed, stubborn SS doctor's attitude."

Lingens believes Mengele eventually lost whatever faith he had in the Nazi cause and mostly became cynical. "He took nothing seriously, neither us nor our situation. He thought conditions in the camp were rotten." Occasionally she says he stirred himself to improve them. But, she notes, he continued to "murder callously." Because he took nothing—including human life—seriously? He surely seemed to take his own life and interests seriously, and continued to do so during his remarkable postwar success in staying alive and free.

Nyiszli has noted that Mengele expended a huge amount of time and energy on research. He approached his studies with a professorial air inscribing entries first in Latin and then in German.

"He could have had a first-rate academic career," says Lingens. "It was really research that interested him. I never understood why he chose the career he did. He did not need to."

None of the inmate-doctors, with the exception of pathologist Nyiszli, whose knowledge was restricted mainly to postmortems, was privy to the exact nature of research or saw the experiments. Mengele once invited Lingens to look at his scientific data. She leafed through several cardboard boxes full of orderly measurements—seemingly innocuous. "When I had glanced at the stuff, he said, 'Isn't it interesting? What a pity all this will fall into the hands of the Bolsheviks.' This was September 1944 and I was flabbergasted not to hear him repeat the usual dribble about final victory everybody else was giving us."

Perl believes the strict secrecy Mengele employed was designed to hide his criminal acts. Lingens now thinks that perhaps he allowed her to glance at his work to make her a witness to the "innocence" of his studies—merely head and body measurements of twins and dwarfs. Mengele was not a fool—he thought ahead.

On the other hand Münch says that in spite of all of their conversations, "Mengele never discussed his research with me or anybody else. He kept it secret. This was to be the basis for his dissertation and he did not want to share the information with anyone." So he said. An explanation for everyone.

Mengele deliberately volunteered to serve at Auschwitz. He came there with the backing of influential members of the scientific community. And he applied himself, in his fashion, strenuously, diligently. He envisioned himself on the cutting edge of genetic frontiers. By his labors he could achieve a monumental breakthrough, something that would somehow justify his rebuff of his father and his murderous activities. Joseph Mengele appears to have been the one person who passed through the gate marked *Arbeit Macht Frei* and believed the legend. Of course his concept of *arbeit,* work, was rather special, and of freedom altogether Orwellian and personal.

What makes a Mengele? . . . obviously there is no easy or single answer. But the beginning was surely in his relationship with his parents. There was the love of a mother who demanded strict obedience. He himself called Walburga a harsh disciplinarian. Did that extend to what we now call child abuse? Not an unlikely supposition . . . psychologists have found that those who have been abused are the ones most likely to visit cruelty on their own children—in Mengele's case the youngsters at Auschwitz toward whom he frequently displayed a kind of parental affection before punishing them so terribly. And does not the story of Oedipus reverberate in accounts of his experiments on children's eyes—surrogates for himself, punished for a forbidden love of mother, hatred of father?

Mengele had rejected his autocratic father by choosing not to follow in his footsteps. And the only acceptable way for him to supplant Karl lay in an extraordinary achievement. His Gunzburg schoolmate Julius Diesbach says, "I think it was his passion for fame that led to his inhuman scientific work, pushed his ambitions to the point where nothing mattered except his experiments."

Clearly Mengele coveted the title of Herr Professor. It would confer upon him his own *permanent* mantle of authority. The power he enjoyed at Auschwitz was transient. Stuck in the rank of captain, he counted for little outside the sphere of the KZ.

Although he disdained business, he managed to retain the involvement of his parents. Karl and Walburga Mengele were ambitious for their firstborn son. While they may have initially regretted his choice of career they certainly had to relish the thought of added glory from a son in the upper echelons of the academic and scientific worlds.

And so they sharpened and intensified his aspirations. He needed to *succeed,* starting as "an extraordinarily ambitious student." Apart from the parental authority figures young Mengele had found new and demanding overseers. In politics he had Adolf Hitler. Intellectually, there was Otmar von Verschuer.

As he frenetically pursued the means to his professorship at Auschwitz the influence of the father-like figures continued. He had fought for Hitler and the fatherland (and had expressed his patriotic fervor with membership in the Steel Helmets and his enlistment in the SA, the Nazi Party and the SS). Now he labored on behalf of the fatherland in its *anus mundi.* A true test. The contact with his intellectual and professional guide, Otmar von Verschuer, was stronger than ever. And even his biological father was part of his scene. According to accounts Karl Mengele came to Auschwitz to spend some time with his son. How much the younger man permitted his father to see is unknown, but one can presume that the visitation could only generate more pressure to succeed.

Mengele's anti-Semitism and his expression of it connects directly with his infatuation with authority. Racism, of course, is a natural offshoot of the authoritarian mind. One race over another, one in authority and control over the other. Mengele's father had made his pact with the Nazis, and certainly offered no resistance to anti-Semitic activities. Mengele's church had achieved its own understanding, some would say accommodation, with the Nazis, declining to speak out against persecutions.

Jekyll and Hyde .

Mengele's professional career depended on the success of the Nazi movement, which held the destruction of the Jews as an integral part of the grand plan.

To a man of Mengele's political bent, the only way the Nazi ideal could prevail was if its authority was not successfully challenged. As an authoritarian, Mengele believed there could only be one relationship among humans, masters and slaves. Consider again his remarks to Ella Lingens when he spoke with dispassion, employing his own logic as it suited his purposes: "The Germans and the Jews are the only intelligent nations in the world . . . it is now a question of which of the two will govern the earth." Later in Brazil Mengele continued to justify the extermination program because the Jews threatened Nazi hegemony. What better way could he have chosen to preserve his preferred form of authority than to apply his energy to the extinction of this alien group, this enemy of the State.

Surely, some might say, Mengele, for all of this, *must* have realized he was committing awful crimes. But the capacity of humans to self-justify, to self-deceive is enormous. Julius Diesbach felt he could plumb the depths of Mengele's mind (and in so doing provides a revealing glimpse of his own): "One has to look at this also from another angle and try to understand it. Beppo may have told himself, 'Here I have an opportunity to carry out investigations. The objects, the people, are anyhow doomed to death. As they will be gassed in any case, maybe I will be able to save the lives of thousands in the future, develop pharmaceuticals that cannot be experimented on with animals, only on humans.' "

But Diesbach fails to consider the random acts of violence visited on inmates by Mengele, to say nothing of the brutality of many of his experiments, which had little if any connection with new pharmaceuticals or life-saving endeavors.

Surely such behavior is aberrant in terms of what we think of as minimally normal behavior. One might say Mengele's behavior at Auschwitz is that of a full-blown paranoid, according to a textbook definition: "A disorder of personality characterized by jealousy, suspiciousness, rigidity, and hypersensitivity; there may be evidence of delusional thinking. The individual usually shows a pattern of chronically unsatisfactory interpersonal relationships with a tendency to place the blame for failures in social interaction on other people."

But the portrait fits too neatly. It fails to take into account the prevailing attitudes of the times that were powerful dignifying and justifying forces for what Mengele was and did. He was *not* a unique loose cannon totally out of the mainstream, including the mainstream of much respectable scientific thinking. The times together with his parental relationship do more for an explanation of Mengele than textbook definitions of neatly compartmentalized psychoses.

Mengele's goals, for all his efforts, receded rather than became more accessible. There was no scientific breakthrough, and as 1944 drew to a close, the terrible Red Army was on the march. Surely, the frustration and rage within Mengele must have been awesome.

Flight

ON NOVEMBER 26, 1944, Himmler, sensing the end, telegraphed Auschwitz to dismantle the death works, thereby reducing mass murder at the camp. A witness places Joseph Mengele at the selection ramp on November 3, perhaps his final performance on the site as the "angel of extermination." On that transport arrived 509 people from Sered, Czechoslovakia. Mengele condemned 461 to immediate death.

One evening about six weeks later, says Marc Berkowitz, placing the time between the Jewish holiday of Hannukah and Christmas, he and a "mixed bag" of inmates—"homosexuals, politicals, and religious persons"—were singing Christmas carols in the washroom. Suddenly Mengele appeared with two other SS men. "He came in from the side facing the Gypsy camp, like a shadow. I don't know how he knew I was there. He had on his full uniform and said to me, 'Take care of yourself. Adieu.' "

Miklos Nyiszli did not even receive a goodbye visit. He woke up one morning to the rumor that Mengele was gone. The most informed guesses place the physician's departure around the 17th of January. Some accounts speak of a chauffeur who drove the doctor away. However, nothing in available records mentions a personal servant. In any case Mengele vanished. About ten days later Russian troops liberated Auschwitz. Only a remnant of the inhabitants were still there, about two to three thousand. Most of the others had been driven westward by the guards. Along the route of march, thousands of prisoners died, succumbing to exposure or bullets from their guards. Marc Berkowitz believes that there were only 180 children like himself who, of the 1,800 in Mengele's "zoo," lived to walk out the gates.

Scattered, early accounts of Nazi KZ atrocities, followed by an increasing number of documented reports from escapees and other sources, led British Prime Minister Winston Churchill and U.S. President Franklin D. Roosevelt to public declarations of the intent to prosecute individuals connected with war crimes. Roosevelt said, "All who knowingly take part in the deportation of Jews to their death in Poland . . . are equally guilty with the executioners." To implement the prosecutions, the Allies formed war crimes units to identify those who participated, to find them and to try them.

Individual countries issued circulars naming wanted persons, as did the United Nations. The name of Mengele can be found as early as May 1945, about the time of V-E Day, and in short order he was listed as a suspect by no less than seven countries for crimes against their citizens.

Unfortunately both the U.S. military government units formed to administer conquered Germany and those charged with pursuing war criminals were disorganized. Personnel changed constantly as citizen soldiers were rotated home to be replaced by newcomers inexperienced in the ways of the army or their assignments. Records were misplaced or unnecessarily duplicated.

Amid all this confusion at least one man investigating war crimes did build a small dossier on Mengele. M. Wolfson, chief research analyst in the U.S. Office of War Crimes, collected several affidavits. One described Mengele as having "frequently punctured the spinal cord, injected both children and adults so that they would fall sick, showing certain symptoms of fever, as a result of which many died." A second statement noted that "Dr. Mengele worked very publicly. He sterilized or gave the order to sterilize women and men and he syphoned blood from people." Wolfson's report delved into the twin-studies and even included a snatch of Mengele's selection style: "Madam, take care, your child will catch cold." . . . "Madam, you are ill and tired after a long journey. Give your child to this lady and you will find it later in the children's nursery."

Wolfson recommended again that "SS Hauptsturmführer Joseph Mengele be placed on the wanted list and that he be indicted for war crimes."

The chief research analyst also uncovered Otmar von Verschuer. Wolfson's file includes a communication from the Berlin office of his organization: "Various records . . . von Verschuer is accused of being connected with experimentation on living human beings in concentration camps, particularly Auschwitz. He is accused of being a Nazi activist."

As a result of references to his role, von Verschuer was interrogated. Questioned about Mengele he tried to exonerate his protege. He suggested to the investigators that the concentration camp doctor had been assigned to Auschwitz against his will and sought a transfer. Wolfson dismissed the premise, recapitulating the adulatory evaluation on Mengele filed by SS Captain Mattes.

Von Verschuer told his questioners that all of the correspondence, papers, and specimens relevant to the work of Mengele had been destroyed. Wolfson and his associates believed that von Verschuer himself burned any incriminating documents to protect himself and Mengele.

The former director of the Kaiser Wilhelm Institute did admit that he engaged in medical studies assigned by the Reich Research Council, but he insisted the research dealt only with legitimate health matters. The Office of War Crimes failed to indict Herr Professor, the mentor of Joseph Mengele.

He remained, though, a subject of interest as he entered into a noisy public dispute with a former colleague. Von Verschuer described his opponent as having been first a communist, then a member of the SS and now with the war over a supporter of the Soviet Union. At issue were papers and equipment which von Verschuer claimed he had retrieved from the Kaiser Wilhelm Institute. Early in 1946 von Verschuer appealed to the Bureau of Human Heredity in London. "I hope that the scientific equipment of my former Kaiser Wilhelm Institute in Dahlem which I saved from the Russians and brought from Berlin–Dahlem to Hesse and then to Frankfurt will enable me to continue or rather restart my research work here in Frankfurt . . . as always our work will center around the tuberculosis research on which . . . I have been working for 18 years . . . I don't give up hope that there will be people in England and America who will help me to continue my scientific research."

Flight

A committee of von Verschuer's peers in 1949 defended their colleague: "It would be pharisaical for us to regard in hindsight isolated incidents in the life of an otherwise honorable and brave man who has had a difficult life and frequently displayed his nobility of character as an unpardonable moral stain." And so German academia declared that the man who coached Joseph Mengele was altogether one of them in spirit and mind.

He eventually won appointment to a professorship of medicine at the University of Münster, both man and university apparently untroubled by his role as a Nazi supporter and theorist and as an instigator of medical experimentation on humans. Von Verschuer held his post at Münster until his death in 1969.

Although a substantial number of witnesses identified Mengele as a tormentor and murderer of Auschwitz inmates, war crimes authorities busied themselves mostly with the trials of the major Nazi officials. Men like Hitler's chief deputy Hermann Goering, Ernst Kaltenbrunner, head of the SS secret service, the military leaders Field Marshal Wilhelm Keitel and General Alfred Jodl, Polish gauleiter Hans Frank, an ardent fan of the *Einsatzgruppen,* all stood in the dock at Nuremberg.

Their misdeeds generated thousands of pages of testimony covering aggression against other nations and a wide range of alleged atrocities. Joseph Mengele's name surfaced on three occasions. Madame Marie-Claude Vaillant-Couturier, a member of a French contingent at Auschwitz, spoke of selections during which Mengele removed twins for experimental purposes. She remarked that at selections Mengele whistled "lively tunes." The Russian Army forwarded a deposition from a nine-year-old boy who said, "During my stay in the camp, Dr. Mengele bled me very frequently." And camp commander Hoess, brought from Poland, mentioned the sterilization work of Clauberg and

Schumann as well as "experiments on twins by SS medical officer Mengele."

According to Telford Taylor, a ranking member of the U.S. prosecution team under U.S. Supreme Court Justice Robert H. Jackson, standard procedure called for further investigation of an individual if derrogatory information turned up about him during the trials. That should have moved authorities to a more intense investigation and search for Mengele, but there is no evidence of any extra effort. Mengele remained just one more name on a long list of non-celebrity war criminals.

Following the trials of the twenty-one top Nazi leaders which ended in the autumn of 1946, Telford Taylor was assigned to prosecute other important segments of German society that participated in war crimes. One trial centered on members of the legal profession. Another targeted people in industry and finance. A third proceeding struck at the men of medicine. Charges were brought against twenty-four physicians. Fifteen were convicted, and seven received death sentences. None of those found guilty served at Auschwitz. The executed included: Karl Brandt, Hitler's Reich commissioner for sanitation and a prime mover in both the euthanasia project and medical experiments; SS medical chief Karl Gebhardt, who personally committed medical atrocities and in 1943 proudly assumed responsibility for his work; Viktor Brack, chief of Hitler's personal chancellery and a supporter of many experiments; Dr. Joachim Mrugowsky, involved in the tests using poisoned bullets; Waldemar Hoven, active in euthanasia.

Joseph Mengele's name failed to appear during the trial. One former colleague fared badly in another court. Dr. Fritz Klein, the middle-aged physician who, except for his implacable hatred of Jews, showed some concern for KZ patients, had transferred from Auschwitz to Bergen–Belsen. At the time he left Auschwitz Klein, perhaps aware the war was lost, made a farewell speech to fellow workers, including some prisoners. Among them Frank Stiffel listened with amazement as Klein said, "I beg your forgiveness for any atrocities I might have committed during my tenure as *Lagerarzt* [camp doctor]. I was forced to follow orders." The grudging *mea culpa* characterized many of the Nazi confessions before courts. It failed to help Klein—the British hung him.

While the Allies conducted their war crimes tribunals, Mengele managed to stay out of sight. His disappearance has presented one of the great mysteries surrounding his career. There is no hard evidence on his whereabouts from January 1945 to 1949 and under such circumstances imaginative tales developed.

The most sensational story of his exploits after he slipped away from Auschwitz centers around a Jewish Pole named Wilma. The adventure begins with Wilma and her brother being raised in Warsaw by their grandfather before the start of World War II. While on a visit to Palestine the prosperous merchant grandfather drinks a beverage sold by a street corner vendor. The brew, laced with methyl alcohol, blinds the old man, who returns to Warsaw, sells his business, and retires to seclusion with his grandchildren. When the Germans overrun Poland Wilma's brother enlists in the despised Jewish security force, a Nazi-sponsored organization formed to police the Warsaw ghetto. The beautiful, blonde Wilma, only eighteen, becomes the mistress of a ghetto black-market kingpin, Hil Tauber. From Tauber she learns how to wheel and deal, meets contacts in the underground. But her luck runs out. Enemies betray her to the Gestapo during the 1943 Warsaw ghetto uprising and she is packed off to Auschwitz.

At ramp selection, Mengele, smitten with her beauty, installs her in his quarters as his "housekeeper." As, in fact, his lover, she soon exerts increasing influence over him. Inmates buy fa-

vors from Wilma with the fees paid by relatives outside the camp
to Hil Tauber, who has escaped the obliteration of the Warsaw
ghetto.

As Rome falls to the Allies, troops invade Normandy on June
6 and the Soviets then launch a massive offensive in the summer
of 1944. Mengele discusses with Wilma possibilities for him to
escape. She convinces him to issue her a temporary pass for a
visit to Warsaw in October 1944. In the Polish capital she locates
a number of Jews who have survived in the city, rewarded for
aiding the Nazis either as members of the *Judenrat* or the security
police. Some now manufacture goods for the German war economy but because they do not trust their masters they also smug-
gle contraband to the Polish underground. Hil Tauber, Wilma's
old associate, has been floating among this Jewish residue,
trafficking with both the Germans and the underground.

But at the moment that Wilma arrives in Warsaw Hil Tauber
is being held by the Gestapo on suspicion of aiding the partisans. The resourceful Wilma, capitalizing on her identification
papers from Auschwitz, convinces the authorities that Tauber is
a key agent for secret missions. The black-market impresario is
not only released but even issued special documents that permit
him extraordinary mobility. Wilma and Tauber arrange to meet
with representatives of the International Red Cross, from which
officials they obtain papers that will enable Polish Jews to travel
to Switzerland, outside the German sphere of power. The pair
sell these permits to Jews who sign promissory notes, payable in
foreign currency after their escape.

Mengele's role in this chicanery is his signature on bogus
medical certificates necessary for an exit permit and for entry
into Switzerland; a certificate from a Jewish doctor, provided any
remained alive in Poland, would be invalid. Polish physicians
refused to treat Jews. Documents with the name of an SS physician carried great weight. Mengele agrees to the scheme after

146

being bribed with a set of ancient manuscripts and on the promise of aid when he leaves Auschwitz. The first customers successfully emigrate to Switzerland. Among them are relatives of Wilma, who are so destitute on arrival that they need support from the local welfare organizations. But before V–E Day the kinfolk amass enough money to buy a hotel near Zurich.

Wilma returns to Auschwitz to fulfill the bargain with Mengele. As the Russian Army grinds toward the camp, the pair sneak away. Once outside the gates they masquerade as a couple of Jewish refugees. Wilma shrewdly navigates their course southeast, knowing their disguise will pass them safely through the Soviet lines. Secure from pursuit by the Nazis, they take up residence in a safe house at Zakopane, a resort in the Carpathians.

By the summer of 1945, with Europe in the throes of a chaotic peace, the couple journeys to Prague, where they prevail on the British to issue papers identifying them as displaced persons from Austria. The idyll continues with a move to Vienna. Red Cross credentials now permit entry into Switzerland. There Wilma claims her due from her relatives, including the management of the hotel near Zurich. She is further enriched through collection of her promissory notes from Jewish refugees in West Germany and Switzerland. Hil Tauber, in possession of a great many more IOUs, never joins them, allegedly being gunned down when he tries to cross the border at Frankfurt an der Oder.

The affair between the Polish Jew and the former SS captain ends. Wilma remains in Switzerland while Mengele briefly visits his family in Germany, then flees to South America by way of Italy.

Such is the scenario that has been reported in print media in the United States and Europe. The primary source is Werner Brockdorff, "an old Nazi," says Frankfurt prosecutor Hans Eberhard Klein, a pursuer of Mengele since 1974. Wilma and Mengele are part of a chapter in Brockdorff's 1969 book, *Flucht vor Nürnberg* (Flight from Nuremberg), in which he summarizes the careers of a number of notorious Nazis.

An unmistakable whiff of anti-Semitism wafts from Werner Brockdorff. The victims appear at least as avaricious and as unprincipled as their oppressors. The basic message is: Everyone behaved badly during the war, so why heap guilt on the losers?

Brockdorff prints addresses, a few names and some dates, facts that seem to lend verisimilitude. He claims to have spoken with Wilma's relatives but does not identify them. He says that a friend of Mengele from South America verified the story.

Still, it is difficult to accept that even in an atmosphere such as that of the KZ that the corruption would permit Wilma to have carried on her business of selling favors at Auschwitz and collecting from relatives in Warsaw. Indeed, Brockdorff talks of 50,000 Jews left in the city after the ghetto destruction. William L. Shirer in his *The Rise and Fall of the Third Reich* places the total number living in the ghetto *before* the final assault at 60,000 (all of the remaining Jews in the city). The Nazis counted the Jewish dead after the three-week battle as 56,000. The surviving net is 4,000. Furthermore, Brockdorff's references to Mengele's escape route to South America are filled with geographical errors.

What is significant about Brockdorff's story—Prosecutor Klein dismisses it as fiction—is that it demonstrates how legend has grown up around Mengele. In the forty years since he escaped an anthology of misinformation and disinformation has been created. Contributors to the falsities include not only apologists like Brockdorff but some of those most anxious to see Mengele on trial.

The less romantic and more accepted version of Mengele's escape has it that he simply decamped on some pretext and headed for the friendly surroundings of Günzburg. With the

148

German Army routed, troops surrendering by the tens of thousands, a resourceful man like Mengele could rather easily have circumvented checkpoints alert to deserters.

In 1945 Irene Mengele rented a small cottage from a farmer at Autenreid, a tiny community several miles from Günzburg, and moved in with Rolf, the son born to her and Joseph in 1944. Many believe that Joseph Mengele hid in this house during the immediate post World War II years. When Hans Eberhard Klein questioned the owner about his tenants he maintained that he never saw any person there other than Frau Mengele. Lawyer Gerald Posner, a Mengele archivist, says he spoke with a person who swore he saw Mengele in the Günzburg *area* during these years. Klein says, "There is no evidence that Mengele was in Günzburg," which is not a flat denial that the fugitive did once reside in Autenreid in the Günzburg area.

Felix Kuballa, a German reporter, put together one account of Mengele's movements after Auschwitz for a 1985 TV broadcast. Kuballa believes Mengele left Auschwitz headed either for the KZ Grossrosen or Bergen–Belsen. While accompanying a transport to one of the camps he probably fled.

Kuballa turned up a witness named Thomas Bergtold, a native of Burgau, not too far from Günzburg. Bergtold told Kuballa that he was a prisoner of war in a British camp near Neumunster. While chatting with comrades about bartering cigarettes for food, another inmate noticed Bergtold's Swabian dialect and inquired about his hometown. After he told him, the newcomer asked if Bergtold knew Günzburg and the Mengele factory. When Bergtold said of course he did, the other man said, "I am Mengele. I come from Günzburg."

The official story given by Rolf Mengele to the magazine *Bunte* after his father's certified death, based on letters and conversations with the doctor, says: "At the end of the war, my unit was located in Czechoslovakia. During the night of the armistice, we fled to the west. In the vicinity of a big city (*Bunte* says Nuremberg) we were taken to a U.S. prisoners of war camp. We were transferred to many camps and then we were released to the U.S. zone."

Kuballa believes his witness Bergtold, in spite of the discrepancy with the account given by Mengele himself. Mengele's account to his son was rather vague on details, so conceivably he fell into British hands as well as American. Furthermore, he may have preferred a story in which he held out until the night before the surrender rather than admit he gave himself up at the first opportunity to the closest Allied troops. His old schoolmate Diesbach, after all, once described him as "not so much a courageous man as a cautious one."

Unlike many of his colleagues, he refused to have the SS tattoo his blood group on his arm, one of the means used by the Allied occupying forces to identify SS troops. The absence of a tattoo did help conceal him. Kuballa also notes that at the war's end there was a need for agricultural workers. Anyone who could convince authorities he was knowledgable in this field was quickly released. Mengele may well have benefitted from the shortage of fieldhands and so been turned loose quickly.

In any case, he made his way to Donauworth, Bavaria, and looked up a student friend, Albert Müller, a veterinarian. Müller's widow remembers when Mengele rang the doorbell. "I opened the door and saw a soldier and recognizing him I greeted him 'Good day, Doctor Mengele.' " He was surprised by her greeting, and although her husband was away she invited him in. When her husband arrived later the two men talked while Frau Müller prepared a meal. She says she heard Mengele say, "All the things you will be hearing about me are lies. Don't believe a word of it. I have done nothing wrong."

Mengele later told his son Rolf that he spent the years from 1945 to 1949 working as a groom on a farm in Rosenheim, near

Munich. He claimed his employer was uninterested in his identity and concerned only that he keep his hands clean. While there is no provable reason to doubt this account it should be remembered that a desire to protect those who sheltered him could have induced lies or concealment of the entire truth.

In the context of the support given to Mengele after he escaped to South America it seems obvious that he must have been in close touch with the folks at Günzburg. But as they did for the thirty-four years after the war until his now presumed death, and another six years beyond, the family, employees of the company, and townsfolk who were privy to information on Mengele remained silent.

Günzburg itself had been spared the battering of aerial bombardment and house-to-house combat during the war. The caretaker government of the Third Reich surrendered just as U.S. troops neared the city. Air raids had destroyed some buildings, but the Mengele factory went largely unharmed. However, shortages of supplies and manpower had reduced the work force to a skeletal 148. Worse still, in June, 1945, the local military government arrested and interned Karl, Jr., exempted from military service to direct the firm's tool manufacturing. Alois, the youngest brother, had served as a soldier and become a prisoner-of-war.

Still, the Mengele tribe came through the war better than those who had opposed the Nazis. One such was the local Catholic priest, Adam Birner. Father Birner came to Günzburg from the Augsburg Cathedral in 1935, well after Joseph Mengele was gone from his birthplace. Authorities sent Birner into exile from Augsburg as a punishment for such opposition to the Nazis as sermonizing against the "criminals" in the government when before a packed church he preached, "He who is a National Socialist is either a fool, a fellow-traveler or a scoundrel."

Allegedly it was members of his own cloth who fed authorities even more damning information on his dissent. The Gestapo carried him off, and on Easter Sunday 1941, the interrogators beat him so badly that the police were obliged to take him from the prison to the main hospital in Augsburg. Forty years later a newspaper dug into the official files to find the notation: "The 43-year-old man who was left laying about for at least 45 minutes without any care died at 7:15 p.m." The signature on the death certificate was that of Dr. Otfried Goerlich, later a physician in Günzburg and a member of the SS. To this day no one knows where the Gestapo buried Birner. And years after the martyr fell, the bishopric of Augsburg informed a would-be chronicler of Adam Birner: "It will be best if you keep him in fond memory but will desist from publicly honoring him." Since no one in Günzburg rose to defend Adam Birner, it is not surprising that no one would rise to denounce the presence of a favored native son—Joseph Mengele.

Anonymous as Birner had become, even less remained of the local Jews. The Günzburg district included the village of Ichenhausen, "Jewtown," to the rest of the good burghers. For hundreds of years Jews had been shunted from Augsburg to Ichenhausen. The rail line between became known as "the Jew chute." The Nazis registered 309 Jews living in Ichenhausen in 1933. There were none left at the end of the war; they either ran or were gassed. (The old synagogue of Ichenhausen now houses fire engines, and the village has had, since 1972, a new street unblushingly christened Mengele Strasse.)

Günzburg served as headquarters for a U.S. military government unit responsible for an area containing a number of towns and cities with a total population of 45,000. The Americans struggled to find burgomasters without Nazi affiliations. People received appointments and then were defrocked as information about their past surfaced. Similarly, efforts to get local businesses and industries into production foundered because the most qualified individuals proved to have Nazi affiliations.

The local population seemed unrepentant. A poll of citizens in the area found they regarded the Nuremberg Trials as "lies made up for propaganda purposes." In the files of the military government unit are letters from local persons who said their neighbors continued to harass them for their anti-Nazi activities.

For example: A pastor wrote describing his efforts to inform advancing U.S. troops of the positions of Waffen SS troops defending the area in the final days of the war. After the cessation of hostilities he was hounded from his pulpit . . . An "artillery association," a reunion of Wehrmacht veterans, held a reunion in Günzburg. The local police attended and the informant advised the U.S. authorities that an inspector's wife was a rabid Nazi . . . Jewish displaced persons, encamped nearby, attended a film in the Günzburg cinema. The newsreel showed the opening of a new synagogue in Munich and spoke of the millions killed in the KZs. A DP said that the audience laughed and when someone yelled "it's too bad such a small number died," the remark drew applause. The U.S. military added insult to such injury with a raid on the DP camp. The American soldiers broke down doors, trampled on religious items, and showed no regard for civil liberties. In fact, the military police showed very little concern for war criminals. The musty records of the Günzburg unit contains only one circular asking for personnel to be on the lookout for a suspected war criminal believed in the area. He was not Joseph Mengele.

True, war criminals were not the chief priority of military governors, whose main mission was to lay the foundation for a new democratic German society. Pursuit of the outlaws was the responsibility of the U.S. Army's Counter-Intelligence Corps (CIC).

In fulfilling its role the Günzburg detachment of CIC found the rehabilitation of Karl Mengele and Söhn compelling. After all, the company had been the largest employer, and its basic products, which the factory continued to manufacture, were just the items needed to help feed Europe and stimulate the economy. When the war ended, the assembly lines of the business were almost at a standstill. But thanks to Karl Mengele's foresight and his position, the company had acquired an enormous pile of wood. The family patriarch had donated some of the lumber to rebuild parts of Günzburg and other places hard hit by bombs. But enough of the huge inventory of wood, plus some carefully husbanded iron, remained, thereby placing the Mengeles in a position to cash in on the postwar rebuilding boom.

The military government records show a recovery that started in July 1945 with an allotment of coal for repair of threshers, grass cutters, and hay lifters. Within three years Mengele executives were protesting against restrictions by the U.S. government that interfered with sales, threatening, they said, an order for 100 threshers from the Soviet Zone.

Karl Mengele had been restored to respectability. Almost ten years after V-E Day the *Günzburger Zeitung* paid the town's first citizen its homage: " . . . during his entire life a convinced fighter for all patriotic causes, a warm friend of the German spirit and German ways." Indeed, the patriot backed the Kaiser until 1918, supported Weimar at least moderately, and faithfully served the regime that took power in 1933. The newspaper added, "He never abused his so influential position for political purposes."

The paper did not consider whether adroit political footwork among the Nazis brought Karl Mengele his influence and his wealth. After all, the prosperity of the company benefitted the town, with a quarter of the work force on the Mengele payroll.

Indeed, the chief burgomaster from 1947 to 1970 was a Dr. Seitz, linked to Karl Mengele in a cordial friendship cemented by Seitz's position as the notary for the company. Seitz did not encourage the start-up of new industries in Günzburg, businesses that might compete for labor or materials or land useful to Mengele. Closer to the Mengele family interests between the critical years of 1947 to 1949, Burgomaster Seitz supervised the police, and it was during these years that responsibility for ferreting out war criminals and prosecuting them was gradually shifted over to the nascent German government.

At the top, then, there was clearly no incentive to look for a suspected war criminal named Mengele. At the bottom, in the *Unterstadt*, there was no fervor either, due to economic self-interest, disinterest and outright hostility to Nazi-hunting.

So it is easily credible that Joseph Mengele could have spent the first years after he fled Auschwitz tucked away in an undisturbed corner of Bavarian Germany, and that Mengele money paid for silence by local people, or even U.S. personnel.

In January 1985, as a result of a petition submitted by the Simon Wiesenthal Center in Los Angeles under the U.S. Freedom of Information Act, the Department of the Army released a copy of a letter dated April 26, 1947 and written by Benjamin Gorby, a special agent assigned to the Counter-Intelligence Corps while stationed at Regensberg in Bavaria.

Gorby's single page memorandum was addressed to the commanding officer of a Vienna-based CIC unit. Wrote Gorby: "This office has received information that one Dr. Mengele, Jos., former chief medical doctor in Auschwitz Extermination Camp, has been arrested in Vienna." His informant, said the CIC agent, stated "to the best of his knowledge Dr. Mengele was arrested in the U.S. Zone of Germany." Gorby suggested the tip be checked out and that if Mengele were located he should be questioned about the fate of twenty Jewish children removed by

him from Auschwitz and taken to an unknown place. Gorby
added that the father of one of the youngsters confirmed that
Mengele had taken the children.

The Gorby letter has made headlines. It has been taken as
proof that the doctor was once in U.S. custody. Indeed, within
a few days of publication two former GIs came forward and said
they thought they remembered a prisoner who fitted the description. Walter Kempthrone, a retired California aerospace
engineer, recounted his experience in July 1945. As a nineteen-
year-old soldier he had guarded prisoners at the Idar–Oberstein
detention camp in the U.S. sector. During a press conference at
the Wiesenthal Center, Kempthorne related that other U.S. soldiers identified a man of five feet, eight inches tall, 160 pounds,
with black hair that he "apparently attempted to bleach" as
"Mengele, the bastard who sterilized 3,000 women at Auschwitz."

Kempthorne, who initially said he had not gotten "a full view"
of the prisoner, has now expanded the scene in which he encountered the suspect. "His appearance scared me, because he
was breathing very hard, red-faced and perspiring like someone
who had just finished a mile run." Kempthorne said the guards
had been tormenting the prisoner, making him exercise in the
midsummer heat. One remarked, "We're getting him in shape
to get hung. This here is Mengele. The bastard that sterilized
3,000 women at Auschwitz."

A second former GI posted to Idar–Oberstein also has
remembered an inmate described as "the sterilization doctor"
who "sterilized 6,000 women." He described the maneuvers
urged on Mengele as "luftwaffe," in which the prisoner rushed
about imitating an airplane.

Aside from the unpalatable truth that the Idar–Oberstein
guards enjoyed their own form of what Auschwitz warders called

"sport" (though with far less deadly effect), the Gorby–Kemp-thorne episode strikes one as suspect. Two years separate the alleged incidents; one cannot support the other. It strains credibility to believe Mengele would have been held for two years without positive identification as a wanted war criminal. The lists bearing his name originated in May 1945, and continued to make the rounds of CIC offices as late as 1948.

It is also difficult to believe that he would have been casually released from Idar–Oberstein in 1945 when even the common enlisted men knew him for having allegedly sterilized "3,000" or "6,000" women. Gorby's suspicion that Mengele was in custody two years later rests on the unsubstantiated word of an informant who hedged his tip with, "to the best of my knowledge." The informant never says he saw Mengele nor does he reveal his source. Gorby has steadfastly vouched for the reliability of his informant in 1985, but the tipster could have been mistaken or received a false lead.

While living in Brazil, Mengele told Gitta Stammer, a Hungarian émigré whose farm he managed, that he had been taken into custody after the war by the Americans or the British—she is vague on which—but was released when he did not appear on any wanted list. Unless Mengele was taken before May 1945, this is clearly not true, since starting that month the circulars all name him. Of course Mengele may well have disposed of identification papers, as did Adolf Eichmann, and used an alias.

There is also the possibility of a breakdown in communications that enabled Mengele to go free. Initially the Americans tried to make the widest possible investigation of potential malefactors. Everyone over the age of eighteen in the American Zone at the war's end was required to fill out a questionnaire designed to screen out war criminals. The task was enormous. Five hundred tribunals with a staff of 22,000 investigators (poorly trained and often less than zealous) examined three million charges. The courts punished 900,000 people, which sounds staggering, except that for most all such punishment meant was removal from a political or civil office.

The Americans compiled a list of 5,000 major war criminals. Fewer than 200 actually stood trial. The British and the French also reduced their prosecutions. The three nations convicted a total of 5,025 for crimes under the Nazi banner. More than 800 death sentences were decreed; 486 persons actually were executed. On the other side of the hardening Iron Curtain as many as 85,000 were tried, convicted, and punished.

Further, a vociferous U.S. lobby decried war-crimes trials. Representative John Rankin of Mississippi, as ardent a racist as anyone in the Nazi legions, announced: "I desire to say that what is taking place in Nuremberg, Germany, is a disgrace to the United States . . . a racial minority, two and a half years after the war closed, are in Nuremberg not only hanging German soldiers but trying German businessmen in the name of the U.S." (Neither German soldiers nor the industrialists who profited from slave labor were hung nor were Robert Jackson and Telford Taylor members of a racial minority.) Senator Joseph R. McCarthy of Wisconsin fought against war-crimes trials for Waffen SS troops who shot down U.S. prisoners at Malmédy. Iowa Judge Charles F. Wennerstrum came home from his labors as a judge in the occupied territory and attacked the war-crimes tribunals. Telford Taylor responded to Wennerstrum: "Your behavior arises out of a warpéd psychopathic mental attitude."

The pursuit of Joseph Mengele then, literally, ran into a dead end. In 1947 Gisella Perl, living in the United States, wrote to the chief counsel for War Crimes in Nuremberg, volunteering to depose information about Mengele. She received an answer signed by Col. Edward H. Young that stated: "Joseph Mengerle [sic] was declared dead as of October, 1946." Oddly enough, both Perl and Olga Lengyel added an "r" in the middle of the doctor's surname in books about their lives at Auschwitz.

Columnist Jack Anderson found a copy of a document dated January 19, 1948, in which Telford Taylor responded to a "request for information regarding Dr. Mengerle" from Washington. Taylor reiterated the report of Col. Young, indeed, perhaps based on that report: "We wish to advise our records show Dr. Mengerle is dead as of October, 1946."

It seems most unlikely that confusion arose because of the wrong sixth letter in the spelling of the name, or that there also was a real "Mengerle" who happened to die in October 1946 and whose name was carried just below "Mengele" on war crimes lists. So how account for such authoritative claims of death? Confusion, breakdown in communications as mentioned, misinformation and/or disinformation. To each his own. In any case, in spite of the death notices, Mengele properly spelled was listed as living and wanted in a circular issued in February 1947, at least four months after he supposedly died.

But even in the face of such inconsistency, there was no passion to find Mengele now. The Cold War was in full swing, and many Americans were more interested in countering what they perceived as the Soviet menace than in retribution. The CIC stopped worrying about the Joseph Mengeles, war criminals, and recruited the Klaus Barbies. Nazi policemens' ancient crimes were deemed less important than their value as intelligence agents. Indeed, one fanciful rumor about Mengele places him in a British-run school for espionage whence he was smuggled out of the country to serve Her Majesty in South America. It is, of course, nonsense; Mengele had no intelligence background and would in any case be a *most* unlikely recruit.

Nor did the Angel of Extermination seem in jeopardy from his countrymen as they assumed responsibility for dealing with war crimes. The newly independent West German government of the late 1940s at first showed no enthusiasm for endeavors along these lines. And when prosecutions did occur, the sentences were essentially slaps on the wrists. Mengele might well have remained in Günzburg several more years awaiting the first sign of a general amnesty or the expiration of a statute of limitations.

Still, reluctant as German law-enforcement officials seem to have been, the heinous nature of Mengele's crimes apparently stirred some action. Preparations were made to arrest him; a citizen of Günzburg supposedly advised authorities that the doctor was in the vicinity.

But even before the remnants of the Third Reich hoisted their white flag, members of the SS had looked to their own future. While untold amounts of booty had been cached, leading to treasure hunts even forty years later, the principal order of business centered on helping one another in the face of the vengeance of the victors. Some SS diehards may have yearned to keep alive the Nazi movement, but most concentrated on a means of saving their skins. They created the *Organisation de Ehemaligen SS-Angehörigen* with the acronym ODESSA. SS internees in Allied POW camps formed a second group, *Spinne,* or Spider. Both organizations set up networks to assist wanted men to escape from Germany. They established safe houses, forged papers, trained guides and go-betweens, plotted routes and techniques for border crossings, and arranged for sanctuaries in Spain and Italy. They also developed outposts outside Europe where Nazi refugees would be helped to establish new lives.

Neither ODESSA nor Spinne operated as formally structured groups. There were no membership cards, no minutes of the last meeting or hospitality chairmen. They worked together as a brotherhood of the defeated with a common interest in survival.

It is believed by some that as Western intelligence units

sought to improve their sources they occasionally joined with ODESSA in helping war criminals to escape. The infamous "Rat Line," which funnelled a series of SS grads to South America serviced the needs of both ODESSA and U.S. intelligence. For notorious example, Klaus Barbie was assisted by the CIC and disguised as Klaus Altmann, with his wife and two children, took the rat-line through Salzburg to Trieste and Genoa. From Genoa, the port-city, they sailed to Buenos Aires. This was in payment for Barbie's espionage activities against European communist agents and organizations. The CIC was well aware at the time of Barbie's war crimes against the French.

Germans employed by the Allies officially manned the borders. Ironically Marc Berkowitz found it much more difficult to leave than his former captors. Several times he was turned back by border guards. Eventually the American army picked him up near Travisio. "The British were pushing the Americans to stop DPs because so many Jews were entering what they called Palestine illegally. A black GI let me go," remembers Berkowitz. "I could have been given a fifteen-year sentence."

Who assisted Mengele at the time is unknown, but the best guess routes him through the slopes of Bavaria into the Italian Tyrol, and on to Rome. Italy, the former ally and then the enemy of Nazi Germany, had become a sanctuary for the fleeing Nazis. Particularly Rome, because of the power of Bishop Alois Hudal, officially the rector of the German Church in the Eternal City. Hudal is a puzzling figure. He had gratified Hitler through his input into the 1933 concordat. The other Vatican representative involved in the concordat was Eugenio Pacelli, who had been annointed Pope Pius XII and governed the Church from 1939 to 1958. Hudal and Pius XII had teetered on a very thin wire during the occupation of Rome by the Nazis. While the Pope equivocated over the persecutions of the Jews he agreed to ransom some Italian Jews with Church gold. He refused openly to condemn the behavior of the Nazis, even though they had violated the concordat of 1933 that he made with them not to persecute Catholics or oppose the Church.

Bishop Hudal, however, did write a letter on his own monogrammed stationery (as opposed to that with the Vatican seal) asking for a halt to deportations of Jews. He argued that arrests of Jews would be "used by the anti-German propagandists as a weapon against us Germans." True, the Bishop raised no moral issues, yet at the time of the roundup that sent Arminio Wachsberger to Auschwitz, Hudal even sheltered a number of Jews in the Monasterio dell'Anima. In his play *The Deputy* Rolf Hochhuth excoriates Pius XII for his temporizing although he praises Bishop Hudal for his letter.

Yet while Bishop Hudal is regarded as having shown more compassion than the Holy Father, he is also the man who opened the doors of his institutions to a horde of escaping German war criminals. Adolf Eichmann, Walter Rauff, chief of the SS in Milan, Otto Reinhardt, governor of Galicia and responsible for the deaths of as many as 800,000 Jews, enjoyed the hospitality of Roman Catholic sanctuaries under the aegis of Bishop Hudal. The most popular hideout was a Franciscan convent on Via Sicilia, just off the famed Roman Via Veneto.

And in 1949 Joseph Mengele, baptized a Roman Catholic and presumably more acceptable than some others, took up residence in the Via Sicilia convent. (His confession would have tested the most devout priest's belief in the salvation of man if not his faith in God). Mengele kept himself invisible in Rome, biding his time. He told Rolf Mengele that Italian police detained him for three weeks, then let him go with apologies. In the summer of 1949 Mengele, equipped with Italian Red Cross Passport 100501, traveled to Genoa. At the time the Italians issued 500,000 such documents. "We received applications for travel documents from all over the place," says an official today.

Flight

"People could travel with our documents, including unfortunately those who misused our confidence and made false statements. Nazis and criminals did not have a rubber stamp on their foreheads."

Mengele's passport identified him as Helmut Gregor, of northern Italian extraction, a mechanic. No one paid close attention to his credentials, even though the photograph on the passport was that of his brother Alois. At Genoa Mengele then boarded a ship bound for Argentina.

Helmut Gregor of Argentina

IN BUENOS AIRES Mengele relaxed. His brother Alois was on hand representing the Mengele company interests in South America. Germans fleeing persecution, looking for new economic opportunities, or fearful of the political climate in Europe flooded into South America, 20,000 arriving in Argentina alone between 1948 and 1953. Buenos Aires had the look of a European city; its citizens could have passed for those of Berlin or Munich, and the country's ruler, Juan Perón, was a man altogether out of the Hitler mold.

As "Helmut Gregor," Mengele moved unnoticed, untroubled

in Argentina, occupying rooms in a handsome house on Avenida Arenales in the so-called Florida section of the city, a neighborhood marked by pristine white buildings, handsome oak garage doors and clean streets. He insinuated himself into local society sufficiently to become a member of a bridge group, which included Jews. They, of course, knew him only as one more refugee from Germany. At home in Günzburg Hans Latserner, a lawyer who represented a number of accused war criminals, had been retained to keep watch over any proceedings directed against Mengele. But during the first years of his life in Argentina there was no effort to find him.

There was one disappointment for Mengele. He had expected Irene to follow him, but she refused. In fact, she had confirmed the fears of her in-laws by failing to conform to the pattern of a Mengele wife. Shortly after her husband decamped, Irene Mengele moved to Freiburg, several hundred miles from Günzburg. The family, upset by such show of independence, had been further devastated by the death of Karl, Jr., in 1949 when he was only thirty-seven years old.

In 1954 Karl Mengele, Sr., felt conditions were safe enough for him to visit his son in Argentina. When he arrived he brought bad news for Joseph—Irene wanted a divorce. Her husband, a fugitive, had little alternative but to agree and the marriage was dissolved by mail. Irene promptly remarried.

Two years later, with all so quiet on the prosecutorial and war-criminal-hunting fronts, Mengele boldly abandoned his alias of Helmut Gregor and obtained an Argentinian foreign resident's permit under his own name. To secure the necessary credentials he went to the West German embassy in Buenos Aires and through its offices requested a copy of his birth certificate from Günzburg. Hans Sedlmeier, an official of the Mengele company from Günzburg, even accompanied him to the embassy to help prove his identity!

Equipped with his new papers, Mengele in 1956 traveled to Switzerland, where he met his son, twelve-year-old Rolf, who was under the impression that he was spending a ski holiday with his uncle from Argentina. The fiction was easy to pass off since Alois, an actual uncle, did live in Buenos Aires. Not until three years later did the adolescent learn that the uncle he had met in Switzerland was actually his father. Also on hand were Martha, his brother Karl's widow, and her son, Karl Heinz.

As for Joseph Mengele, he could travel to Europe in 1956 under his own name, and no country had issued an arrest warrant or served an extradition notice anywhere. Remarkable but true. Mengele proceeded to live comfortably if not conspicuously. He even went so far as to have his name listed in the Buenos Aires telephone book. One widely circulated account has it that he performed abortions and that in 1959 a woman died because of his surgical error. The police, so the story goes, arrested Mengele but allowed him to leave after two hours when a friend arrived with a bribe. Nazi hunter Simon Wiesenthal and the late Ladislas Farago, an author, as well as several news magazines have printed this story. Argentine police records, however, show no evidence of Mengele being tied to abortion. Although termination of pregnancy is illegal in Argentina, a Catholic country, it has long been practiced rather openly by midwives there. So it does seem rather unlikely that Mengele would have resorted to backroom illegal abortions, thereby risking problems with authorities for very little reward (midwife services were widely available at a nominal fee).

There was, of course, a need for income, and early on the family doled out money through its offices in Buenos Aires. The fugitive may have also brought a large sum with him. And when father Karl came for a visit he likely did not come empty-handed. In 1957 a company called Fadro Farm was registered in Argentina for the purposes of selling chemicals and pharmaceuticals. Capitalized at $1 million, Fadro Farm listed Mengele as a partner. Clearly the Mengele company advanced his share of the investment. It is also assumed that Mengele further enhanced his income by sales of Mengele farm equipment to South American customers.

In 1956 Mengele received some interesting visitors in Buenos Aires—Martha Weil Mengele, the widow of his brother Karl, and her son Karl Heinz. One account has it that the patriarch of the family, during his 1954 meeting with his son, had advanced the notion of a marriage to Martha. Whatever, in 1958 in Uruguay, the couple did indeed marry, the groom using his original name. The union, ironically, had a distinctively Judaic quality, it being a tradition among Jews for a brother to take into his family a sibling's widow or, if a bachelor, to marry her. On a practical basis, a marriage to Martha provided a convenient and natural means to siphon funds to Joseph. At the same time, by such a marriage the family protected itself against the possibility that Martha might remarry and her inheritance in the company business pass into the hands of an outsider. The Mengeles had already protected themselves against any problems involved in a legacy to Joseph when he formally renounced any claims to an inheritance, thereby negating in advance any prosecutor who might try to impound his portion of ownership. And presumably in return the family guaranteed to support him. Significantly Rolf Mengele, whose mother took another husband, never became an official of the company as did Karl Heinz and Alois's son Dieter.

Trouble from the past reared its head in the form of Hermann Langbein, who had been sent to Auschwitz as a political prisoner. Langbein had fought with the Loyalists in Spain in the 1930s and after the *Anschluss* (Hitler's forced merger of Austria and Germany) was ticketed to a KZ. As a clerk at Auschwitz, Langbein was in a position to collect damning details on Mengele's life. In 1959 Langbein was serving as general secretary of the International Auschwitz Committee, composed of alumni intent on perpetuating the memory of the Holocaust and seeking out its perpetrators. When Simon Wiesenthal asked Langbein for any information on Mengele, the general secretary advised the Nazi hunter that Irene Mengele's divorce suit had been filed in Freiburg, Irene's place of residence and the last legal German one for Mengele. The files in Freiburg gave up some letters from Mengele to his attorney, Laternser, and on these appeared Mengele's address in Buenos Aires.

Langbein and Wiesenthal, both Austrian citizens, now pressured the West Germans for action against Mengele. Their efforts paid off with an arrest warrant issued by the Freiburg state prosecutor on June 7, 1959. Subsequently, the Bonn federal government requested the extradition of Mengele from Argentina.

Argentina rejected the first writ because Mengele no longer lived at the given address. Unless the West Germans produced the correct location, the Argentinians would refuse to take any action. Obviously officials in Buenos Aires were reluctant to move on the case; certainly the police in Argentina could have tracked down Mengele earlier, particularly since he used his own name.

Wiesenthal contacted a friend in Argentina who supplied the doctor's last two known addresses, and on December 30, 1959, the hunt narrowed to a single house located at 968 Virrey Vertiz in the Vicente Lopez section of Buenos Aires. Wiesenthal's account is that he advised Langbein, who in turn notified West German prosecutors.

The legal machinery proceeded at a snail's pace. Early in January 1960 a second request for extradition came from Bonn. Argentine officials dallied; one even suggested, presumably with a straight face, that the charges against Mengele might be considered *political,* for which extradition would be improper. Historically, even in clearly criminal cases extradition from South American countries has been difficult to obtain, and for years Brazil was a well-known safe harbor for U.S. embezzlers and swindlers. The reluctance to turn over war criminals was really not that exceptional. Interpol, for example, the international police organization, has steadfastly refused to cooperate in the apprehension of war criminals on the grounds that the offenses could be considered only political activities.

The result of the delays was to give Mengele's friends in Europe and South America time and the opportunity to warn him that he was in jeopardy. Rallying around were the Mengele executive Hans Sedlmeier and a German World War II hero, Colonel Hans Ulrich Rudel, the most decorated soldier of the Third Reich. Rudel had enlisted in the Luftwaffe in 1936, and as a bomber pilot flying mainly on the Eastern front was credited with destroying 519 tanks, 150 gun emplacements, 800 combat vehicles and damaging three large ships and seventy smaller craft. Shot down five times, he earned such decorations as the Gold on Oak Leaf with Sword and Diamonds and the Knight's Cross of the Iron Cross—the only man to receive the award in World War II. Rudel's last crash cost him a leg and put him in a prisoner-of-war camp. After his release he became a representative for various manufacturers, including Siemens, the electronics company that once had a factory at Auschwitz. Rudel's territory included South America, and although he was never listed as a war criminal he was a notorious right-winger and had helped Argentine dictator Juan Perón build his air force.

Among Rudel's customers was the Mengele company, and in the course of business he became well acquainted with the company's executive Hans Sedlmeier, who had become the company's designated contact for handling the affairs of Joseph Mengele. Mengele himself said that he met Rudel in Argentina, but it was Sedlmeier who asked Rudel to use his good offices on behalf of Mengele.

By 1959 Juan Perón had been ousted from power, but Rudel was still operating and was close to Alfredo Stroessner, the son of a Bavarian immigrant to Paraguay. General Stroessner had become President Stroessner in 1956 and ruled his fief of two million people with an iron fist. In 1959 Eugenio Jiminez y Nuñez held one of the three seats on the Paraguayan Supreme Court, among the duties of which was approving or disapproving petitions for naturalization. Jiminez was approached by a lawyer named Luis Martinez Miltos who, in the locutions of the Mafia, had some very dear friends at the top levels of Paraguay's power structure. A former ambassador to Brazil as well as once minister of Justice and Labor, Miltos knew Rudel well and moved easily now between government and private enterprise. In addition Miltos bore the deserved reputation as a Nazi—in fact, his acceptance into the country's ruling Colorado Party was delayed because of his ties to the NSDAP in Paraguay during World War II.

Remembers Judge Jiminez: "Miltos told me that it was urgent that I expedite the papers for a German doctor seeking citizenship." Jiminez knew nothing of the applicant but says he thought it odd that a physician had chosen to live in a rather unpopulated area where, except for some Germans, the natives did not even speak Spanish, using the Indian language of Guarani.

Miltos seemed to have arranged everything. A young Asunción lawyer, Cesar Augusto Sanabria, had been selected to submit the appropriate brief. Sanabria's father was an old compadre of Werner Jung, a naturalized German who owned a hardware store. Jung, a former Hitler Youth leader, had emigrated to Paraguay before World War II to help prepare the continent for the victory of Nazi Germany. Jung called Sanabria and asked him to come to the store to meet his client.

"He was a slim, dark man, had a moustache," recalls Sanabria, "with a space between his upper front teeth. He did not look like a German." There actually was almost nothing for Sanabria to do. Mengele had been well prepared: he was equipped with all of the necessary documents attesting to the facts of his birth; he had the proper statement demonstrating his economic integrity, a deposit slip from the Central Bank in Asunción for 5,000 guaranis (about $35.) He also had two Paraguayans ready to swear that he had lived in the country for at least five years. His witnesses were Werner Jung and Captain Alejandro von Eckstein, a 1930 emigree from Estonia on the Baltic Sea. Von Eckstein had fought alongside of the then Captain Stroessner in the great Chaco War between Paraguay and Bolivia from 1932 to '35.

After two or three brief meetings with his client Sanabria submitted the papers. The statements by the witnesses were, of course, perjury. Mengele had not lived in Paraguay for five years and von Eckstein admits he only met the doctor in 1957 or 1958. In October of 1959 Paraguay issued Mengele a passport and five weeks later "José Mengele" was a citizen. And since the laws of Paraguay forbade extradition of a citizen, *José* Mengele seemed to have acquired an impenetrable shield.

The next month, in November of 1959, Karl Mengele, Sr., died. It has been reported—not proved—that Joseph, or José, in an act of filial piety and at considerable risk, returned to Günzburg for the funeral. Petra Kelly, the leader of the left-wing Green Party in West Germany in 1985, and oddly enough born in Günzburg, maintains that according to information she received from three nuns Mengele hid out in a convent. Wiesenthal has said, "The whole town knew he was there, except the police." That is the extent of the evidence.

The notoriety eventually generated by the officials in Bonn did put a crimp in Mengele's commercial activities in South

America, his partners now informing him that his name was a liability and cutting him out of the company. And while the West Germans tried to capture Mengele through conventional international channels, a daring and unorthodox plan was being mounted by another interested party—the State of Israel. Busy forging a state from the small resident population in 1948, augmented by a deluge of immigrants from Europe after World War II in the face of determined British resistance, the Israeli government had little time or resources to devote to the hunt for war criminals. By 1960 Prime Minister David Ben-Gurion believed it was time for retribution. He summoned Isser Harel, chief of the Mossad, Israel's intelligence organization, and directed him to capture escaped Nazis for trials to be held in Israel. Israel had passed a law authorizing its government to try anyone who had committed crimes against the Jewish people even if such crimes were committed before the establishment of the Israeli state and regardless of where they were committed.

Although some accounts have it that Mengele was the first target, the number one object of Isser Harel's attentions was former SS Lieutenant Colonel Adolf Eichmann, Heydrich's traveling salesman assigned to peddle the Final Solution.

Harel says, "At the beginning of the fifties . . . I devoted some of my spare time to studying the history of the Holocaust. I was especially interested in the fate of the war criminals who were mainly responsible for the destruction of European Jewry. Two names stuck out, Adolf Eichmann, who was responsible for the implementation of the 'Final Solution,' and Dr. Joseph Mengele, the 'Angel of Death' of Auschwitz . . . I placed Eichmann and Mengele at the head of the Mossad's wanted list. Eichmann, because he generally was responsible for the destruction and because through his capture a trial would be held, thereby exposing the events of the Holocaust of Jews in Europe."

Like Mengele, Eichmann had availed himself of facilities provided by sympathetic Vatican officials. He too was housed in

Rome, where he obtained a passport endorsed by the Vatican and which identified him as mechanic Ricardo Klement, born in Bolzano of German parents—a carbon of the "Helmut Gregor" background.

A West German, Dr. Fritz Bauer, Chief Prosecutor of Hesse, pierced Eichmann's disguise. Bauer, unlike some of his colleagues, aggressively pursued war criminals with good reason. He was a Jew, a former Stuttgart judge imprisoned by the Nazis before escaping to Sweden. Bauer gleaned his clue to Eichmann's whereabouts from a West German intelligence agent who had penetrated ODESSA. Bauer forwarded the tip to Isser Harel, and agents of the Mossad discreetly swept Argentina.

This was difficult because Eichmann exercised great caution. He stayed out of sight, changing his address frequently. However, the Argentine police were aware of Ricardo Klement's true identity, and while they had no reason to apprehend him, they did keep him under surveillance.

Mossad agents worked for positive identification of Klement as Eichmann. Secretly, they photographed the suspect from a number of angles and shipped the pictures to Tel Aviv and to Germany to be checked with persons who had known Eichmann. But he had aged badly, and Klement seemed too old to be Eichmann. The photographic results were considered inconclusive, until a picture of March 21 caught Klement bearing a bouquet of flowers to his home. The date coincided with Eichmann's marriage anniversary. For the Mossad this quirky detail was persuasive. Preparations to spirit Eichmann to Tel Aviv began.

Harel says his appetite for the operation increased when Commander Jorge Messina, Director General of the Argentinian Central Intelligence Agency, supplied the Israeli agents with a memo stating that Klement "has been seen with another high-ranking Nazi in the neighborhood of La Gallareta, in the province of Santa Fe. The description of that other man corresponds to that of Joseph Mengele."

The prospect so tempted Harel that he decided to go to Buenos Aires himself to take personal charge of operations. When some Israeli officials fretted over the enormous costs of sending a special jet to Buenos Aires to carry Eichmann to Israel, Harel says he replied, "To make the investment more worthwhile we'll try to bring Mengele with us as well."

Eichmann lived on Garibaldi Street in Buenos Aires. One morning the commando team watched him board a bus to work and then waited until about 6:30 p.m. As the unsuspecting Eichmann stepped off the bus and began the short walk to his house, a pair of Mossad operatives approached, one from the front, one from the rear. They grabbed Eichmann and hustled him into a car whose motor was running. The whole operation took possibly thirty seconds. Eichmann managed to cry out once, but the car sped off before anyone noticed what had happened. Eichmann was taken to a previously arranged safe house.

Harel then deputized an agent to interrogate Eichmann about Mengele. The strategy called for Eichmann to be told the Israelis already knew the doctor was in Buenos Aires and he should now give them the exact address. Eichmann did not deny that he knew Mengele but he steadfastly insisted he knew nothing about his whereabouts, claiming he had no knowledge that Mengele was even in South America. Harel refused to believe him and ordered a more intensive interrogation. Eichmann then broke to the extent of saying he feared for the lives of his wife and children.

Harel in turn wondered if Eichmann really believed any aid given to the Israelis would provoke vengeful acts against his family or whether they would simply be cut off from financial help. Operating on the latter assumption, the Mossad chief tried to bring Eichmann around with a promise to support Eichmann's wife and children if he gave Mengele's address. Eichmann still refused. "I felt that his obduracy stemmed not from any sense of loyalty but from sheer funk," Harel reported in his memoirs, dictated or written in Hebrew and which therefore may suffer from a clumsy translation. But continued pressure on Eichmann did finally bring the reluctant disclosure that Mengele had lived in a boarding house run by a German woman named Jurmann.

With this lead, Harel now tried a new tack. His agents found an Israeli couple spending some time in their former home country of Argentina. Both were fluent in Spanish and could pass for natives. The husband, Binyamin Efrat, told Harel that he "had heard of Mengele but didn't know much about him." Efrat's ignorance of Mengele's career indicates the surprising lack of information about him published in either Argentina *or* Israel as late as 1960. After Harel filled in the high—low—points of Mengele's career the Efrats agreed to assist the Mossad.

The husband and wife team proceeded to reconnoitre the neighborhood in Vicente Lopez where Mengele reportedly lived and learned from local residents that a North American couple supposedly lived at the Virrey Vertiz address given for Mengele. Harel speculated that Mengele might have used that story as a cover now that the West Germans had issued a warrant for him.

Binyamin was then instructed to approach a local postman and say that he was looking for a long missing uncle who supposedly lived in the area but whose address he had lost.

"And what was your uncle's name?" the mailman asked.

"Dr. Menelle," answered Binyamin, mispronouncing the name as per instructions from Harel.

"Dr. Menelle? Oh yes. There was a person by that name in the neighborhood. He lived over there"—the mailman pointed to the suspected house—"until a few weeks ago." Binyamin pressed him for a forwarding address but the postman said he had not received one. Further checking at the post office for Dr. Mengele—the correct name was now used—brought the frustrating response that while he had indeed resided at the house in question he had left without filing a new address.

Harel, in his book *The House on Garibaldi Street,* reports that another possible lead on Mengele was a garage in Vicente Lopez where Mengele reportedly kept several lathes. Binyamin visited the workshop and asked for some special lefthand screws such as could be turned out by lathes owned by Mr. Gregor (the original alias employed by Mengele). A secretary asked Binyamin to wait while she checked with her superiors. She came back briefly, seemed to scrutinize him and then disappeared to the rear of the shop. Finally she came back to say that no one knew of any "Gregor and that lathe work was not done there."

Harel was sure from such behavior that Mengele was indeed known to the garage workers—the delay and the checking meant that only certain authorized people were to know of Gregor and Binyamin failed to pass muster.

Harel now ordered one final effort. Binyamin managed to inveigle himself into the Vicente Lopez house and found that the people living there had recently moved in, just as the postman had said. Mengele was gone. Harel could stall no longer. A drugged Eichmann, passed off as a man injured in an accident, was bundled aboard an airplane and flown to Israel for trial.

Eichmann was abducted in May 1960. As word of the derring-do of the Mossad spread, people involved in the apprehension of war criminals began to talk about the death two months earlier in Argentina of an Israeli woman named Norita Eldodt who had been found dead at the foot of a precipice in Bariloches, a resort in the foothills of the Andes. It had originally been listed and accepted as an accidental fall, but now in the context of the adventures of the Israeli agents and the narrow escape of Mengele foul play was suggested.

Bariloches had long been popular with the German expatriate crowd. Indeed, the area resembled the European Tyrol, attracting a large German resident community. Others of German extraction frequently spent vacations at the resort. Mengele reportedly stayed in Bariloches on a number of occasions, including during March of 1960 under the name of Dr. Fritz Fischer.

Which was also when Norita Eldodt was there. (Her name has been variously given as Nora Eldoc and Nourit Eddad as well.) An employee of the Israeli trade mission in Cologne, ostensibly she had come to Argentina several months earlier to see relatives who had taken refuge there before the outbreak of the war.

According to Simon Wiesenthal's *The Murderers Among Us,* "One evening in the ballroom of a local hotel, she suddenly found herself face-to-face with Mengele. The local police report does not say whether he recognized her. Mengele had 'treated' thousands of women in Auschwitz. But he did notice the tattooed number on her lower left arm. For a few seconds the victim and the torturer stared at each other silently. Eyewitnesses later testified that no word was said. A few days later she did not return from an excursion into the mountains. The police were notified. Several weeks later, Miss Eldoc's bruised body was discovered near a crevasse. The police made a routine investigation and ascribed her death to a mountain climbing accident."

In 1974 came the late Ladislas Farago's *Aftermath,* a book in which the central figure was Martin Bormann, alive and well in South America, with Mengele featured as the second lead. In this account the scene at Bariloches takes on the trappings of a drama of sex and murderous intrigue. Mengele has become quite smitten with Nora Eldoc. A romance flowers with luncheon tête-à-têtes, cocktails, dinner, and dancing. One day he and Eldoc hike into the hills. A few hours later three men, Mengele and his two bodyguards, arrive at a cafe on the road back to

Bariloche . . . one of them rushes in shouting in Spanish with a heavy German accent: "A terrible accident! The woman who was with us fell off the cliff!" After three days a search party finds her broken body under a promontory. Farago explains that one of Mengele's associates had broken into her room, "had come upon her secret, and it tolled her inevitable doom." In the false bottom of her suitcase the aide found her Israeli passport. Farago did not equivocate. He quoted from an alleged Argentine police report that described her as a member of the Israeli Secret Service who had come to Bariloches with a group of Israelis who stayed at a different hotel. "It would have been logical to send Nora to set up Mengele for the kill," says Farago. "They correctly gauged the soft spot in his armor, his weakness for the opposite sex. A strange man would never have had a chance to get through to him and observe the routine of his daily movements from such close quarters. A pretty woman could and Nora did." Curiously, Farago did not accept the story of Wilma, the Jewish mistress, who helped Mengele escape, and which fits the alleged pattern of a "soft spot."

Werner Brockdorff, the creator of Wilma, offered his own explanation for the death of Norita Eldodt, although he lists her as Judith Aldot. Brockdorff claims that those Jews who had escaped from Poland, first by cooperating with the Nazis and then availing themselves of the services of Wilma and Mengele, desperately feared Mengele's death. To protect himself the doctor, says Brockdorff, warned: "I have deposited sealed envelopes at five different places. Should something happen to me, giving the impression of an unnatural death, these envelopes will be opened. And there will be a wave of suicides from the U.S.A. to Israel. They will protect me as long as I shall live."

Still according to Brockdorff, when Nora or Judith left for Argentina, persons with access to Israeli intelligence and who considered themselves vulnerable to Mengele's "sealed envelopes" contacted conspirators in Argentina. A former member of the Flemish SS, identified by Brockdorff only as "Albert," struck up a friendship with the Israeli woman. Mengele stayed out of sight. It was Albert who took her for a fatal hike into the hills.

The stories of the encounter between Eldodt and Mengele enjoyed widespread credence thanks especially to Dr. Michael Bar-Zohar, an Israeli government official and himself the author of several books including *The Avengers,* which depicts pursuits of war criminals. Farago credits Bar-Zohar as his source, and indeed the Israeli graphically describes the murder: The victim has gone into the hills with two guests, but not Mengele. "During the day, the three arrived at the top of a precipitous cliff which offered a magnificent view of 'the Switzerland of Latin America.' Suddenly one of the men slipped behind Nora Aldot and gave her a terrific blow on the back of her neck. Then he and his companion threw her over the precipice."

One would have thought that the dramatic effects in these versions, replete with dialogue, should perhaps have been sufficient to raise warning flags to news magazines in Europe, South America and the United States. Not so. They all swallowed the basic story. (Then again one must not forget the distinguished journals that bought and published Hitler's supposed secret diaries.)

It was left to enterprising Argentine journalists in 1961 to trace events and find that, in fact, Norita Eldodt had left Germany in 1933 for what was then Palestine. She was never in a concentration camp, had no tattoo number, and did not know Mengele. She had come to Argentina to see her sister, from whom she had been separated for many years. While in the country she met a group of young Jewish Argentines planning a stay in Israel. They asked her to coach them in their Hebrew and to educate them about Israeli culture. When the group decided to spend ten days in Bariloche as a combination vacation and study period for the trip they invited her to come along. Since she was a last-minute member of the party it was necessary for her to stay at a different hotel. The Argentine reporters interviewed several of the group, who described in great detail the climb into the hills, how people became separated and how poorly marked the trail was. When Norita did not appear immediately after everyone had descended, no one was especially alarmed because it was assumed she might have gone into town on her own or was back at her own hotel.

Perhaps the most telling argument against the notion that this was a crew of secret Nazi agents is that the entire group posed for pictures in Bariloches, including Norita Eldodt frolicking with a man wearing a bear costume. Hit teams do not customarily sit for the camera. No one, for example, has ever seen pictures of the team that kidnapped Eichmann.

With the recounting of the Norita Eldodt adventure as recently as the week that Mengele's body was discovered the troublesome pattern of disinformation and misinformation emerges. Nazi Brockdorff sought to denigrate the victims, painting Jews as Mengele allies. Nazi antagonists, consciously or otherwise, tried to speed up pursuit of Mengele by putting new, even more lurid crimes on him (a sort of coals to Newcastle exercise). Over the years both the defenders of this war criminal and his antagonists have been unwitting collaborators in laying down a thick smoke screen that obscured his whereabouts and distorted his character.

Misinformation, Disinformation and a Little Light

THE PACE OF THE MENGELE PURSUIT picked up as, on July 3, 1960, a court in Buenos Aires issued an arrest order, almost one year after Bonn's original request to detain the fugitive. The Argentine writ bore the signature of Federal Judge Jorge Luque, appointed by President Pedro Aramburu in 1956 as part of a cleanup of the Perón-corrupted courts.

A diminutive, gnomelike man, Luque proudly traces his lineage back to a priest who ministered to Pizarro's conquistadores engaged in the rape and conversion of Peru. Luque says he wanted to demonstrate to the world that the Argentine courts functioned on the basis of law, and like many of his countrymen, he had been offended by Israel's abduction of Eichmann, which he felt violated his nation's sovereignty and its court's authority.

"It was not fair or correct for the Israelis to kidnap Eichmann," he said, but conceded "it was logical. There had not been any request from Germany for his extradition. And we would not have recognized one from Israel. He had not committed his crimes there. The State did not even exist when he acted against the Jews. But the Germans had given us a proper request for the extradition of Mengele. My aim was to find him, put him in a safe place, and then let the courts resolve disposition under the rules of law, deciding whether he should be returned to Germany. In this way we could convince people to have confidence in Argentine justice."

He dismisses as invention a Ladislas Farago account in which he so burns with zeal that he commands the borders sealed. "A judge does not have that power." He also denies that Bonn authorities fed him false addresses for Mengele. Luque laughs as he points to an acknowledgement by Farago of his help. "I never even saw him."

Mengele apparently was apprised of Judge Luque's diligence, staying away from Argentina and settling down in Paraguay. Occasionally he spent days at the home of Werner Jung on Avenida MacArthur, a few blocks from Stroessner's presidential palace and the U.S. embassy. Much of the time Mengele lived on the hacienda of a German rancher, Alban Krugg, in Hohenau, about fifty miles from the capital city of Asunción.

The Belgian Nazi, Alfonz Dierckx, who met Mengele then, says the doctor was known as "Herr Fritz" or "Señor Fritz" to the local people. "He was a silent person," according to Dierckx, who said Mengele rarely alluded to his past but once confided that he was being persecuted for carrying out his duties during the war.

Von Eckstein, the military man who had falsely sworn that he knew Mengele as a Paraguayan resident for five years, says that between 1959 and 1961 he saw the doctor once or twice a month. "He would drive into Asunción in a jeep. Once he came with his wife, a blonde woman. Mengele was very simpatico, a scientist who spoke very little. Nobody had said he was a criminal. I knew him as a doctor. Then in 1961 Dr. Planas [Alberto Planas], the chief of police investigations, came to me and said, 'Look here, I've just had five Israelis visit me and they say they are looking for a war criminal.' I answered, 'What have I to do with that!' Planas told me, 'It is your friend Mengele.' I was shocked. To me Mengele would not kill a mosquito. I told Werner Jung and after that I did not see Mengele, except once he came on a visit in 1964 or '65."

Needless to say, having been tipped off by Jung to the Israeli hunters, Mengele now determined safety lay underground. His disappearance from public view clearly dates to a helpful message relayed to Jung by von Eckstein.

Precisely who the five alleged-to-be Israelis represented is uncertain. Their sponsors were not identified. Meanwhile, in any case, Isser Harel remained on the case. Mossad units scoured South America checking out possibilities for an Eichmann style coup against Mengele. In 1962 the agents pinpointed Mengele's hideout as somewhere in the triangle of territory where Paraguay, Argentina, and Brazil meet. Harel zeroed in on two locations. One site was a German-owned farm near Encarnación close to the border. Unfortunately, says Harel, surveillance could not verify Mengele's presence.

"It was very reasonable that Mengele did take refuge there," says Harel, "but not all the time. The farm was protected by armed guards. There of course was the option of an armed raid on the place in order to try and find and identify Mengele but that was impossible. We discovered, not without suffering casualties [never identified] while checking, that to take him would be a costly operation. It meant fighting our way into the Paraguayan jungle and fighting in a hostile heavily guarded area a cruel battle in order to take him with us. It would have generated a severe conflict with Paraguay. We also had to take into account that if we failed—whether because Mengele was not there or because of failure of the raid—we would not succeed in capturing Mengele for quite a while to come. In the meantime we had other information that Mengele had gone into hiding in German populated territory in rough conditions about forty kilometers from São Paulo in Brazil. We got this information from a Nazi agent who turned during our work in this area."

But again the Israelis could not confirm Mengele's presence at the site, and they abandoned operations involving the São Paulo sighting. In fact, Mengele was in Brazil during 1962 but living at Serra Negra, a good hundred miles from the city of São Paulo, not the twenty-five or thirty suspected by the Mossad.

The Mossad plots against Mengele in the 1960s in a sense illustrates some dangers of success. The intelligence agency had snatched Eichmann without losing a man. Most of the world approved; for once even the Soviets backed Israel in the United Nations Security Council when Argentina lodged an official protest. As Jorge Luque remarked, the strike against Eichmann was logical if not lawful. Bonn, however, was trying to snare Mengele by lawful means. Still, unwilling (not without at least historic reason) to assign good faith to the Germans, and perhaps carried on the crest of their own derring-do, the Israelis refused to employ conventional means and so perhaps stymied some productive results. Information to Bonn on Mengele's possible hideout might have brought an extradition petition to Brazil; a search by Brazilian police might have uncovered the fugitive even if he were not at the precise location tagged by the Mossad; and a hue and cry in Brazil might at the very least have caused Mengele to surface while looking for a new refuge.

There is little question that the kidnapping of Adolf Eichmann did frighten Mengele as well as some other Nazi fugitives in South America. Tales of Israeli hit teams and abduction squads circulated widely. Harel says, ". . . other wanted war criminals began to leave their hiding places. Many of them began to see Israeli commando units chasing them all over the place. We did not even try to calm them down. On the contrary, we increased their feeling of terror and fright as much as possible."

The campaign was stimulated by the likes of Farago, Bar-Zohar, and Wiesenthal, who offered a variety of plots to snatch Mengele. Dates and details do not quite coincide, but one much bruited adventure is set in 1964 at the Hotel Tirol near Hohenau.

"It was a hot, dark night," begins Wiesenthal's *The Murderers Among Us.* "Half a dozen men had trailed 'Dr. Fritz Fischer' to Suite 26 to the hotel. I later met some of them. They had formed a Committee of Twelve. They were twelve survivors of Auschwitz. Some had become wealthy and had donated considerable money for the purpose of bringing to justice some of their former torturers."

Wiesenthal then writes that six of the group drew the assignment in South America. "They were to seize Mengele alive and bring him to Frankfurt am Main where preparations for the Auschwitz trial were being made." (Actually that trial began in 1963 and by 1964 was coming to a close.) "A few minutes before one A.M. the men entered the lobby of the Hotel Tirol, ran up the stairway, and broke open the door of bedroom 26. It was empty. The hotel owner informed them that 'Herr Dr. Fischer' had left in a hurry ten minutes earlier, after getting a telephone call. He had been in such a hurry that he hadn't even bothered to take off his pajamas. He had put his suit over them, raced down the stairway, and disappeared into the night."

Bar-Zohar quotes Wiesenthal in *The Avengers:* "I know about those men. They came to see me, here in my office. . . . This Committee of Twelve had plenty of money and planned to kidnap Mengele, to take him to a yacht and judge him when out at sea." Bar-Zohar goes on, reporting that a few days after the raid on the Tirol the Brazilian police found the body of a young man. He had been shot in the head and had died "during a gun battle that night with the Nazi war criminal's bodyguard."

According to Farago, the vigilantes consisted of twelve young Brazilian Jews. Two of the group crossed the Paraná River on a reconnaissance mission. "They were next seen with their throats cut from ear to ear, floating down the river, their arms outstretched as if crucified."

Farago also concludes his saga of Norita Eldodt in this fashion: "Nobody died in the search for Eichmann. But Nora was the fourth known casualty of the hunt for Mengele. [The pair from the Tirol would make it six by Farrago's count.] The protective wall he had built around himself could be pierced. But nobody who pierced it lived."

As cited above, on one occasion Isser Harel said that the search for Mengele cost the Mossad "casualties," yet at another time he said that under his stewardship the agency never lost a life while pursuing Mengele. Among the best-kept secrets of intelligence units are their own failures; their successes tend to leak to the media. It has been said that nobody ever retires from the Mossad, even if he or she submits pension papers, and perhaps whatever Harel said should be viewed in that context, even though he did formally resign in 1963 after a dispute with Prime Minister Ben-Gurion.

Farago, on the other hand, mixes reputable sources, many of which are still alive at this writing, with seeming fantasy. Having published credible books before *Aftermath,* including a well-received biography of General George S. Patton, and having been an intelligence agent himself, Farago has been accepted as a reliable source on Mengele. But *Aftermath* is suspect, among other reasons because of its premise that Martin Bormann escaped to South America after 1945. A wide variety of experts on the lives of Third Reich leaders are well convinced that Bormann died in 1945. *Aftermath* concludes with the author at Bormann's bedside in a tiny hospital run by Bolivian nuns. Farago also implies an interview with Mengele when he describes his appearance in the 1970s and offers colloquial quotes from Mengele. Benno Weiser Varon, a former Israeli ambassador to Paraguay, had been interviewed by Farago, and questioned the author about his claim that he located Mengele in Paraguay and negotiated over the price of an interview. Farago told Varon that Mengele demanded $30,000 but that he snapped, "You're not worth that much, Dr. Mengele." Supposedly the unabashed war criminal then offered a Mengele byline for a book on twin-research for $100,000.

During a publication party for *Aftermath,* Farago told Varon he had met with Mengele. The diplomat inquired whether the exchange cost the requested $30,000. "Of course not," said Farago. "It was my faked interest in his twin-book that made him receive me." Varon asked why, if he had indeed seen Mengele, he did not indicate that the quotes in the book came directly from the doctor to him. Farago, a charming and witty fellow, replied with a straight face, "Had I quoted him directly, he could have sued me for payment."

The notion that the object of a search that, according to Farago, had already cost the lives of six people would have emerged from the dark shadows of the Paraguayan outback to plead in court for his rightful due—a mere $30,000—may be Ladislas Farago's most impressive mind-boggler.

Shortly before he died Farago told Varon that after he published a series of articles in British newspapers claiming to have found Martin Bormann, Simon and Schuster, a book publisher, offered him a substantial advance for a book predicated on a live Bormann. Perhaps in order to avoid a demand to return the money the author felt obliged to be creative about details on Bormann and added in accounts of Mengele as a bonus?

Another imaginative account about Mengele was offered by Erwin Erdstein, a Viennese-born refugee in South America. Erdstein insinuated himself into Brazilian police work. Known as "Dr. Erico," he represented himself as a scourge of war criminals. In his book *The Fourth Reich,* Dr. Erico recounted a tale of a trap set for Mengele in 1968. As Dr. Erico sought to ferry Mengele to Argentina into the hands of police, Paraguayans boarded Erdstein's boat to liberate the captive. "Mengele and his friend broke for safety," writes Erdstein. "I raised my gun and fired four bullets at Mengele. They struck him in the chest and side. He turned toward me, stared at me with a surprised expression and I shot again. This time it was a direct hit in the throat." Erdstein says he watched the Paraguayans fish Mengele out of the water. "His body was limp and I knew he was dead. He had been in the water at least five minutes."

Farago, this time a critic, concluded that if Erdstein shot anyone it was probably a smuggler. Confronted by Farago, Erdstein reportedly shrugged and admitted he apparently killed the wrong man—which hardly offsets the claims in *The Fourth Reich* of explicit dialogue with Mengele. As Dr. Erico, Erdstein's bailiwick was São Paulo. Had he actually had an effective network of informants, as he asserts, should he not have known or at least uncovered some evidence that almost under his nose hid the man he claimed to have shot down?

Like Hitler, Mengele's all too real satanic crimes elevated him to the heady atmosphere of a mythic figure. Not surprising, then, that as such he invited, indeed perhaps required, some highly colorful, and perhaps colored, accounts of his life and death.

With the West German government stolidly filing legal writs for his arrest and the Israelis stalking him, Mengele abandoned hopes of an open life. His brief marriage to Martha collapsed. It had never been a matter of passion on his part. He described her as "home-loving, religious, withdrawn into herself." She disliked being tucked away on a ranch in rural Paraguay. Around 1960 she chose to return to Europe, where her son Karl Heinz was a student. Martha settled first in Switzerland, then took up permanent residence in Merano, a town in the Italian Tyrol with many expatriate Germans, very few Jews, and a nearby Mengele factory.

The last actual witnesses had observed Mengele collecting his citizenship papers in Paraguay. The subsequent absence of hard information on him made possible, perhaps inevitable, the creative stories about him. But simply because he had dropped out of public view did not mean a lack of sightings. For example, a woman who said she survived Auschwitz had married a proprietor of a jewelry store in Asunción. One day in 1965 a pair of men entered the store. They spoke English and as she waited on them, the woman was dumbstruck. She suddenly recognized "Schöne Joseph," the person who with an insouciant wave of his hand spared her life twenty years or so earlier. Only after the customers left was she able to tell her husband that she had just seen Joseph Mengele.

During the same year, Eckhard Briest, the German Ambassador to Paraguay, acting on instructions from Bonn, raised the extradition matter with Paraguay's President Stroessner. The dictator refused to become involved on the grounds that Mengele held Paraguayan citizenship. Briest suggested that the papers had been obtained fraudulently, Mengele had falsely sworn residence for five years. Stroessner banged the desk with his fist. "Once a Paraguayan, always a Paraguayan." The incident terminated Briest's effectiveness, and Bonn was forced to recall and replace him. Another fifteen years passed before Bonn mustered the courage to ask again for Mengele's extradition.

Former Israeli Ambassador to Paraguay Benno Weiser Varon believes the accounts of the woman in the jewelry store and the incident that signaled the end of Ambassador Briest's career in Asunción. Varon actually arrived in Asunción in 1968 to take up his post under extremely sensitive conditions. A self-styled polemicist, Varon, like Mengele studied medicine. But while Mengele went on to infamy in his profession, Varon fled the Nazis in Vienna three months before completing his medical course and took refuge in Ecuador, where he became a journalist, the first syndicated columnist in that country.

"In 1946, because of my background, the Jewish Agency [then acting as the representative of the Jews in Palestine] drafted me to convert Latin Americans to the idea of a Jewish state," recalls Varon. "There were fifty-seven countries in the United Nations in 1948 and twenty of them were from Latin America." After establishment of the State of Israel, Varon accepted a post with the Jewish Agency in New York.

Because of his background and perhaps because some astute Israeli official perceived that the witty, intelligent, and entertaining Varon was the sort who could captivate, the former medical student was selected as ambassador to Paraguay at a critical moment. The country had suddenly assumed major importance because, under the rotating policy of the United Nations Security Council, Paraguay for two years would hold one of the ten votes delegated to the smaller powers. "I was sent there with one purpose," says Varon. "To win Paraguay's support for Israel in the Security Council. No one in Tel Aviv ever said anything to me about going to Mengele's sanctuary."

Officially Varon received no communications concerning Mengele, but in Asunción he was given a minimum of two tips a week on the whereabouts of the fugitive. At first he dutifully forwarded the information. But when he received no response from home and as he realized that everyone gave a different address, he took the position that since Israel was not officially in search of the Auschwitz doctor, the proper recipient for material was the German embassy. However, when even the U.S. ambassador pressed him to listen to a tipster, Varon felt that the sponsorship promised a legitimate finding. The suspect turned out to be six feet, four inches tall. No amount of plastic surgery could have so stretched Mengele.

Periodic announcements stating that Mengele roamed freely in Paraguay came from Tuviah Friedmann, a Haifa-based freelance Nazi hunter, and these reports did haunt Varon. After newspapers repeated Friedmann's accusations, the Paraguayan foreign minister would summon Varon. The tightly controlled Stroessner government could not understand how a private citizen such as Friedmann could utter calumnies against another country without the connivance of the Israeli leaders. Varon notes that the foreign minister, Dr. Raul Sapena Pastor, never disputed Friedmann's allegations. He only complained about the unfriendly attack on his country.

In a moment of undiplomatic exasperation, Sapena Pastor said, "Whatever Mengele did, he did as a German, in the name of Germany. You know our country. Do you believe anybody can hide here without people knowing who he is and where he is? This is not a matter for diplomats. This is a matter for commandos."

Whether this was an invitation for an extralegal expedition, Varon could not determine. But if the Mossad was still active, Varon says he was unaware of their movements. And still no word came for him to look for Mengele or any other war criminals. The original mission to Paraguay was, however, successful —the country backed Israel in every Security Council vote.

It seems interesting to note that no U.S. ambassador has reported scenes of this nature with the Paraguayan foreign ministers. Neither the State Department nor the White House ever risked the wrath of Stroessner with calls for the apprehension of a war criminal holding Paraguayan citizenship. Still, one U.S. agency, the CIA, did start to file reports concerning Mengele. In June of 1972 the first of these called attention of top officials to the "activities petty criminal [name blacked out] hid out at farm owned by one FNU [first name unknown] Mengele." It continued: "According [source name blacked out] Mengele resides in town of Encarnación, where he is known as Dr. Henrique Wollman. Report suggests he and others heavily involved in narcotics trade." (Henrique Wollman was an alias that has been put on Mengele by a number of sources.) The agent added that an attempt was being made to confirm whether the Mengele mentioned was the same "Auschwitz Concentration Camp doctor and notorious war criminal." It cited a 1965 broadcast from Rio de Janeiro in which former SS member Alfred Frankel told Interpol that Joseph Mengele had been seen in Encarnación and that he enjoyed the protection of Stroessner.

A followup CIA report seven weeks later adds more details. It dates Mengele's arrival in Paraguay as "first time, around 1951 and lived alternately Paraguay, Brazil, Argentina and Uruguay." The memorandum specifies a number of locations in Paraguay, and it repeats a rumor that he worked as an auto mechanic a few miles from the Brazilian border as well as some gossip that he lived on a "well-guarded ranch either near Encarnación or in Chaco [in eastern Paraguay]." The vagueness of the findings tends to erode confidence in the efficacy of the intelligence.

A four-page report concerning Mengele in Paraguay bears a June 7, 1974, date and describes a number of sources questioned about him. It starts with an account of "a former German soldier by the name of Federichi" who "had been beaten to death last year by Israeli terrorists who thought he was Mengele. Federichi's wife lost portions of one of her ears and her stomach was cut open as a result of the beating." The widow, it says, wrote a letter to the German ambassador requesting a pension since her husband had served in the army. The CIA correspondent noted: "These people . . . came from East Prussia at the end of WW II in an attempt to get away from political activities."

The West German prosecutor in the Mengele case since 1974, Hans Eberhard Klein, professes no knowledge of this incident. Nor have any Paraguayans in the government or in the press heard of the alleged murder of Federichi.

The June 7, 1974, CIA dispatch goes on to list a series of encounters with individuals who supposedly dealt with Mengele. In every instance names are blacked out, making it impossible to verify the statements. One person managed an establishment the name of which is obliterated; he is, however, described as "a former pro-Nazi who reportedly knew Mengele very well . . . said that the last time he saw Mengele was in 1970. Mengele had been a frequent guest and visitor and had resided in the nearby German community called Hohenau on a farm owned by"—name blacked out. The location sounds very much as if it were the Hotel Tirol, site of the alleged raid by the Committee of Twelve. The source appears to be a Belgian Nazi, Armando Raeynarts, who operated the Tirol. The owner of the farm very likely was Alban Krugg. The CIA agent also drew from the source: "Mengele was a nice person, that he had provided medical assistance to many people at no charge; that Mengele most frequently played a card game called Scat; that he never talked politics." One should consider the source of this tribute.

A second informant acknowledged that he was still a Nazi at heart, hoping for the rebirth of the movement in Latin America. He reluctantly admitted he could contact Mengele if necessary, but after a chat with some German publications a few years ago, a Paraguayan [position and name blacked out] "came to his house and advised him he had better keep his mouth shut on this matter." He remarked that Mengele was still in the vicinity but traveled with bodyguards.

A third confidant claimed that Mengele had undergone cosmetic surgery and appeared much younger than his age. He too advised that Mengele lived in a house guarded by "armed heavies."

And a fourth insisted he had seen Mengele's police file. Most interestingly, among its documents was a 1973 application for a Paraguayan passport. A one-year-old photograph of the doctor was supposedly part of the police dossier. If the information was correct, the dates are significant, as will be explained later.

Back in the United States that first report from the CIA naming Dr. Henrique Wollman, believed to be Dr. Joseph Mengele, as linked to a suspected narcotics dealer circulated slowly, very slowly, among appropriate agencies—the Drug Enforcement Administration, the U.S. Customs Service, the National Security Agency. These offices searched their files but could find no support for the proposition that Mengele was engaged in the dope trade. And in 1979, seven years after the report that first tied him to drug trafficking, the CIA advised its restricted circles that "the Mengele/narcotics connection mentioned . . . has been withdrawn from consideration for publication in the International Narcotics Review. It is the opinion of this office that the article, although a tantilizing [sic] bit of information, is based on very circumstantial and unsubstantiated evidence and does not warrant publication as finished intelligence." Indeed, one of the chief sources had even talked about Mengele as a roommate of Martin Bormann.

With Israel concentrating on the cultivation of South American good will, the Germans frustrated by Mengele's disappearance and alleged Paraguayan recalcitrance, and the U.S. disinterested or fumbling, the only real heat on the fugitive came from amateur and privately funded Nazi hunters.

Among the first of these to gain renown was Tuviah Friedmann, Israeli Ambassador Varon's cross. Born in 1923 at Radom, Poland, Friedmann says he escaped after several years of captivity in the Belzec concentration camp. During his incarceration, however, Friedmann claims he managed to eavesdrop on General Kurt Boetsche and his deputy, Wilhelm Blum, commanders of the KZ, as they reminisced about their hometowns, and was able to commit their addresses to memory.

After V–E Day Friedmann traveled to the cities where Boetsche and Blum lived, denounced them to the occupying authorities, and both men were promptly shipped to Poland, where they were convicted as war criminals and hung.

Friedmann, flushed with his first success, opted to make a career out of pursuit of war criminals and volunteered to serve as a secret agent for the victors, infiltrating prisoner-of-war camps, passing himself off as one more luckless soldier, and collecting intelligence on Nazi war criminals, including names and addresses, for occupying military government units.

As an employee of the Jewish Agency in Vienna, Friedmann interviewed displaced persons, cajoled them into revelations of Nazis active in their home areas, sometimes trading food parcels for scraps of information. He gathered photographs of suspects, showed them to victims of war criminals. He checked lists of city residents and, according to his account, uncovered numerous wanted men as well as some who should have been. Most of the war criminals uncovered by Friedmann were arrested by Soviet and Polish authorities, and a good many of them went to the hangman.

By 1950, with the State of Israel now in being, the Jewish Agency no longer needed a Vienna office and Friedmann migrated to Israel, bringing along the files accumulated in Vienna. Yad Vashem, the Jerusalem memorial to the Holocaust, employed him for a time, but he annoyed some of his associates by continuing to operate as a one-man posse. The function of Yad Vashem was and is to maintain remembrance of the great horror, not to serve as a headquarters for forays against war criminals. Eventually Friedmann separated from the institution.

After the capture of Adolf Eichmann an array of folks stepped forward to claim credit for their roles in the operation. Among them was Friedmann, and indeed *Time* magazine initially prepared a long story on him as the unsung hero, though further checking by *Time* considerably diminished Friedmann's role.

While some journalists and TV broadcasters continued to regard Friedmann as a reliable source, law-enforcement authorities were less convinced. Yet, when Friedmann started to campaign for the capture of Joseph Mengele he still managed to draw coverage in the newspapers, to the distress of Benno Weiser Varon in Paraguay. Friedmann asserted that Mengele was Stroessner's personal physician, a contention that drew an irate denial from officials in Asunción. Varon doubts that Mengele ever met Stroessner, and Colonel von Eckstein, admittedly not always reliable, declares the pair never met; in this instance he would seem to have little reason to be less than forthcoming. Friedmann also maintained that Mengele had made several trips to Miami under assumed names, and in 1979 agents from the U.S. Attorney General's office futilely waited at the Miami International Airport with a warrant for Mengele's arrest, insisting that they were acting on "more than just a tip." Friedmann even claimed that Mengele had retired to Florida to bask in the sunshine, presumably along with some of his aging victims.

A self-inflicted blow to the Nazi hunter's popularity with American officials came when he announced that U.S. authorities had yielded to alleged requests from West Germany not to arrest Mengele because Bonn no longer wanted war criminals extradited and tried.

Taking up a Nazi hunting career at the same time as Friedmann was Simon Wiesenthal, the son of an officer killed in action during World War I while serving with the Austrian forces. Educated as an architect, Wiesenthal struggled to make a living as a mechanic before World War II in the Polish city of Lvov. First the Soviets overran the town, then they seized his stepfather and shot his stepbrother. The German army drove the Reds out, only to turn the resident Jews over to the murderous local Ukrainians. Several times Wiesenthal himself faced execution, and on one occasion only the tolling of the church bells halted a team methodically shooting a group that included Wiesenthal.

Wiesenthal spent much of World War II in a series of KZs before being liberated from Mauthausen by the Americans in May of 1945. Wiesenthal himself says that as much to offset the peculiar apathy that came over so many after the early exhilaration of liberation as the desire for justice, he volunteered to assist the war crimes offices. As he accumulated evidence for trials at Dachau, he realized that he had discovered a calling.

In 1947 he opened his own Documentation Center in Linz, and a few years later set up shop in Vienna—and not because he was welcome there; to the contrary, because he wasn't. The Austrians had taken the position that theirs was an occupied country, a victim of Hitler, like other nations. In so doing they conveniently ignored their 99 percent yes vote on the issue of union with Germany. Money and the prevailing postwar winds brought their new enlightenment. From the start Austria resisted restitution payments to victims of home-grown Nazis. Instead it boldly demanded compensation from Germany, putting itself on an equal basis with, for example, Israel. Germany's chief of state, Konrad Adenauer, reportedly answered, "If the Austrians want something, we'll send them the bones of Hitler" —who was, after all, Austrian born. Nonetheless, Bonn paid over 321 million marks to its former partner-in-crime. Much of the money went to Austrians who had lost property or jobs because of the war, which in effect translated into a situation whereby local Nazis received payments for losses incurred because they supported the Third Reich. Payment, *not* punishment. And the Austrian citizenry backed its government. Public opinion weighed heavily against war crimes trials. A series of acquittals brought cheers and flowers for the accused. Wiesenthal, who may be given to certain excesses of zeal, was not exaggerating when he said that for all of the criticisms that can be leveled against West Germany, it tried much harder to achieve justice for Hitler's victims than Austria. Austria, he decided, deserved him, and so he proceeded to hunker down in Vienna, a permanent thorn, he hoped, in the Austrian conscience.

A burly, gruff man with a hound-dog look, Wiesenthal operates from a cluttered office whose filing system seems chaotic but whose proprietor can lay his hands on wanted documents almost as swiftly as a computer retrieves items from its memory banks. Attacking as he does Austrians sympathetic to the Nazis, Wiesenthal attracts threatening letters. An alarm system protects his building, and the guard at the door demands visitors present their credentials. Supporting his efforts is a Simon

Wiesenthal Center in Los Angeles with offices in New York as well.

Toughened by beatings, torture, and a death sentence, Wiesenthal also knows how to brush aside hostility with a ready wit. In one instance a group of young Germans known as the Teutonica Society, with all that label implies, invited Wiesenthal to speak. Before he could begin, however, a heckler stood up and said, "Herr Wiesenthal, we know all about you. You eat a Nazi for breakfast, have a Nazi for lunch and then another Nazi for your dinner." Answered Wiesenthal, "You are wrong, my young friend. My religion forbids me to eat *Schwein.*"

Wiesenthal has assumed an impressive record, credited, he says, with having caused the arrest of more than 1,000 war criminals. He tracked down the Gestapo agent that arrested Anne Frank and her family. He annoyed the East German government by exposing Nazis alive and well in their employ. He nagged the West German government to extend its statute of limitations on war crimes and supplied information that led to the arrest in Brazil of Franz Stangl, commandant at Sobibor and Treblinka. He claims to have exposed Eichmann in Argentina, but Isser Harel says he played no role.

Wiesenthal has on occasion erred. In his book *The Murderers Among Us,* he located Martin Bormann near the frontier of Argentina and Chile. A few years after publication, however, he recanted. "All those stories about him being seen alive are just a myth. We know beyond all reasonable doubt that he committed suicide in Berlin in May 1945."

Success and attendant fame also seem to have created a delicate ego. When Varon praised the Nazi-hunter couple, Serge and Beate Klarsfeld, Wiesenthal expressed hurt feelings, and some European reporters have suggested that Wiesenthal at times behaves as if he were the only reputable source for information on the likes of Mengele.

He has always used the media effectively, reasoning that publicity washes fugitives from their cover and goads governments to clean house. He has also been creative: When 1979 was designated by the United Nations as The Year of the Child he wrote the U.N. Secretary General Kurt Waldheim urging pressure for the capture of Mengele because his crimes were so much against children. Not an unreasonable proposition, given Mengele's exploitation of children in the death camp.

He has also, to keep the ledger in balance, been given to extreme claims, such as one announcing that through mobilization of his contacts in South America, Mengele would be in custody within forty-eight hours. The arrest, of course, never occurred. Wiesenthal did, though, keep the chase for Mengele alive by his periodic announcements of sightings in Chile, Brazil, Argentina, Peru, and at a half dozen locations in Paraguay. In *The Murderers Among Us* the author reports two instances, one in the Greek Islands and the other in Spain, where he barely missed apprehending Mengele. From the evidence gathered after the unearthing of Mengele's remains in the Embu cemetery it appears that the fugitive was never in either place.

Wiesenthal was also among the first to offer a reward for Mengele, promising $50,000 for information leading to his capture and $10,000 to the welfare fund of the police department in the country where the doctor was detained. This extraordinary bounty offered by a private organization for the war criminal further helped to keep the Mengele story alive.

The French husband-and-wife team of Serge and Beate Klarsfeld emphasized confrontations and risk taking, challenging and guiding the conviction of those who committed war crimes against their compatriots as well as others. In 1979 their work led them to South America, where they began a campaign to apprehend former SS Colonel Walter Rauff, a key figure in gas van exterminations, as well as the notorious Klaus

Barbie, the Gestapo chief in Lyons, who was later to be linked with Mengele.

Also looking to South America was the British Granada Television, which traveled to Paraguay in 1978 to produce a feature, "The Hunt for Doctor Mengele." The show sketched Mengele's career and concentrated on his presence in Paraguay. Drawing on material from Isser Harel among others, the voice-over narration depicted Mengele as practicing medicine some distance from "Krugg's fortified farm." The Grenada TV program also offered a clip made by a Brazilian purporting to be Joseph Mengele. The face differs markedly from that of the person who spent the final seventeen years of his life in Brazil and has been certified as drowned at Bertioga Beach. But that picture of a frowning, close-cropped, trim, mustachioed, hatless man in shirtsleeves was used repeatedly as the last known picture of Mengele. Even when Mengele's remains were uncovered at Embu, *Time* magazine used it on the cover. The photographic strip was described as having been shot at Eldorado, Argentina, in 1966. During this period of his life Mengele, according to the Stammers, always wore a hat and jacket, making the representation even more dubious.

Granada TV reinforced the notion that Mengele was living in Paraguay with the statement: "Three German ambassadors, including the last one, Helmut Hof, told us that President Stroessner himself ordered Mengele to keep away from the capital Asunción and change his name and appearance." Also used to underscore Mengele's alleged whereabouts was an interview using hidden cameras. The subject, an unregenerate German immigrant, Enrique Mueller, widely known in Asunción as "Nazi Mueller," held forth before the camera that he saw Mengele "every week, every month . . . We meet regularly every month to play cards." Mueller remarked that he had seen Mengele only four weeks earlier.

CBS's "60 Minutes" offered its own segment on the hunt for Mengele, which in turn evoked a telegram from U.S. Ambassador Robert White to the secretary of state in April of 1979: "Since my arrival seventeen months ago I have interested myself in the Mengele case to the extent that I have held discussions with government officials, six or eight foreign reporters, several ambassadors and members of the Jewish community regarding the whereabouts of Nazi war criminal Joseph Mengele. Government officials admit that Mengele formerly lived in Paraguay but state that he left the country many years ago and that his whereabouts is unknown to them. None of the various ambassadors of European countries admit to any certain knowledge if Mengele lives in Paraguay or not. Members of the Jewish community also plead lack of knowledge. The journalists who have visited me have come here with the intention to locate Mengele and to photograph him. To my knowledge none has uncovered any proof that Mengele is here. Several believe that he is here, nonetheless. And one or two are of the opinion that he resides in one of several German communities scattered around Paraguay. But these are opinions and not facts . . . if Mengele wanted to live in Paraguay, the government would permit him to do so."

Ambassador White's clear statement about the absence of any substantiation for claims of Mengele enjoying sanctuary in Paraguay went unheeded. Those who desperately, and understandably, wanted Mengele to face his day in court continued to lend credence to nearly every scrap of news about Mengele. The nature of the Paraguayan government closed off free inquiry. The country's unchartered wilds and the strong Nazi-supportive German community encouraged speculation that Mengele would be safe there. Some of the misinformation about him was also due to nothing more than simple error . . . A German

refugee approximating Mengele's description would be identified as the fugitive; people gossiped about Mengele, turning
hearsay into fact.

But some of the evidence of Mengele's whereabouts derives
from a more sinister source, deliberate disinformation fed to the
CIA, the Mossad, and even the hidden cameras of Granada TV,
by people bent on helping Mengele avoid justice.

Shortly after he arrived in Buenos Aires, Mengele, under the name of Helmut Gregor, rented rooms in this house on Avenida Arenales in the Florida section of the city.

Credit: Gerald Astor

Hans Ulrich Rudel, Nazi Germany's most decorated soldier, speaks at a rally of the Right Wing German Reich Party in 1953. Rudel worked for several West German companies in South America where he helped many war criminals, including Klaus Barbie and Mengele.
Credit: Wide World Photos

This picture, taken in 1956 in Buenos Aires, was used on Mengele's passport which was obtained with help from the German Embassy.

This house on Virrey Vertiz in the Vicente Lopez section of Buenos Aires is the last known residence of Mengele in Argentina. The Mossad plotted to kidnap Mengele from this house when it abducted Adolf Eichmann in 1960.
Credit: Gerald Astor

The Mengele factory on the outskirts of Günzburg was built after World War II. The original plant, which is still in use, is in the center of town.
Credit: Gerald Astor

Wolfgang Gerhard, an Austrian, befriended Mengele in Brazil and gave him his identification documents. He posed for police documents as a youthful refugee from Europe in 1950 and then in 1976 when he made a quick trip back to São Paulo to renew the residency permit on which Mengele substituted his picture.   Credit: Wide World Photos

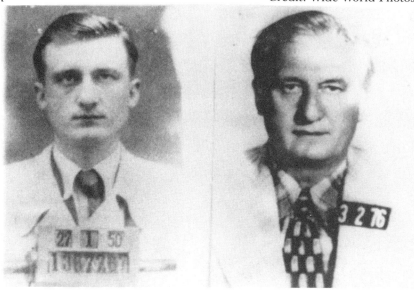

A lookout tower built by Mengele rises from the farm house at Serra Negra, Brazil, where he lived with the Stammers from 1961 to 1969.
Credit: Camara Tres, Black Star

The five room house (rear view) occupied by Mengele at the time of his death in 1979 on Estrada da Alvaranga in El Dorado, a suburb of São Paulo. Because the house was unoccupied for six years after his death, the exterior is run-down.
Credit: Gerald Astor

Rumanian born dwarf twins Elizabeth Moscowitz and Perla Ovitch were part of a circus family of ten people, seven of whom were dwarfs, deported to Auschwitz. When Mengele saw them he gloated, "Now I have work for twenty years." Moscowitz and Ovitch survived and at a mock trial of Mengele in 1985 testified that he forced them to perform naked before an audience of SS.
Credit: Richard Nowitz, Black Star

XII

The Nazi Ambience in South America

THE EASE WITH WHICH MENGELE concealed himself, the failure of governments or local citizens to denounce him, and the help given him is puzzling only if one is ignorant of South American ethnic and political currents.

A strong German presence dates back well before World War II. In 1940 Paraguay numbered 30,000, Brazil 900,000, and Argentina 200,000 residents who were either born in Germany or descended from Germans. The immigrants from Europe created their own communities, resisting assimilation. The cities of Blumenau, Hohenau, Novo Hamburgo, Nueva Germania,

Westphalen all have echoes of the origins the settlers wanted to preserve, much as North American colonists created New London, Gloucester, and New Amsterdam. The difference, however, is that the Latin American emigrés established themselves amid the established Hispanic society while the newcomers to the northern hemisphere put down roots in a largely unsettled land.

The South American Germans retained their own language and in many communities in South America it prevailed over Spanish. Prior to the outbreak of World War II the Germans actively sought to indoctrinate the values of the Third Reich through hundreds of German schools. For example, in 1936 Brazil registered 50,000 pupils in 1,260 German schools; Argentina had 58 institutions for 7,276 students, Chile 44 with 4,902, and tiny Paraguay was fourth with 31 schools and 1,161 youngsters enrolled.

The Nazi Party was also alive and thriving. To Paraguay belongs the dubious honor of being the location in 1929 of the first branch of the NSDAP, composed mainly of Germans and a few Paraguayans. This is four years before Hitler gained power. Like toadstools, Nazi parties popped up all over the continent during the 1930s.

By the start of hostilities in Europe, the local Nazis were in a good position to support Germany. In spite of Franklin D. Roosevelt's Good Neighbor Policy, many South Americans still considered the United States a gringo bully. Pro-German propaganda and espionage enjoyed a fertile soil. In Brazil dictator Getulio Vargas openly championed the Axis powers, altering course only when German U-boats sank Brazilian ships and killed Brazilians.

The German embassies in South America operated spy rings using resident local Germans. *Abwehr,* the intelligence arm of the German military, collected vital information on U.S. imports and shipping. German diplomats wrote checks for millions of pesos made out "to the bearer" to pay for the agents. In Brazil Alfred Winkelmann, a naturalized German, and Féderico Eisendecher, born in Brazil of German parents, were imprisoned as Nazi spies. In Paraguay authorities, once aware of the fading fortunes of the Third Reich, arrested a group of people celebrating the death of President Roosevelt.

Following V–E Day the exodus of Germans for South America paralleled, on a smaller scale, that of the Jews to what became Israel, an exodus that included many bona fide Nazi war criminals. Rabbi Henry Sobel of Congregation Israelita Paulista, whose 2,500 families make it the largest synagogue in São Paulo, estimates that 5,000 ex-Nazis fearing prosecution made their way to South America. As many as 300 of them hid out at one time or another in Paraguay alone. But no country held a monopoly. SS mountebank Friedrich Schwend, a currency manipulator, settled in Lima, Peru. Walter Rauff found a home in Chile. Eduard Roschmann, a Nazi *Gauleiter* for the territory of Latvia, shuttled between Argentina and Paraguay. Herbert Cukurs, a Latvian Nazi, Franz Stangl and his deputy Gustav Wagner lived in Brazil. Eichmann and Joseph Schwammberger, chief of the Przemysl KZ in Poland, took refuge in Argentina. Klaus Barbie opted for Bolivia. And of course Mengele lived in Argentina, Paraguay, and Brazil.

The pursuers of war criminals have debated whether the hunted benefitted—and still do—from an organized conspiracy, an ODESSA or *Spinne* (La Arana in South America). Indeed, immediately following the discovery "with reasonable scientific certainty" of Mengele's body in 1985, São Paulo Superintendent of Police Romeu Tuma told Associated Press correspondent Stan Lehman, "I believe an ODESSA type of organization exists for protecting escaped Nazis. Latin America was a good choice. It was far removed from the events of the war. Many foreigners already lived here and there is a certain naivete among the people."

Subsequently Tuma backed off from his affirmation of an ODESSA. Rabbi Sobel is dubious of a structured conspiratorial network. Instead, he speaks of Brazil's traditional ethnic harmony, its tolerance for many ideological viewpoints, and its hospitality to all foreigners and newcomers.

A reasonably telling argument, it seems to this author, against the existence of ODESSA can be made from the case of the man who made the "organization" famous, Eduard Roschmann. A Sudeten German, SS Captain Roschmann terrorized the Latvian Jews in Riga and was believed responsible for the deaths of some 30,000. In 1948 he fled to Argentina, where he used the name Dr. Félipe Erlich Prat. Roschmann became notorious in 1972 after novelist Frederick Forsyth made him the principal villain of his novel, *The ODESSA File*. Forsyth, who is said to have obtained much of his background from Simon Wiesenthal, spins a plot that centers around Roschmann's attempts to revive Nazism in Germany.

On October 26, 1976, West Germany formally requested without success Roschmann's extradition from both Argentina and Paraguay. In 1977, while traveling from Buenos Aires to Asunción on a passport in the name of Féderico Wegener, Roschmann complained of chest pains. The sixty-three-year-old Roschmann was brought to an Asunción charity hospital by a man who identified himself as Señor Rios. After seventeen days in a ward, Roschmann died of a myocardial infarct. Señor Rios visited the patient several times before he expired; staff members said Rios looked like a German rather than a Hispanic, but since he disappeared as soon as Roschmann died his identity was never revealed. Wegener was identified as Roschmann only after his death, largely because the former SS officer was distinguished by the absence of three toes on his right foot, two from his left.

Roschmann's end, it would seem, does in itself tend to mitigate against an ODESSA. Consider that he was taken by his companion to the worst institution of its kind in Asunción—a hospital where medical students learn their trade practicing on the indigent. When he died Roschmann had no money, and none appeared even anonymously, and so he was consigned to a pauper's grave. Would not a structured, powerful, and well-financed ODESSA have done better for one of its more esteemed members?

The argument against ODESSA-like cabals is, it would seem, rather strengthened by the lack of any hard facts after some forty years. A genuine conspiracy would almost surely have been penetrated by undercover agents or exposed by a disgruntled informant from within. After all, even the Mafia has yielded to spies and members who have been turned by law-enforcement agencies. Likewise the CIA, the KGB, the FBI, etc. Following the discovery of Mengele's skeleton in Brazil, Sepp Wolker, the West German consul in São Paulo said, "I think Mengele survived so long precisely *because* [author's italics for emphasis] there was no formal network."

That is not, of course, to say that war criminals such as Mengele did not receive genuine aid and comfort in South America. To the contrary. The Germans who arrived before World War II have always considered the war-crimes charges as Allied propaganda, the lies manufactured by the victors against the losers who have been barred from writing their version of history. The prewar residents who supported the Nazi movement accepted the postwar immigrants as members of the brotherhood and sisterhood of the defeated-in-battle-only. The cause, for them, remained viable. Further, refugees from Eastern Europe, oppressed by communist regimes, strengthened the conviction that whatever its faults, the Third Reich at least stood firm against Bolshevism.

Mengele was shielded and comforted by a string of individuals sympathetic to his background, and sharing the opinions of Alejandro von Eckstein, the Paraguayan perjurer who called the communists the true menace and then proceeded to point out that "most of the Jews were Communists in the Red Army. . . . Who killed the Russian Imperial Family? Commissar Sverdlov, another Jew. The greatest war criminals were the Communist. They killed millions, millions disappeared and the principal Communists were Jews."

Von Eckstein, though a colonel, is a mere factotum in the military command, taking his cues from his old comrade in the Chaco War, President Stroessner. Edgar L. Ynsfran, the minister of the interior during the early 1960s, and as such supervisor of the police, says he spoke with President Stroessner after the extradition papers first arrived from Germany in 1961. "They bring us problems which are not our problems," said Stroessner. "That is a European problem, not one of ours." His indifference hardly surprises. He once scoffed at the figure of six million Holocaust victims.

The prevailing viewpoint of the Nazi refugees is summed up by Alfonz Dierckx, the Belgian who befriended Mengele while the doctor lived in Paraguay. "Nothing is said of Hiroshima, Nagasaki, Dresden and the other German cities where thousands of women, old people and children were made homeless and whose lives were lost because of the pitiless bombings of the Allies. Winners lay blame on the conquered to assuage their own consciences. The losers are made war criminals."

While the TV team from Granada may have been misled into thinking Mengele lived in Paraguay, it did capture the attitudes of the local Germans. "Nazi Mueller" insisted Mengele was "just like you or me. All he did then was his duty. What Americans do today are the same bloody experiments that Mengele carried out then." Prodded further, Mueller added that he believed Mengele did commit the acts he was accused of but he also said, "I would be prepared to support it myself. What we were trying to do then was to rid ourselves of society's cripples. . . . When I look at them all today, the way they all run around here, all I can say is that Mengele didn't do anything more than scratch the surface." (*Also spracht* Euthanasia some thirty-five years after Nazi Germany's defeat. Some viruses never die.)

Wilhelm Sassens, another war criminal on the run, declared, "I met Mengele the first time in 1949. He was a brilliant man from an intellectual point of view, a good philosopher, historian and a good medical man." Werner Schubius, also speaking for Granada's cameras, could not believe Mengele was guilty of the crimes attributed to him. "When we met him, we said he can't possibly have done that. I'm convinced of that. If he had done something, it is only because he was acting under orders [Eichmann's rationalization as well]. I can imagine Mengele only as a human being . . . like everybody else, modest, educated, very well educated, much more than we are." Armando Raeynarts, the Belgian who served in the Waffen SS during World War II and then escaped to Paraguay where he opered the Hotel Tirol, dismissed charges against Mengele: "What was this man accused of? He was a doctor in the camps. We always hear the rubbish [murders of Jews] that you probably know was written in the newspapers."

A native of Paraguay, a businessman who deals with Germanic visitors from Brazil and Argentina, says the Nazi spirit is not even deeply buried. "A lot of them are still Nazis at heart. You need only talk to them a while before you realize that if they had it to do all over again they'd do the same thing. They still think highly of Hitler." And a German diplomat stationed in Brazil says that the thousands of Nazi refugees there brought with them the philosophical baggage acquired during the Hitler years. Instead of discarding the ideas, they have held onto them as ties to the old country, the fatherland.

For the most part the climate experienced by Mengele in South America, while hospitable to Nazis, did not cause a definable resurgence of the movement. During the 1970s and early 1980s, the authoritarian governments of Bolivia, Chile, and Argentina in particular did make common cause with a small band of expatriate Nazis to ensure rule by the extreme rightwing, and this includes Klaus Barbie; but the sins of the South American governments in regard to Nazism are largely those of omission rather than commission . . . In no case did a Latin American ruler, junta, dictator or even democratically elected chief of state expel a known war criminal as an undesirable. At best they acceded to legal requests for extradition, and the deportees are few.

Not surprisingly, Argentina had been the first refuge chosen by Mengele. Juan Perón welcomed fascists. If Perón and his spiritual descendants could have maintained control, Mengele might well have finished out his days among the one million residents with Germanic roots. (Even today, Buenos Aires still has restaurants that especially cater to Nazis.) But, of course, the Argentines ousted Perón, and Mengele could not trust Perón's successors.

He picked Paraguay as his next stop because of Rudel's connections and the 200,000 people born in Germany or descended from immigrants from Germany. Stroessner, too, extended the hand of friendship to old Nazis. Further, the apparent stability of dictatorship reassured Mengele. (Changes in government were to be the downfall of the likes of Klaus Barbie.) However, the arrival of Israelis looking for him under his own name required a new address.

The Nazi Ambience in South America

Safety now lay in anonymity. Brazil, particularly by hindsight, had to seem a perfect place. In geography Brazil dwarfs other Latin American lands: it is nearly as big as the United States; there are sparsely settled areas, well removed from the media and poorly policed, where a man can live without inquiries about his identity.

The Brazilian indifference to ideology and the tradition of sanctuary for immigrants guaranteed to the 3.6 million inhabitants of German extraction the opportunity to closet themselves and retain the culture and ideas they brought from home. Mengele had only to change his name, nothing else. No one in Brazil fussed over the presence of war criminals or Nazi refugees. The selection of Brazil was obvious; only the details for hiding Mengele remained a problem.

XIII Senhor Pedro and the Brazilian Conspiracy

PREPARATIONS TO SHELTER MENGELE once again became the responsibility of Mengele's South American godfather, Colonel Rudel, who plotted in conjunction with Hans Sedlmeier, the Mengele executive and dispenser of largesse for all of the Joseph Mengele operations. Both men, of course, fully accepted the Nazi ideology, so assistance to Mengele combined business with pleasure.

During his travels Rudel had met an Austrian named Wolfgang Gerhard. Born in Leibnitz, in 1949 Gerhard left Graz, Austria—a crossroads for escaping Nazi war criminals on their route to Italy—for South America. A former Hitler Youth member and soldier during the final years of the war, Gerhard sailed for South America from Genoa, a route much like that of Mengele, except he debarked in Brazil. Romeu Tuma, the head of the São Paulo police, has described Gerhard as a "fanatical Nazi." He was indeed a fellow who never lost faith in the cause for which he fought. A ne'er-do-well, Gerhard frittered away time trying to organize meetings of Nazi sympathizers and printing literature for the movement that he shipped from Brazil to other parts of the world. He once said his dream was to throw an iron hook into the carcass of Simon Wiesenthal and drag the Nazi hunter for miles behind a car. Considered a wild romantic, his passions also included art, music and poetry (appropriately, he wrote a complete cycle of verses celebrating the moon). Gerhard also liked to drink and group-sing.

When Rudel proposed that Gerhard be recruited to find a refuge for Mengele, the family, with whom all arrangements were checked out, expressed doubts. Gerhard's business failures and his fondness for alcohol indicated, they felt, a poor security risk. They also predicted that Gerhard would blackmail them. Apparently, however, Rudel convinced the family to accept Gerhard. Perhaps they were won over by the Austrian's willingness to do the job for nothing, considering as he did that helping Mengele was an honor beyond price. And the relatives in Günzburg never missed an opportunity to do things on the cheap.

So Gerhard was enlisted, and proceeded to nominate as potential hosts for Mengele a family he had known since 1956. They were Geza Stammer and his wife Gitta, who had emigrated from Hungary in 1948. A civil engineer, Geza spent World War II as a student, then teacher, and in the latter days of the war his university had been transported to Germany. As Gitta Stammer told the author, the couple left Hungary "because we didn't

like living under Communists. We had three years of it." Asked
about her attitude toward Nazi Germany, Gitta laughs uncer-
tainly, "Hungarians admired the Germans from a distance, do
you understand? We felt it was all very well for them to build a
great nation for themselves but it didn't help us. We were always
anti-Communist but we've never belonged to any party. We're
conservative, not of the right or left."

When thirty-one-year-old Wolfgang Gerhard met the Stammers at a gathering of Hungarian refugees in 1956, Gitta was
thirty-six and her husband a few years older. Gerhard made no
effort to hide his political sympathies, but in those days, says
Gitta, no one inquired into the past history of other refugees.
She thought of Gerhard as highly educated and intelligent.
Thereafter the Stammers and the Austrian saw each other from
time to time, and it seems likely that a man of such fervid convictions as Gerhard sufficiently investigated them to determine that
they were at least fairly sympathetic to his beliefs.

The Stammers had arrived in Brazil with little more than the
clothing on their backs. At first they lived in a one-room São
Paulo apartment, assisted by a Hungarian Catholic organization.
Geza Stammer worked in a soil-analysis lab and on land grading,
and eventually they saved enough to buy an eleven-acre farm—
primitive conditions, no electricity—on the dry plains of Nova
Europa, about 200 miles from São Paulo.

In the fall of 1961 Gerhard paid them a visit and remarked to
Gitta Stammer, "Wouldn't it be good for you to have someone
to help you?" Geza was, after all, away from home for long
stretches of time. He added that he had "a friend his own age"
looking for a place. In October Gerhard came round with his
friend, a thin, pale man with callused hands. Gerhard introduced him as Peter Hochbichlet, the son of a Swiss farm laborer.
He arrived, remembers Gitta, "with two medium-sized suitcases, clothes and books." He explained that he needed a place

where he could "restore himself." Indeed, he looked as if he had been ill.

The boarder, known as Senhor Pedro to the locals, now occupied a room in the house with the Stammers but with a separate entrance. He did odd jobs about the place, delivered calves, and showed a rare skill when he performed surgery in a cow. After about a month Hochbichlet declared himself well satisfied with the arrangements and asked to stay on with the Stammers permanently.

Some of the farm laborers were not fond of Senhor Pedro. "I didn't like him. He liked to boss people around and he didn't know anything about farming," said one of them. The Stammers were also somewhat dubious, but he overcame their objections, announcing that he would be their partner in finding a new and better place to live.

By December 1961 the Stammers and their boarder had relocated to the town of Serra Negra, one hundred miles from São Paulo. Peter, as the Stammers called him, busied himself with the construction of a stone observation tower, using a local mason who followed "Peter's" exacting specifications.

From the eyrie, the surrounding area lay open to the eye in a breathtaking panorama, and Peter spent long hours perched in the tower. Gitta Stammer noted that he never went outside without a hat and coat, both arranged so that very little of his face showed. She now says she thought of asking about his background, but Gerhard had advised, "It's better if you don't know about his past." The agent of the conspiracy obviously wanted to conceal the fugitive's true identity until it was certain that the Stammers could be fully trusted.

Friction grew between the Stammers and Peter. He seemed unable to resist an urge to dominate. He intruded on the lives of his hosts and was overbearing toward the farm employees and the domestic help. Gitta Stammer recollects that in 1963 she came on a magazine article with photographs of the notorious Dr. Mengele. There is a strong suspicion that the conspirators may have deliberately planted the magazine to bring the situation to a head. In any event, struck by the resemblance to Hochbichlet, his furtive behavior, and his knowledge of medicine, Gitta says she confronted him, "This man looks a lot like you. You have a lot of mysteries." He paled, said nothing but left the room. That evening he admitted to the Stammers that he indeed was Dr. Joseph Mengele.

The Stammers claim that they now asked Gerhard to take him away. Indeed, they contend, for the next eleven years they tried to rid themselves of their guest-helper. At the time of this first request a newcomer appeared at the Stammers'. Short, plump and well dressed, the man, known to the Stammers only as Hans, had come from Europe. It was Sedlmeier in the role of bagman for the Mengele family interests. He asked the Stammers to have patience, and doubtless encouraged their forbearance with cash. Gitta Stammer says that Hans gave Mengele $2,000 and on a subsequent inspection of conditions handed him an additional $5,000. However, Hans and Peter went for some long walks together and so conceivably the sums could have been greater.

Any diffidence—always out of character—on the part of Mengele seems to have disappeared once the Stammers knew his identity and accepted him for it. He proceeded to try to organize the household according to his rules. Says Gitta: "He said we were too soft with our children"—an echo of his own strict upbringing and his devout authoritarianism. "He was always telling us to sack this servant or that one and that we were too slack with them. He would argue with my husband, 'Why didn't you ask for more money to do that job!' "

According to Gitta, Mengele's disparaging remarks about her husband made her angry. "I said to him, 'You're such a great man, why do you live in hiding! Your fellow countrymen who had the courage to live openly stood trials and some were hung. Our fellow countrymen, the non-Communists, were killed by the Russians. They were real men. they didn't hide.' " There was a brief flashback to the *Obersturmführer* Mengele of Auschwitz, who brooked no resistance. He raised his arm as if to strike her but then stalked out of the room.

After another similar conversation the outraged Mengele yelled, "If you want it that way, then we'll have the law of the jungle," slapping his side as if to indicate the presence of a pistol. Geza Stammer, in his sly fashion, seemed bent on provoking Mengele, questioning his ukases during dinner and usually igniting his nasty temper.

The squabbling often ended, according to Gitta, with another plea to Gerhard to relieve them of their burden. "Wolfgang would say he would take Peter to Egypt, Morocco, or Libya. All he needed was time to obtain the necessary documents. He would say, 'Just wait a little longer, a few more months. You must understand, it's not easy to find anyone. Nobody wants him.' "

That nobody wanted this most notorious Nazi war criminal must not only have been a great burden for Gerhard but also a source of chagrin—Gerhard, after all, continued to think of Mengele as an authentic hero, a warrior-scientist unjustly persecuted.

But chagrined or not, to his requests for understanding and patience Gerhard added some threats. He spoke of the danger in going to the police, who in all probability would charge the Stammers with a crime for assisting a criminal. He pointed out that their two sons might suffer, and he also implied that any betrayal of Mengele might well create dangerous anger among the large German population in Brazil, a group, he said, that favored the Nazi cause.

Gerhard, as the Mengele family back in Günzburg worried,

was inclined to recklessness, and from a weekend cabin at Hapecerica da Serra, near the town of Embu, he tried to reinvigorate the Nazi movement in Brazil, holding meetings in his cabin that could have attracted the attention of authorities. And when in 1967, acting on information from Simon Wiesenthal, the São Paulo police under Romeu Tuma seized Franz Stangl, the former commandant of KZs at Sobibor and Treblinka, Gerhard became so distraught he decided "I must do something for him." (It was Mengele himself who related this to Wolfram and Liselotte Bossert, Austrians who later befriended him.) Gerhard informed Mengele he intended to go to the police and vouch for Stangl as a respectable law-abiding citizen. Mengele told Bossert he advised Gerhard, "This could be another trick," and finally convinced Gerhard not to do anything rash that would open him up to investigation by the police. Certainly, Mengele reasoned, he could hardly afford to have his closest confidant expose himself through an ardent defense of a well-known war criminal.

So Gerhard was reined in and Mengele was able to go on living undisturbed with the Stammers for seven more years. In 1969 the Stammers and Mengele moved from Serra Negra to Caieiras only twenty miles from São Paulo, their house sitting on a two-acre plot. They had given up farming.

Gitta Stammer offers this explanation for the extended sanctuary she and her husband gave Mengele. "We were frightened. We knew we were doing something wrong. But you live so long with someone under one roof it becomes a habit. It is difficult to denounce them. We didn't like Peter." (Interesting that even after the whole world knew Hochbichlet as Joseph Mengele, she continued to refer to him as "Peter.") "He was often unpleasant but he was never cruel to us. He could be playful [a characteristic he also exhibited at Auschwitz] but mostly he complained."

The truth? The background of the Stammers, refugees from

Communist rule, suggests at least passive if not active membership in the Hungarian fascist movement of the 1940s. As suggested earlier, Gerhard would never have trusted them otherwise, which in turn meant they could accept Mengele as, like
themselves, a victim of communist persecution. Besides, and not
incidentally, Mengele through Sedlmeier and probably other
go-betweens distinctly improved their fortunes.

There is also the not unreasonable possibility of an affair
between the Hungarian woman and the doctor. She was only
forty, he fifty when they met. Her husband Geza was absent for
long periods of time. Wolfram and Liselotte Bossert have insisted to *Stern* writer Manfred von Conta that the pair were
lovers. The romance only ended, say the Bosserts, when Gitta
reached her menopause, could no longer achieve orgasm and
was no longer interested in the doctor as a sexual partner. The
Bosserts' remarkable ignorance of female sexual function, while
of passing interest, does not negate the possibility of an affair
between the two.

Gitta Stammer steadfastly denies any liason. She also professes total ignorance of any sexual activity by Mengele. "He
would go for long walks, but otherwise I don't remember any
opportunities for him, or else he was extremely discreet." She
does recall that he enjoyed looking at the legs of the maids, and
amid a cache of medicine uncovered six years after Mengele's
death the police found a packet of Brazilian-manufactured con-
doms. One was missing. (In that same batch of medical supplies
were several capsules at first presumed to be suicide-pills, in the
SS-tradition of Himmler and Goering, and later revealed to be
distinctly un-Wagnerian laxative suppositories.)

Lover or not, "Peter" continued to make life difficult for the
entire family. "Our oldest son did not like him at all," says Gitta
Stammer. "Peter was always telling him what to do, giving him
tasks. My son would say, 'He's not my father.' "

Mengele also taunted his hosts about their origins. "He would say," says Gitta, " 'You are typical Hungarians. We were never true partners during the war.' " When Wolfgang Gerhard and Wolfram Bossert, the Austrians, would visit the Stammer home they would sit as cronies with Mengele disparaging the ethnicity of their hosts while extolling the superior virtues of the German "race." "They would say we were just Hungarians," says Gitta, "only the Germans were honest and hardworking . . ."

Belief in his essential Teutonic superiority was not a joking matter to Mengele, who never relinquished his faith in the master-race concept. He held in contempt all *other* peoples, aliens, with equal vigor. He retained his anti-Semitism, denigrating Jews as *alien* to Germany. As the State of Israel, the home of his most dangerous enemies, actual and imaginary, struggled through two more wars, Mengele grudgingly acknowledged, "They are in a difficult situation." He of course did not support them and managed to twist the issue into a racial one: "Even though the Arabs and Jews are both Semites, they fight. It's brother against brother, like Germany against England when both are Saxons."

Mengele volunteered his considered opinion that the site chosen for a Jewish homeland was a poor one both for its climate and the presence of hostile people. He said he favored settlement of the Jews on the island of Madagascar (the former French colony in the Indian Ocean that had become the Republic of Malagasy). The Madagascar plan actually was a figment proposed by Himmler and his associates before implementation of the Final Solution. It was absurd and impractical but it served as a cover for the real intentions of the Nazis.

To the people of the land where he now made his home he granted a mild compliment. Brazilians, he said, had good hearts, even though they were "superficial, undisciplined." He despised the connotations of such expressions as *"amanha"* (tomorrow) and *"mais ou menos"* (more or less). For Mengele the truth was an absolute and its enforcement couldn't wait for tomorrow.

Mengele claimed he accepted *pure* blacks, of whom there are very few in South America, but he condemned the mixture of black blood with others, and to one of the maids remarked that slavery should never have been ended.

Mengele, once the Stammers saw the light and accepted him, along with his largesse, into their lives, allowed the family to listen to the radio or watch television after dinner, and it was on such occasions that he delivered himself of his endless, unqualified opinions. He knew nothing of the United States other than what he had read, seen on TV, or heard from others, which did not prevent him from all-knowing analysis. He told Gitta Stammer that he believed the geography of the country was worth seeing and regretted that the war had prevented an opportunity for him to see the United States as an exchange student, but he grumped loudly at what he considered the American way of life. Democracies, he lectured, brought everyone down to the lowest common denominator, to the level of the masses. "Everyone is equal, too many things are permitted in democracies." There were not enough enforced rules for him. It all boiled down to "a question of business, a person was worth the amount of money he had." That last is an interesting comment in view of his claim that he admired his father as a self-made man who built his own fortune, a man whose value to him was therefore based on his accumulation of wealth.

Mengele despised societies "where anyone can do what he likes and doesn't respect authority." What sort of state did he praise from his hideout in Brazil's hills? That with "a strong government that looks after the entire nation." The ideal was the regime of Adolf Hitler, who made Germany a great nation after it had become so weak. His adoration of the Führer remained constant. Either Wolfgang Gerhard or the Bosserts had given him a tape of a Hitler address which Mengele reveled in, reliving his early worship of the Führer in Munich.

"He never hid his admiration for Hitler," recalls Gitta Stammer. "He said Hitler was an extraordinary person, a man with so little education who could organize things so perfectly. He said many people adored Hitler." Other leaders came off less well by comparison. Juan Perón, whose government had shown such easy tolerance for war criminals when Mengele arrived, received fair marks for some accomplishments but Perón's achievements, said Mengele, were more myth than fact. Eva Perón, on the other hand, earned unstinting praise as "a great woman." Winston Churchill was despised for having "shopped England," for having sold out its aristocratic heritage. Indeed, Mengele said he admired the British people as "reserved, disciplined, loyal good soldiers" and liked their sense of tradition—the Nazis had to invent theirs. John F. Kennedy was rated as intelligent but "not nice." The basis of this rather mild disdain is unclear. He liked, however, what he saw of Charles de Gaulle, an authoritarian figure without the slackness he perceived in other leaders.

Above all Mengele seemed to abhor the new Germany. Hearing something on TV or the radio, reading one of his German-language newspapers, Mengele would exclaim, *"Ach, ach,* this regime. It isn't serious. All it wants is to make money, to have prosperity, just leveling people."

He also favored the Stammers with his views on a variety of other contemporary events. On the occasion of the first heart transplants by Dr. Christiaan Barnard in South Africa, Mengele was only moderately impressed, predicting, correctly, that the patients would not survive long and observing that the technique was not a permanent answer. The U.S. landing on the moon and the exploration of space drew one of his few grunts of total approval. "Fantastic" was the word he used. He devoted most of his reading to books and articles on biology, plants, and animals. He also enjoyed accounts of concerts. The only medical subject that seemed to grip him was cancer. (He offered none of his professional skills to the people around him. "If someone was sick and wanted advice," says Gitta Stammer, "he'd say, 'take an aspirin.' ")

Mention of Auschwitz was always *verboten,* Mengele explaining that when he accepted assignment to the KZ he pledged never to speak about what happened there. And of course the doctor was not one to break rules.

Like Mengele, the Stammers were not churchgoing Catholics. Mengele, though, said he still considered himself a member of that religion and told the Stammers that while the purpose of the Church in itself was "to bring people to something good, the hierarchy is outdated. In modern life there is no place for this sort of religion." Pope John XXIII with his *Pacem En Terris* and his democratization of the Church hardly could have inspired Mengele to place faith in the rulers of the Roman Catholic Church.

It seemed to the Stammers that there was no subject on which Mengele did not have a forceful opinion. "Seventy percent of the United States military doctors are Jews and it is the same with psychiatry. There is a spiritlessness, a negativism. This is our shit-time, formed by those little groups which control the mass media." *Also spracht* Mengele, not to mention some people to this day who speak of the "Jewish-controlled" media.

Mengele even extended his analyses to his benefactor Rudel: "The opinions of Rudel are nothing but the result of all of that stupid material pouring down on young Germans since 1945." Actually his snit with Rudel had to do with a number of things. He had doubtless learned how Rudel charged the Mengele company exorbitant sums for the products he sold to it, figuring the excess profits were justified by his services for the family black-sheep. Further, Rudel was not reluctant to express strong opinions himself. At a party in Paraguay, Eugenio Jiminez remembers him loudly holding forth on why the Germans lost the war: "From the first day we were directed by a crazy man, a fool." Rudel, the professional soldier, also expressed scorn for the Waffen SS, Mengele's branch of service. "They took the best weapons," said Rudel, "but they were not real soldiers."

Such opinions could hardly have endeared Rudel to Mengele, and in passing, the doctor offered the Stammers a final judgment on his patron: "As a soldier and a pilot, Rudel was excellent. As a man, he was not my type."

The Mengele company's deal with Rudel had been ended in 1969, but the former Luftwaffe colonel still was inclined to help the fugitive. And in 1971 a situation developed in which Mengele appeared to need special help. The bizarre string of events led to a complete break with Rudel and also in the process helped unveil another war criminal in hiding.

Mengele appeared safe enough in the Caieiras hideaway regardless of the bickering with the Stammers. Wolfgang Gerhard would somehow patch up disputes and keep the household from disintegrating. But Gerhard had his own troubles. His wife Ruth, whom he had met in Brazil, had developed cancer of the stomach; his firstborn son, christened Adolf, was suffering from bone cancer. And although adept as a fixer, a manipulator for Mengele, Gerhard had stumbled through one business failure after another. Now his small textile printing plant could not support the family's needs, and desperate both for money and proper treatment for the sick members of the family, he decided to pack up and return to Austria.

With the prospect of no more Gerhard on the scene and the Stammers finding the irascible doctor increasingly insupportable, the Mengele family turned to Rudel for help. The ex-Luftwaffe ace proposed that Mengele shift his hideout from

Brazil to Bolivia, specifically that he join forces with the "Butcher of Lyons," Klaus Barbie, then living under the name of Klaus Altmann.

Rudel had done business with Barbie in Bolivia as well as another SS-refugee in South America, Friedrich Schwend, the officer who among other projects directed the scheme to counterfeit British currency. Schwend operated from Lima, Peru, and engaged in several financial transactions with Barbie.

São Paulo police chief Romeu Tuma says he cannot find any evidence that Mengele traveled out of Brazil while he lived there, but Gitta Stammer remembers several trips made by Gerhard and Mengele that lasted from three or four days to as long as a week. The times seem too short for visits to Europe but are easily long enough for jaunts to Paraguay, Bolivia, and Peru. And so the woman in the Asunción jewelry store could have seen him in 1965, as could have von Eckstein.

Whether Mengele ever met with Barbie in Bolivia can only be conjecture, but there are strong reports of his presence in Peru. Hedda Schwend, the widow of Friederich, who died in 1980, reportedly mentioned to a woman acquaintance in the Lima German embassy that Mengele had visited her husband with Klaus Barbie in Lima. During 1971 the Peruvian police also claim that Mengele met Schwend both at his home and at a fashionable restaurant.

To the annoyance of Rudel, however, Mengele refused to move permanently from Brazil, would not risk the uncertainty of Bolivian security. He may also have considered that with Klaus Barbie he could hardly continue to dominate those around him. Barbie had his own profitable enterprises in Bolivia; he had helped train the country's intelligence agencies in the techniques of interrogation he had used against the French Resistance, and he freely wheeled and dealed with the highest officials in the Bolivian government. Barbie also was someone not likely to be susceptible to the bully-boy tactics Mengele used to overwhelm the Stammers.

When Mengele finally refused to accept what Barbie considered his generous hospitality, Barbie was so offended that he committed a huge indiscretion—giving an interview, using the name of Klaus Altmann, to a reporter from the newspaper *Estado da São Paulo.* The gist of his remarks amounted to a statement that "I am a man, one who does not hide." The result was to pinpoint his location and expose himself to his nemesis—Nazi-hunter Beate Klarsfeld.

Mengele's refusal to join Barbie in La Paz also so angered Rudel that he broke off all dealings with the doctor. It was left to the resourceful Gerhard once again to save the situation, this time by introducing Mengele and the Stammers to Liselotte and Wolfram Bossert, whom he had met in 1956, the same year he first encountered the Stammers. There was clearly no doubt about the impeccable credentials of the Bosserts. Wolfram had served as a corporal in the Wehrmacht during World War II and had retained his faith in the Nazi cause. Mengele and the Bosserts hit it off immediately, and the Bosserts gave some relief to the Stammers by taking Mengele out for trips and chatting with him regularly and at some length.

Gerhard now did wind up his affairs in Brazil, made his final call to his mother's grave in Embu, then with his family flew home to Austria.

The year was 1971, and while the introduction of the Bosserts provided occasional respites from the squabbling in the Stammers' household, shouting confrontations still occurred. After one argument Wolfram Bossert hurried to Caieiras to play peacemaker. He took Mengele aside, he says, and reminded him that he was only a guest in the house. Since the Mengele family appeared to have advanced the money for the Brazilian real estate, Mengele was hardly pacified. "Half this is mine," he declared, referring to the property. Indeed, in a letter to the family in Günzburg Mengele talked of collecting $25,000 from the sale of a house in Brazil. There was another eruption after the family sent a car to Geza Stammer, who promptly traded it in for a larger one complete with chauffeur. The extravagance of course turned Mengele apoplectic, the notion of Stammer profiting at what he considered his expense setting off a blistering tirade.

Not altogether consistently, Mengele would also grumble on occasion to the Stammers that his family in Günzburg had abandoned him, then would revert to bravado, saying, "I don't need money, I can live without money and support myself."

Rolf Mengele, for his own purposes, now claims the family kept Mengele on an allowance of only $100 to $150 a month, but that does not include the lump sums delivered by Sedlmeier or the outlays for real estate. In any event, according to Gitta Stammer, Mengele was not a man who cared much about possessions or luxuries. He enjoyed, she said, woodworking and made his own bed, table, and chair. Money could not, in fact, have a real value for him; after all, if he spent lavishly he would have become conspicuous and thereby risked discovery.

Mengele was not only a trial for his hosts in Brazil but also pained his relatives in Germany. After his brother Alois returned to Germany on their father's death to run the company, he came across letters written by Mengele to Karl Heinz, his nephew and stepson by marriage to Martha. In the correspondence Mengele instructed the young man in his own philosophy and theories of behavior. Appalled, Alois wrote to his brother demanding he cease any communication with Karl Heinz. Mengele fired back, saying in effect who are you to tell me whom I can write to. Although the family continued to support their black sheep, locked away in Brazilian obscurity, the ties between the brothers were broken.

Senhor Pedro and the Brazilian Conspiracy

Unchastened, Mengele still tried to exert control over anyone within reach, even if only by mail. He designed, for example, a complete educational program for one of Hans Sedlmeier's children. Even though the boy was only in secondary school Mengele decided the youth should become a theoretician in the law and even prescribed the topic for a *doctoral* thesis. In one letter he plaintively inquired about his candidate's school grades: "I'm already waiting many weeks in vain for notification of the results of your exams."

As for the Günzburg contingent, he complained in a letter, "Why don't they ever send a book that they have liked, for my opinion. Analysis of political situations does not interest me. I am more interested in information about their own activities, plans, hopes . . ." It seemed the only real safety for a paranoid like Mengele lay in a world he could completely control.

The conspiracy that kept Mengele's whereabouts secret relied on mail drops, Gerhard's and the Bosserts' in Brazil, Sedlmeier's in Germany. They also devised a code. In correspondence Mengele was referred to as "P" while Rolf was designated "Ro." The house at Serra Negra was "Situ one" and Caieiras "Situ two." About Rudel, known as "the good comrade," Sedlmeier delicately informed the Bosserts, "We will have no more contact with the good comrade because of his own priorities." (Which presumably meant the high price Rudel was charging the Mengele company for manufacturing supplies.)

Unknown persons who presented themselves to the family or its representatives in Germany and claiming acquaintance with the Brazilian cabal were photographed and the pictures airmailed across the sea for checking. The same procedure, in reverse, was applied to anyone who approached the group in Brazil and announced themselves as connected with Günzburg.

In 1974 the Stammers and Mengele at last split up. The Stammers bought a plot of land on a São Paulo hill, rented a nearby house, and started to construct a large enough place to accommodate themselves, their two grown sons—officers in the Brazilian merchant marine—and prospective daughters-in-law. Mengele, under the protective supervision of the Bosserts, remained at Caieiras for a few months, then moved to a five-room house in a São Paulo suburb—El Dorado.

CHAPTER

The Final Years

MENGELE HAS BEEN PORTRAYED in some reports about his life in Brazil as constantly fearful of capture or assassination by Jews. One of the maids has said he slept with a Mauser pistol at his side. Gitta Stammer never mentions this. She describes him as more suspicious of everyone than frightened. In this instance his seeming paranoia was well taken—there were indeed people out to get him.

Gitta further reports that whenever a flurry of news about Mengele appeared in print or there was talk of him on radio or TV he would openly become agitated and show signs of stress, but the discussion of him ebbed as well as flowed and he would relax as his name disappeared from public view.

Still, he was always bedeviled by anxiety and developed a nervous habit of biting off the ends of his mustache and swallowing the hair. The result was what doctors call a bezoar or the equivalent of a cat's hair-ball, and the condition required surgery to remove the material from Mengele's rectum.

Wolfram Bossert says, "He was a man of complexes, frightened of leaving the house. When he went anywhere in a car he would hide his face with his hands. The result was that he actually drew attention to himself. He had that complex that everyone was looking at him. I told him that he was making himself conspicuous and I started to take him out in public more often, to the cinema, window shopping. It was a tremendous effort for him. He sweated with tension."

The Bosserts also assigned their two children a role in bringing Mengele out of the closet. For several weeks they took him on the São Paulo metro, riding from one end of the line to the other as a way of trying to combat his agoraphobia, his fear of going out. Unlike the Stammers' sons, the Bossert youngsters developed an affection for Mengele, and he in turn made a small boat in which he paddled them about on the nearby Billings reservoir.

The small house in El Dorado on Estrada da Alvaranga consisted of two bedrooms, a living room, a parlor, kitchen, and bathroom. On the plot of land behind the house Mengele built a small structure suitable for household help, including a bedroom, dressing room, and bathroom. Near the ceiling in a section of wall panel he constructed a drop, a concealed space where he could stash papers and where the police, six years after his apparent death, were to find his stock of medicines.

Once a week Wolfram Bossert came for dinner. With Bossert, Mengele maintained his self-appointed role as mentor and leader. Bossert has agreed that his place was that of the inferior, the pupil. "Since he didn't have anyone else to talk to, he spoke to me about his family, told stories about his family history. He was a very cultured man, very educated. There was hardly a subject about which he did not have knowledge. [Or else acted as if he did.] And so I learned a great deal from him. He represented to me a very important stage in my education and development as a person."

For Mengele, concern about discovery did not slacken, and in one instance the family in Günzburg exacerbated matters. Mengele had sent a request for some trinkets that he might dispense as Christmas gifts. (While living with the Stammers he occasionally handed out candy at Christmas, an echo of his days at the KZ.) The Mengele company routinely gave away pen knives as favors to its customers and now shipped a box of these to Brazil. To the doctor's astonishment, and anger, the pocket knives all were inscribed with the Mengele factory legend, hardly suitable for distribution by a person seeking to conceal his Mengele identity. Mengele shot off a request for items minus incriminating inscriptions.

Another far more serious threat to Mengele's safety followed. When Wolfgang Gerhard had said his goodbyes to Mengele he had also handed him his Brazilian foreign resident identity card. It then became a simple matter for Mengele to peel off Gerhard's photograph and replace it with his own. Nothing, of course, could be done about the discrepancies in the physical description on the document or the fingerprint, but with the appropriate picture the card would, Mengele felt, pass casual inspection. But in 1976 the authorities decided to change the entire format of the identification paper; now there was no possibility that Mengele could present himself to officials and pass himself off as Gerhard.

A request for Gerhard's help was transmitted to Europe. Unfortunately for Mengele, the Austrian now harbored a grudge against the Mengele family, even if not against its refugee in El Dorado. Desperate for money as usual, Gerhard in 1973 had concocted an idea for a business with Polaroid cameras. However, to start the venture he needed an estimated 30,000 marks, some $10,000. When he went to Günzburg to ask for the money the Mengele family felt confirmed in their feelings that at heart he was a blackmailer and refused to see him, offering only a handout of 1,000 marks, a few hundred dollars.

Gerhard was outraged. He wrote to Bossert about his troubles and insisted that it was his money that had paid for the first move of the Stammers and Mengele from Nova Europa to the much more comfortable place at Serra Negra.

Hans Sedlmeier, the Mengele executive, was given the job of placating Gerhard and despite his grievance convincing him to perform one more service for the Mengeles. The urgency placed on Gerhard's cooperation certainly speaks volumes about the absence of any well-organized ODESSA-type conspiracy. The family could not even arrange for the forgery of a foreign-resident's permit, though other amateurs acquired papers with astonishing ease.

Sedlmeier shrewdly asked Gerhard to meet him in Salzburg, then took him for a small excursion, a pilgrimage to the site of the Führer's home, a move calculated to soften up the Austrian, a man who had once hung a swastika in place of a star on top of his Christmas tree. After much talk in such a seductive ambience Sedlmeier did manage to persuade Gerhard to travel to Brazil to secure the renewal of the needed document.

Gerhard arrived in São Paulo on January 10, 1976, and went through the procedures required for obtaining a new permit. No sooner did he possess the paper than Mengele, using a picture taken the same day as Gerhard's, substituted his face for Gerhard's. Gerhard lingered only long enough to visit the cemetery at Embu, where he spoke with the manager about reserving a grave next to his mother's for an aged relative. Having thereby made plans for Mengele's interment, Gerhard returned to Austria. Two years later, in 1978, he died under distinctly mysterious circumstances. The official explanation was that while standing alongside his automobile he had fallen and struck his head, and then while unconscious had suffered a fatal heart attack.

In this same year Mengele's health started to decline seriously, which led to the introduction of new, if unwitting, members of the conspiracy. Liselotte Bossert taught kindergarten in a local São Paulo school, and through her job she and her husband had met one of the parents, Ernesto Glawe, an Argentine-born textile engineer. His antecedents were in Hamburg. The Bosserts introduced Glawe to Gerhard, and Glawe now says he was bemused by Gerhard's veneration for Hitler and preaching on the return of Nazism. Glawe contends that he always thought of him as "a little unbalanced mentally."

Nevertheless, when during his brief 1976 stay in São Paulo Wolfgang Gerhard asked Glawe to look in occasionally on an elderly Austrian, the textile engineer agreed because, he has said, "I like to help my fellow man." Mengele, going now by the name of Peter Gerhard, was so introduced to Glawe.

Accompanied by his son Norberto, Glawe proceeded to visit Peter Gerhard periodically, sharing conversation, biscuits, and chocolate. Peter volunteered very few details about his life except to say he had been a doctor with the German Army, recounting a few anecdotes about wounds at the front. Glawe says he suspected Peter had some secrets, and then one day was surprised to see the Bosserts appear; he says he had not been aware they also knew Peter Gerhard.

On May 17, 1976, Norberto Glawe and his fiancée were bidding the older man goodnight when suddenly his speech slurred and his physical movements became uncoordinated. After telephone calls and consultations with his father, Norberto, along with Wolfram Bossert, drove Mengele to a small hospital where he was diagnosed as a stroke victim. He was admitted only after he deposited an American one hundred dollar bill to cover the initial costs. Actually the payment was a violation of Brazilian law since all transactions were required to be made in cruzeiros. More significant than a minor currency transgression was that Mengele had the bill at all. How many more he owned and who supplied them was and is unknown.

While Mengele recuperated in a hospital bed, Norberto Glawe moved into his house on Estrada da Alvaranga. When the patient came home, Norberto stayed on as a kind of male nurse. He describes Peter as "egocentric." There were arguments, possibly because the young man had made such free use of the house. He even held a backyard barbecue to which he invited his friends, including the younger son of the Stammers. Unlike his older brother, Miklos Stammer had never been annoyed by Peter when he lived with the family. In fact, when Gitta Stammer confided the truth about the long-term guest just before her two sons entered the Brazilian naval academy, Miklos's response was, "I never knew we knew anyone famous."

Actually, says Norberto, Mengele appeared to enjoy the party. "He was very attentive to the young ladies," but the festive spirit evaporated quickly. The host's "authoritarian" behavior drove young Glawe away. Later his father claims to have noticed a catalog for Mengele farm equipment about the house and began to suspect Peter might be the celebrated doctor.

In any case their services were no longer needed because Mengele now had a new aide, Elsa Gulpian, who cooked and cleaned and took him on trips into São Paulo. They ate in restaurants and went to movies. Blonde and thin, in her thirties, at the time, she now denies any sexual relationship. She worked for "Peter Gerhard" until 1978, when she announced that she was leaving to marry. When Mengele asked her to stay and live with him, she asked if he would marry her. He balked. That he was still Martha's husband probably did not enter into his calculations. He simply could not risk a wedding because that would entail presenting himself at the registry with his foreign resident permit.

Some accounts have it that he was in love with Elsa Gulpian. More likely it was the relationship of a lonely aging man, desperate not to lose a reliable caretaker and part-time companion.

In fact Joseph Mengele never developed any kind of strong relationship with *mutual* respect. His marriage to Irene, "the only woman I ever loved," was sixteen years chronologically, but, wed in 1938, there were only two years before he entered active service with the Waffen SS. Thereafter, until 1945, he and Irene could only have been together for the brief intervals of his leaves, and from the end of the war until 1949 he was in hiding. After he went to Argentina the mails were the only contact. The arrangement with Martha seems singularly empty of any passion, and she stayed with him in South America for not more than two years.

Nowhere in his history, not among his schoolmates, not in medicine, not in the military, or at Auschwitz has any confidante ever been found. A series of acquaintances, Diesbach, von Verschuer, Rudel, von Eckstein, the Stammers, Gerhard, the Bosserts, Elsa Gulpian mark his pathway like street lamps rather than places where he stayed for sustenance and a genuine exchange. Men like Gerhard and Bossert apparently considered him worthy of close to veneration. They accepted his ex-cathedra pronunciamentos, however banal and unknowing. But his inability to open himself to others in a mature relationship built on equality and mutual respect must have made Mengele an inadequate lover, a seeker only of his own satisfaction. This weakness of character, also typical of a paranoid personality, kept the doctor from valuing the lives of others. He had no feeling for other human beings, and as a consequence could tinker with the minds and bodies of men, women, and children, send them to their deaths without conscience or qualm.

If anything, the Mengele of Brazil is more closed off than the one who terrorized Auschwitz. Hans Münch has said Mengele at the KZ was a man with a wide interest in things, a person with whom one could discuss things and offer opposing views. That person was no longer evident in "Peter Gerhard."

Mengele's opaque quality characterized his efforts to communicate with his son Rolf. Brought up under the influence of a stepfather, Rolf had become a lawyer, and except for the vacation in 1956 had no communication with his father until after one of Sedlmeier's forays to South America. Letters then passed between father and son. The conspirators used a mail drop in Augsburg. A man named Schweigart was the addressee but inside an outer envelope would be a sealed one marked "Herr H." Sedlmeier then distributed the letters to the appropriate parties. Sedlmeier also sent letters from Germany to either the Stammers or the Bosserts.

In one letter the father wrote, "On the one hand I can never hope from you for understanding and sympathy for the course of my life. I on the other hand have not the slightest inner cause to 'justify' or to make apologies for any decision, any actions, or any relationships in my life concerning the relevant arguments . . . my tolerance has an exact limit, namely, in that which concerns indisputable traditional values and what I must fear for those who are close to me and the community of my people." Mengele never wavered from the conviction that he had behaved properly in defense of "indisputable traditional values." And, indeed, in terms of the Germany of his day, the argument can be made that he did—hardly an exoneration of

Mengele so much as a condemnation of his time. Having thus justified his role in mass murder he concluded the letter "with many heartfelt Christmas greetings."

He repeated the theme of blameless service in another letter: "I have not the slightest reason to make excuses for myself for what I did . . . What I did was done for the utility of our people."

Mengele, having found himself without blame, proceeded to lecture on the failings of others, castigating, for example, Albert Speer, Hitler's architect and master builder, for his memoirs, which criticized Hitler and the Nazi regime. Mengele told his son that Speer had failed to realize that the Nazi era would be regarded by historians of the future as one of the most splendid since Alexander the Great.

Rolf now says that as he matured and then studied law he became less accepting of the word from Brazil and engaged in transatlantic disputes through correspondence. Eventually dissatisfied with this dialogue by mail, Rolf decided to confront his father in person and made no attempt to disguise himself, traveling with a passport issued in his own name in 1977. His only address was the Bosserts', Rua Missuri 7, São Paulo.

Wolfram Bossert then agreed to drive the son to a reunion with his father at Alvaranga. "The street where my father lived," says Rolf, "was here and there in dreadful condition. There was no pavement [by 1985 the road was hard-surfaced], just hardened dust that whirled up, potholes, and dirt. To the left and right of the road were kilometer-long slums, the famous *favellas.* Wolfram Bossert stopped in front of my father's door. The house was really not more than a wood hut. I was tired and worn out." In fact, *favellas* spring up wherever there is open land; the nearby presence of one does not mean an entire area is a slum. Also, the Alvaranga house was not made of wood; it has a smooth stucco finish . . . "The first thing I perceived," he says, "was a feeling of strangeness. But then I saw how my father

trembled with excitement. I saw that he had tears in his eyes."
Rolf says the house was small and poorly furnished—one bed,
one table, a few chairs and a closet, and because there was only
a single bed, Rolf says, his father slept on the floor, giving the
son the bed. Actually the Alvaranga cottage consisted of five
rooms, and Mengele had constructed a shed for servants separate from the house.

"The man that stood before me in 1977," Rolf says in *Bunte*
(the German publication to which he provided the serial rights
for his experiences), "was a haunted creature." His father was
fearful, depressed and talked of suicide. His low spirits were not
signs of repentence—his father, says Rolf, felt no guilt. He did
not expect to appear before judges because, as he told Rolf,
"There are no judges. There is no guilt." There were only those
bent on revenge.

The image of a haunted, depressed person contrasts with the
many photographs made by the Bosserts. In these Mengele appears smiling, jovial, as though enjoying his life. Indeed, when
the Stammers by chance bumped into Mengele, Rolf, and Rolf's
wife in the São Paulo post office, Gitta Stammer says her former
tenant seemed extremely happy as he introduced the young
couple. Elsa Gulpian also discerned a cheerful mood as Mengele
introduced her to a young man he identified as his nephew.

Until the Bosserts entered his life Mengele avoided the camera. The picture-taking was part of Wolfram Bossert's campaign
to draw Mengele out if his shell, but the fugitive trusted Bossert's discretion, apparently convinced the photographs would
not fall into the wrong hands. Not so with the maid Elsa Gulpian,
who took her employer to her sister's wedding. Not until later
when she looked at the work of a photographer hired to record
the festivities did she realize that not a single shot of Mengele
or Peter Gerhard existed. He had removed himself from range

whenever the photographer turned the camera in his direction.

So the photographs reveal an elderly man enjoying himself at family get-togethers, playing the role of grandfather to the Bossert youngsters and beaming in the presence of Rolf and his wife. The portraits taken by Liselotte capture the stern, almost fierce look of a man unashamedly staring the world down, altogether appropriate to the man who could say, as reported years later by Hans Sedlmeier: "I never killed anyone. I only decided who was fit to work," and who could tell his son that, although he did send people to their deaths as part of his job at Auschwitz, there was no guilt or wrong-doing in his actions.

Whatever the degree of aberrant rationalization and self-deception there may be here, it seems necessary to remind ourselves that Mengele's behavior at the KZ, his research, and the concepts and philosophies of race superiority behind it were *not* unique but reflected, though in extreme degree, the mainstream science of Germany at the time. The temptation is great, even among distinguished psychiatrists such as Robert Jay Lifton, to focus on the sick personality and what makes it to the relative exclusion of the cultural and environmental sickness that Mengele so terrifyingly, but accurately, reflected.

For all of his photogenic appearance of good health and strength, Mengele was fading. His stroke left Mengele with a twisted left hand. Then in 1978 an angry rash erupted on his face and body. Ointments did not assuage the discomfort of what today sounds very much like a case of shingles. He also suffered fits of depression and grew noticeably weaker, nearly falling down in the street.

According to the Bosserts, early in February 1979, they invited him to accompany them for an outing at a cottage they had rented at Bertioga Beach, forty miles north of São Paulo.

Though reluctant at first, Mengele agreed. He remarked to his last maid, Ines Mehlich, "I'm going to the beach because my life is ending."

At Bertioga the sand-shelf slopes very gently into the sea. One can walk hundreds of yards without reaching a depth greater than the waistline. On February 7 Wolfram Bossert, the children, and Mengele waded into the Bertioga surf. Mengele walked far enough for the water to reach his belt level. Bossert was distracted for a few moments and took his eyes off the older man. Suddenly, one of the children cried out.

Mengele either fainted or stumbled, tumbling under the water. Bossert rushed to him. He claims that he almost drowned trying to save the victim. Taken from the ocean, Mengele failed to respond to resuscitation efforts. His body then lay on the beach for nearly two hours, guarded by a policeman before an ambulance arrived to transport it to the coroner's offices in Santos.

José Mendoza, the São Paulo coroner, says he observed a whitish froth about the nostrils and mouth of the corpse, telltale symptoms of drowning victims. With that evidence and the statements of witnesses he saw no reason to perform an autopsy. Mendoza routinely signed the death certificate, based on the identification papers subsequently handed to him. He never, however, had an opportunity to examine the body while in possession of the dead man's documents. On a weekend he would deal with fifteen to twenty drowning victims, and the volume of business deterred close scrutiny of each case in the absence of anything suspicious.

On the following day the body of "Wolfgang Gerhard" in a closed coffin was brought to the Embu Cemetery, to be interred next to the remains of Gerhard's mother. The cemetery officials at the gravesite all knew Wolfgang Gerhard from his regular visits to the tomb of his mother. When the administrator of the burial grounds asked if the casket might be opened in order for him to pay his last respects to an old acquaintance, Liselotte Bossert burst into a near-hysterical fit of tears. Seeing how upset she was, the official backed off out of fear of causing her even more distress. And so Mengele's being buried as Gerhard managed to pass undetected. As for Wolfram Bossert, he was not present—his efforts to save his friend had left him bedridden for several days.

The world, of course, knew nothing of Mengele's demise, but word spread among the conspirators. There was a second trip to São Paulo by Rolf Mengele forty-eight hours after his father's death. The Bosserts' account of the drowning and the burial apparently satisfied the son that his father truly was dead. Rolf gathered up papers, books, and photographs belonging to his father and returned to his home and offices in Freiburg, Germany. Curiously, the house on Alvaranga was to remain unoccupied for six years.

One other event related to Mengele occurred in August of 1979 when the government of Paraguay formally revoked the citizenship awarded to José Mengele. The reason was that he had been absent from the country for more than two years, dating back to 1961. "Once a Paraguayan, always a Paraguayan," in Stroessner's words, no longer applied to Joseph Mengele.

Discovery

IN 1979 THE CONGRESS of the United States had attempted to influence Paraguayan President Stroessner when fifty-seven of its members petitioned him to extradite Joseph Mengele. Senator Jesse Helms of North Carolina had offered the Senate a resolution calling on Paraguay to act against Mengele. Now that Paraguay had taken away the citizenship, Wiesenthal said it was because the country feared a cancellation of U.S. aid, but the maximum granted to Paraguay was $4 million and some years the appropriation amounted to as little as $50,000, hardly sufficient to influence even a small nation. So long as landlocked Paraguay had the misfortune to be surrounded by non-communist states, it was ineligible for large sums of U.S. aid. After all, what was there to save it from?

Paraguay was not the sort of place that knuckled under to criticism by outsiders, though insiders rarely spoke up. Its officials were offended by the Granada TV show. Interior Minister Sabino Montanaro said, "That film was fiction—something like this movie about Brazil," referring to *The Boys From Brazil,* which featured Gregory Peck as Mengele cloning ninety-four Hitler offspring. Mengele had been thinly disguised as "The White Angel" in another movie, *Marathon Man.* Ambassador Varon, with a smile, suggests that Americans became especially outraged about Mengele only after they saw his character in *Marathon Man* try to murder Dustin Hoffman.

In any event, Paraguay was now intent on keeping its records on Mengele closed, records dealing with his naturalization having disappeared from the files of Paraguay's Supreme Court early in the 1960s. Suspicion points to Luis Martinez Miltos, then chief justice. For years Mengele had been the topic of informal discussions in Paraguay because of the world's insistence that he was hiding there. Edgar Ynsfran, former minister of the interior, particularly recalls a conversation with Rudel after Mengele vanished from the country: "I asked him where Mengele was. He assured me that Mengele was no longer in Paraguay. I pressed him for more details and he told me, 'He had been on a ranch in the Chaco'" (the region near the Bolivian border).

Ynsfran persisted, "But where is he now?"

"That I cannot tell you," answered Rudel.

Ynsfran flattered the war hero, complimenting him as a "good friend of Paraguay." Rudel at last relented. "He is in Brazil."

Ynsfran says he never revealed this conversation "because no one ever questioned me about Mengele." Curiously, he passed on the clue to a reporter from the Cox newspapers a week or so before Mengele's body turned up at Embu in 1985.

In retrospect it seems fairly clear that high-ranking officials in the Stroessner government had learned of their adopted citizen's passing. More than coincidence lies behind the timing of Paraguay's revocation of Mengele's citizenship. As long as he was alive, Paraguayan officials offered him the protection of their citizenship and passport. If Nazi-hunters had traced him to Brazil, he could have retreated to Paraguay, but after he died the Paraguayans had an opportunity to show themselves responsive to the clamor for cancellation of his citizenship. It was an empty gesture that fooled the world. But except for lifting his citizenship the Paraguayans gave no hint of the disposition of Joseph Mengele. Misinformation and disinformation continued, often featuring prominent individuals.

Having played a major role in rousting Klaus Barbie from Bolivia to face trial in France, the Klarsfelds mounted a combined effort against Walter Rauff in Chile and Mengele in Paraguay. West Germany had asked Chile to send Rauff home in 1961, but a court ruled he was exempt because of the statute of limitations. Early in 1984 Beate Klarsfeld, employing tactics that had proved effective against Barbie, mounted a demonstration in front of the palace occupied by the Chilean president, the authoritarian August Pinochet. For the ten years since the beginning of the Pinochet regime no Chileans had been allowed to demonstrate on any issue within sight of the president's offices. But Klarsfeld, joined by forty women from the "Committee of Relatives of the Detained Disappeared," marched into the plaza facing La Moneda, the palace. A few spectators cheered from the windows of a nearby hotel as Klarsfeld unfurled a banner reading, "General Pinochet—why are you waiting to expel Walter Rauff?" Other signs proclaimed that "Chile must not protect war criminals," and "Rauff must be tried for the deaths of 97,000 Jews."

Previously the local Jewish community had been somewhat diffident about protests, out of fear of what Pinochet would do to them on the grounds of alleged political disruption. Similarly Paraguay's Jewish community worried that demonstrations against Mengele might be interpreted as anti-Stroessner. In mitigation, they, after all, had to live there. The Chilean Jews, however, did accompany Klarsfeld when she put on a demonstration show in front of Rauff's home in an affluent suburb.

For a government notorious for its low tolerance to dissent, the Chilean authorities responded moderately, briefly detaining Klarsfeld for failing to secure permission to demonstrate and then suggesting she sign a statement committing herself to refrain from public ations or risk being deported. Beate Klarsfeld responded, "All of a sudden the person who is demanding the expulsion of a man that killed 97,000 people faces the possibility of being expelled." Rauff saved the Pinochet government further annoyances by expiring of natural causes. (Prior to that, it should be noted, he visited Germany in 1960 and 1962, using his own passport, and no attempt was made to detain him.)

From Chile, Klarsfeld flew to Asunción, proceeding on the premise that Mengele was alive and well in the Paraguayan outback. She explained the strategy: "First you have to locate him. Then you have to mobilize public opinion against him. He is alive in South America, but he is not living openly or traveling around. Mengele is not like Rauff. Rauff had a phone number in Santiago, Chile. You could telephone him. Klaus Barbie went to German clubs in Bolivia. He was seen singing Hitler songs and making *sig heils*. Mengele is very careful. He is really afraid and not living openly." She was at least correct about the lifestyle of Mengele, but she employed the wrong tense. In her defense, everyone except a few conspirators and officials in

Paraguay assumed Mengele was in Paraguay. The same people who had revoked his citizenship and presumably knew he was dead assured her, "If we find him, we will arrest him and extradite him to Germany."

Meanwhile groups at work with Simon Wiesenthal were busy on another front. Rabbi Marvin Hier, head of the Simon Wiesenthal Center in Los Angeles, had filed Freedom of Information Act requests with government agencies asking for the release of any documents referring to Mengele, joined in the effort by his deputy, Rabbi Abraham Cooper.

One response was a copy of the 1947 letter written by Benjamin Gorby in which he said an informant claimed Mengele was being held by a unit of the U.S. Army. The newspapers, magazines, and TV broadcasters accepted and built that thin, unsubstantiated belief into a headline fact. Gorby, located in Israel, stoutly defended his letter.

The opportunity to campaign against a despicable target with no constituency was not unattractive to U.S. politicians, including senators Alfonse D'Amato of New York and Arlen Specter of Pennsylvania, the latter chairman of the Juvenile Justice Subcommittee of the Senate Judiciary Committee, who held a hearing on the matter. One does not question the sincerity of the senators' feelings about Mengele, but the relevancy of Joseph Mengele to a committee enquiring into U.S. juvenile justice is rather difficult to discern. Further, the investigation did not focus on legislation to protect American children or their involvement with law enforcement, but sought information on the alleged release of Mengele from U.S. custody in 1947, the hearings rehashing the Gorby letter, and the indistinct memories of the pair of former soldiers at the Idar–Oberstein internment camp in 1945. Senator Howard Metzenbaum of Ohio and Senator Specter interrogated witness Lieutenant General William Odum, assistant chief-of-staff for intelligence, for not having pursued the case on his own initiative, and there were demands for the names of those responsible for releasing Mengele thirty-eight years earlier. If indeed Mengele had been in custody, those involved more than likely were dead or long retired. What, then, was the point?

Rabbi Hier added further headlines with his documents—CIA reports from Paraguay in the 1970s that linked Mengele as "Dr. Henrique Wollman" with traffic in narcotics. Rabbi Hier declared that the West Germans had in custody on drug smuggling charges, a Paraguayan named Ricardo Riefenstaph who said he had roomed with Mengele. Prosecutor Hans Eberhard Klein in Frankfurt, in a position to interrogate Riefenstaph, found no evidence to tie Mengele to narcotics, and surely Klein would have been pleased to come up with some evidence to enhance his position. *Stern* magazine writer Manfred von Conta says he was contacted by several people in prison who claimed information about Mengele. Investigation revealed they wanted to trade invented tales for lesser sentences or for money.

These various people in the rediscovering Mengele business did not furnish perspective by citing the appraisal of authorities on the alleged linkage between Mengele and dope as "tantalizing," "very circumstantial," "unsubstantiated" "and does not warrant publication as finished intelligence." Indeed, the CIA, not overly shy or conservative in such matters, in 1985 labeled it little more than vague rumor. Senator D'Amato also told ABC–TV he would soon release more information on Mengele, but when the author telephoned his office he was advised that all of the material was obtained by the Simon Wiesenthal Center. A request to Senator Specter for any additional details he might have brought no response at all.

North of the border in Canada, a flurry was caused by a document that mentioned one "Joseph Menke," who sought to emigrate to Canada. Intelligence forces questioned whether

Menke might not be Mengele. Canadian editors, like their U.S. counterparts, played up the story. Prime Minister Brian Mulroney announced a "vigorous investigation." Within a few weeks the tempest vanished as authorities determined that Menke was not Mengele and that the doctor had never attempted to enter Canada.

Not to be outdone by the legislative branch in the Mengele business, the administration of President Ronald Reagan struck off on its own. Attorney General William French Smith ordered agencies under his jurisdiction to investigate not only the question of whether U.S. forces released Mengele from custody after the war but also to search for him around the world. Charged with the twin quests was Neal M. Sher, head of the Office of Special Investigations, a division assigned to hunt war criminals in the United States. Sher dispatched U.S. marshals overseas to collect information, though it is unclear how the U.S. Department of Justice had jurisdiction in a case where the crimes were committed in another country and none of the victims at the time were American citizens. Senator Specter did cite a precedent from the nineteenth century, when U.S. marshals traveled to South America for a desperado, but his crimes had been committed in the United States.

Considerable fanfare characterized a joint conference of West German, U.S., and Israeli law enforcement officials seeking the seizure of Mengele. The agenda and discussion were top secret, but from Germany Klein insisted that in the past he had been handicapped by a lack of intelligence from South America, a strange claim in view of the millions of German expatriates living there. He also said that the CIA and the Mossad possessed much more effective instruments for gathering information.

In review, the operations of the various law-enforcement agencies tend to strike one as more damage-control missions than meaningful pursuit of the fugitive. The West Germans had, after all, been on the case for twenty-five years with little to show for it beyond some writs for extradition and testaments from Auschwitz survivors. Hans Klein, in charge of the case for ten years, had several times invoked in extenuation German law's protection of the family, Article 52 of the German Penal Code, stipulating that close relatives, including fiancées, have the right to refuse to testify. Klein, however, did not seek to interview members of the family to draw *voluntary* information, according to Dieter Mengele, who along with his cousin Karl Heinz Mengele had directed the family business since the death of Joseph's brother Alois, Dieter's father, in 1974. And certainly law-enforcement officials could have interrogated Hans Sedlmeier and investigated his movements. A long article in the magazine *Der Spiegel,* published in April of 1985, named three people who could be presumed to know Mengele's whereabouts. Martha, the estranged wife, who likely would indeed have invoked her privileged legal position (her one published response to questions about her husband's criminal past was "rubbish"). Alfredo Stroessner, another, was unavailable to Klein and claimed to ABC that he was ignorant of Mengele. The third person listed was Sedlmeier. Wiesenthal says he urged investigation of Sedlmeier. One would think that phone taps and passport checks might well have revealed compromising trips by Sedlmeier and Rolf Mengele.

The Israeli representative at the tripartite meeting of Mengele hunters was Menachem Russek, a police officer assigned to track Nazi war criminals. Russek was described in *The Jerusalem Post* as possessing "a huge pile of information about the man, including his fingerprints and a chart of the fillings in his teeth." The writer, however, failed to note that the dental records were more than forty years old and marginally useful. Russek also found himself in a defensive position. Pursuit of war criminals by Israel had, as mentioned, slacked off as the country fought three wars and contended with terrorists. In the interests of state survival, concerns about the likes of Mengele had been dampened. As former Ambassador Varon explained, Israel attempted good relations with Paraguay, although a known sanctuary for war criminals, because of what Stroessner's representatives could do on behalf of Israel at the United Nations. It would have been bad manners, and more importantly a negative signal to other countries if Israel had turned on its ally. Russek also had to be sensitive about charges that Mossad, Israel's intelligence agency, had perhaps bungled opportunities to seize Mengele.

The first concern of the Americans was that in Joseph Mengele they had another Klaus Barbie case, wherein a known war criminal was hired by U.S. intelligence for espionage against the Red menace. Allan Ryan, Neal Sher's predecessor in the Office of Special Investigation, has said that of the 10,000 war criminals who managed to enter the United States after World War II, fewer than 100 were brought to court and of these only a handful were deported. Investigation might only emphasize this performance by immigration authorities and the Justice Department. One immediate action of the U.S. team had been to shut off information, the Attorney General silencing all government sources. Requests for documents under the Freedom of Information Act brought such stock answers as: "This agency has been instructed by the Department of Justice at this time not to release any information directly or indirectly involving Mengele or the government's present criminal investigation of Mengele." Or: "In our view the release of any information concerning Mengele from any time period, including information dating to the period of World War II, would interfere with and potentially impede investigation." Such a closed door position was an open invitation for further misinformation and disinformation.

Officials in Washington were, one can assume, worried about the reputation of the United States in this matter. Neither the

White House nor the U.S. Department of State under any administration had ever denounced Mengele or applied pressure on a country where he supposedly resided. Interestingly, Senators D'Amato and Specter, both Republicans calling for the capture of Mengele, did not embarrass their leader, President Reagan, by asking why his administration had not moved against Mengele.

To continue the chronicle of the trackers, Beate Klarsfeld had returned to Asunción to further press her case. Accompanying her were Menachem Rosensaft, a member of the Children of Auschwitz Survivors (his mother and father had both been imprisoned there), Bishop Francis Mugavero, the Roman Catholic head of the Brooklyn, N.Y., diocese whose participation lent an air of ecumenicism, and Brooklyn District Attorney Elizabeth Holtzman. Herself Jewish *and* a twin, as a member of Congress she had sponsored the formation of the Office of Special Investigation. Additionally, some said Ms. Holtzman might have had further reasons to be interested in the case, such as a possible rerun for the U.S. Senate seat occupied by Alfonse D'Amato. In any case, once again the Paraguayans proved polite but firm in their insistence that Mengele did not live there anymore. They did offer a concession, though: the outsiders could monitor the efforts of the government to find the person they said was not there.

The Mengele hunt was further stimulated by an expedition to Auschwitz of survivors on the fortieth anniversary of the liberation of the camp. Among those making the pilgrimage were Marc Berkowitz, Ruth Eliaz, who had killed her own newborn, Vera Kriegel, who saw the "wall of eyes" in the doctor's laboratory. From Poland the group traveled to Israel, where a tribunal staged a mock trial. Dignitaries present included Gideon Hausner, the prosecutor of Eichmann, Simon Wiesenthal, former Nuremberg trials prosecutor Telford Taylor, and historian Yehuda Bauer.

In the wake of such events came a deluge of publicity as journalists now descended on both Günzburg and South America. Indeed, the search for Mengele became a kind of cottage industry. Hotels in Asunción housed a steady stream of reporters, writers, and TV journalists. Alejandro von Eckstein priced his offerings at between $1,500 and $3,000. ABC–TV interviewed him, and he chauffeured Gerald Posner, a New York lawyer, about the country. Posner announced that he had amassed a collection of 25,000 pages of documents on Mengele and had interviewed 200 people in South America. He became something of a voice of authority for *Time,* among others, though there is no evidence his 25,000 pages were closely examined for their value.

Posner also talked on ABC, declaring that Mengele had lived in Asunción "for nearly five years" and that a family (Alban Krugg's survivors?) last saw Mengele "in 1982." It turned out that Mengele had been dead for three years. Posner completed his ABC piece with: "I have evidence that I believe is trustworthy that Dr. Mengele in the last eighteen months has visited both Brazil and Chile"—an active year for a corpse. Posner also said he was writing a book with John Ware, the producer of the Granada TV film in which "Nazi Mueller" regaled the interviewer with tales of Mengele in Paraguay in 1978.

More equivocal and disingenuous before ABC–TV's cameras was President Alfredo Stroessner, who told correspondent John Martin, "I will be very sincere," said Stroessner. "I don't know where he is and we cannot find out where he is."

The prevailing mood of the hometown, Günzburg, to all of this was resentment—not toward its fugitive son but to the reporters who came to town to chronicle him, his family, and his background. Unfair, was the consensus, to blame the town for the sins, if any, of the man. After all, they would say, he left at nineteen and never came back. The town's reputation concerned them far more than the deeds of its most notorious resident.

Journalists searching for material uncovered *A Little Piece of the Home Country,* published in 1983 and written by Joseph Baumeister, a local schoolteacher and folklore scholar, which contains an address to Dr. Joseph Mengele that shows a sentiment far from neutral about his town's ex-resident:

"Germans clung to Germany, and so did you when you were young. Now that the war was a fiasco, you and the German people stand accused . . . Luther cried, 'Burn the synogagues!' In the schools the outcry was that the Jew knows only 'Juda!' Everywhere it was said that both the Gypsy and the Jew were parasites, not enjoyed by any nation."

And Baumeister went on to say, "Already in school he was known for his good deeds," and scoffed as impossible that such a person could "degenerate into such a monster. To me," declared the schoolmaster, "those who were condemned by the German people are much baser still than the Nazis altogether, because they still today claim payment from Germany even though, as is said, they are criminals!" In short, the victims were to blame.

Behind the chair of the Günzburg mayor hung a painting of a foggy riverscape with the English motto: "Only those who are invisible can do the impossible." The inscription took on heavy irony for the incumbent Rudolph Kopper, whose anti-Nazi credentials could not be questioned. His father was executed by the Nazis a few days before the end of the war, and Berlin-born Koppler is himself a left-of-center politician. Still, Koppler felt the presence of the invisible man, "a monstrous shadow," in his words. "Slowly a legend is forming, Koppler said, "all the world over that Günzburg is the stronghold of obstinate Nazis. Günzburg is neither worse nor better than other cities." Koppler also scorned those like Baumeister.

Koppler produced a 1965 statement of Alois Mengele when the brother of the war criminal said that based on his upbringing in their parents' home he could not believe Joseph was capable of perpetrating the terrible crimes, but Alois added, "If somebody comes whom I can trust and tells me that he really shot or tortured children with his own hands, I immediately will separate myself in my mind from my brother." It may be that the letters to Karl Heinz, their nephew, which Alois read, convinced him that his brother was capable of the acts of which he was accused.

When reporters managed to reach the youthful nephews of Joseph Mengele, who ran the company, they received answers similar to Alois's statement. Karl Heinz allowed that Auschwitz with all its terrible deeds existed but characterized the evidence against his uncle and stepfather as "thin." Dieter Mengele was asked by ABC what he would say to his uncle if he could speak with him. "I would say he should come here and really stand up and say I did it or I did not and take away these terrible pressures from us."

In the interview Dieter declared, "I think he's dead. First of all, he's seventy-four. If it's true what I'm reading that everybody's looking for him, they would have found him if he's still alive." Karl Heinz also told reporters that he believed his uncle had died.

It is difficult not to believe that both of them indeed knew that Joseph Mengele was long dead, and their seemingly ingenuous assertions may have been the first tentative efforts to reveal the death, a revelation that was becoming increasingly necessary because of the mounting pressure on them. (During this period, Rolf Mengele was unapproachable.)

Dieter reflected the heat felt by the family in his interview with

ABC's John Martin: "I don't know why everybody is stepping on my family and the whole town is getting responsible for a man who is born here and lived here eighteen years and then he's gone. There's no truth at all that Joseph Mengele got any money or does have any share of the company. That's absolutely not true."

Karl Heinz adamantly denied that the company provided any support for Joseph Mengele, and professed no knowledge of payments from a fund created to cover what would have been his uncle's inheritance. "How and if such arrangements were made by my grandfather, who died in 1959, I do not know. I never had any contact with Joseph Mengele. I never knowingly have seen him. We do not pay anything and we never paid, not even on a Swiss bank account." Any assertions to the contrary he called "stinking lies."

To lie to the press is not, except to the press, a crime, but the statements by the nephews do not square with the truth. Both the Bosserts and Rolf Mengele say the family (without specifying the actual persons) funneled $100 to $150 a month to the fugitive. Certainly Hans Sedlmeier was not the source of the $7,000 in cash cited by Gitta Stammer, but Sedlmeier was an employee of the Mengele company. His expenses were one more tab for the upkeep on Joseph Mengele. The real estate in Brazil was financed by the family; the car received by Geza Stammer was bought by the family and undoubtedly the airplane tickets that brought Wolfgang Gerhard back from Austria to obtain new credentials for the wanted man were purchased by the family. Lesser, but still an untruth, is Karl Heinz's contention that he had no contact with his stepfather. Surely the letters that so excited Alois contradict him. And the company executive Hans Sedlmeier publicly acknowledged his meetings with Joseph Mengele. In fact, Sedlmeier volunteered Mengele's defense against all accusations: "I personally have killed, injured or physically harmed no one," adding that he had not selected Jews for the gas chamber but only "to work in the arms industry."

The reward money for Mengele skyrocketed. The Simon Wiesenthal Center in Los Angeles announced that an anonymous group had pledged $1 million to those responsible for the legal arrest and subsequent extradition of Mengele. The government of Israel offered an additional $1 million, and the same sum was vouchsafed by the *Washington Times,* the paper owned by the Unification Church of Rev. Sun Myung Moon. Altogether the price on Mengele's moldering head had reached $3.4 million. The originator of the large bounty, Simon Wiesenthal, now deprecated the value of rewards: "You can't buy an entire country." With everyone convinced that the fugitive was being protected in Paraguay, it is difficult to understand how reward money could have played any role. Paraguay was not the sort of place where someone could make a citizen's arrest of a war criminal. But the high price for Mengele continued to make headlines and the evening news.

Against this backdrop the fortieth anniversary of V–E Day, peace in Europe, May 8, 1985, approached. As a gesture of friendship, reconciliation, a political debt—the purposes have not been altogether clear—the White House scheduled President Reagan for a ceremony at a German military cemetery in Bitburg. Overlooked or ignored were the forty-seven graves of Waffen SS troops. In the face of strenuous protests, President Reagan explained that among the current German population there were "very few alive that remember even the war and certainly none of them who were adults and participating in any way." Actually, the Berlin Document Center, a repository of captured German files administered since 1953 by the U.S. State

Department, contains dossiers on 4.5 million living West Germans who were Nazi Party members. All were adults when they applied for membership in the Party.

The president sought to mitigate the furor by calling the dead soldiers victims just as much as those consumed by the Holocaust. It was a breathtaking comparison, made all the more difficult to accept in view of the fact that several of the SS dead were not teenage boys but veterans from units accused of massacres of war prisoners.

When Elie Wiesel made his dramatic appeal to President Reagan not to go to Bitburg he invoked the horrors of the concentration camps ". . . Cut off from the world with no refuge anywhere, sons watched helplessly their fathers being beaten to death. Mothers watched their children die of hunger. And then there was Mengele and his selections . . ." But not even the shade of Mengele or the eloquence of Wiesel could deter what many European and some American observers perceived as a political ploy by West German Chancellor Helmut Kohl facing elections at the time in the Bitburg area.

On May 25, 1985, the Paraguayan newspaper *Hoy* published a brief interview with Alfonz Dierckx, who matter of factly remarked that Mengele, whom he knew through Alban Krugg, had lived in Brazil and died there in a drowning accident. He provided no further details and said he had remained silent out of respect for the confidence accorded him by Krugg, who died in 1982. Dierckx's statement went unnoticed by the world press and the Nazi hunters. According to Ralph Blumenthal of *The New York Times,* the West Germans had two months previously intercepted a letter from a German resident of Paraguay, Gert Luk, to Manfred Roeder, a guest at a 1978 Hitler birthday celebration at the Brazilian Hotel Tirol and now residing in a West German cell on a thirteen-year sentence for planning bomb attacks on immigrants. Luk informed Roeder that "Uncle" had died some time before "on the beaches of Brazil." The West Germans theorized that "Uncle" was Mengele, but Brazilian officials said they could not check out the tip. Their excuse: "Which beach? We have 17,000 kilometers of beach."

In the United States, however, the Office of Special Investigations brought an Auschwitz survivor to Washington to look at pictures of an elderly man sitting beside a swimming pool. The witness seemed satisfied that the subject was Mengele; the pictures were made in 1984 in Paraguay and probably came from a photographic set splashed across an Italian magazine.

On May 31, 1985, investigators from the West German Criminal Police knocked at the door of the home of Hans Sedlmeier in Günzburg, and produced a proper search warrant. The now retired Mengele company executive and his wife were apparently taken by surprise. He dashed for a jacket hanging in a closet, but an investigator managed to retrieve from a pocket his 1985 address and telephone book, some of whose entries were in code.

Hidden in a room used by Sedlmeier's wife, were photocopies of letters to and from Joseph Mengele, as well as correspondence with the Stammers and the Bosserts in Brazil. According to reporter Blumenthal, Sedlmeier was unaware of the photocopies made by his wife and raged at her, "How could you do that?" as investigators scooped up the material.

Because many entries in the seized papers were in code and telephone numbers lacked area dialing codes interpretation of the data was impeded, but the West Germans were able to determine that the key lay in São Paulo, Brazil.

The detectives under São Paulo police superintendent Romeu Tuma allegedly investigated an address written as Guararapes 650. That number did not exist but a few doors up the cross-street of Missouri lived an Austrian couple named Wolfram and Liselotte Bossert. After a few hours of questioning the Bosserts broke down and admitted that their friend Peter Hochbichlet was Joseph Mengele and that he had been buried at Embu in 1979. That was on June 5, 1985. The next day the police rounded up Gitta Stammer; her husband Geza was at sea, a passenger on a ship commanded by one of his sons.

On June 7 the Brazilians, accompanied by a horde of reporters, photographers, and TV cameramen, exhumed the body that had been buried as Wolfgang Gerhard. One investigator brandished the remains of the skull for the cameras, and observers, including forensic scientists, feared that the casual digging might damage bones and make identification even more difficult.

Within a few days an impressive international team of specialists was on the scene prepared to aid the Brazilian experts. At first the reaction of many Nazi hunters was skepticism. In Israel, Isser Harel and Menachem Russek both expressed doubt. The Klarsfelds suspected a hoax. Wiesenthal was dubious. Gerald Posner appeared on TV to say he had contacted a source in São Paulo who told of the coroner's insistence that he had buried a fifty-two-year-old man in 1979; Mengele, of course, would have been much older.

There was good reason to be wary. Jorge Luque remembered a "dead" Mengele in Paraguay that proved out to be a Czech doctor. Erwin Erdstein had claimed that he killed Mengele in Brazil during the 1960s. In 1970 a report had come from Asunción that Mengele had died; the corpse bore the name of Flores. The Institute of German–Paraguay Relations had reported Mengele's demise in Bolivia in 1976; the body was cremated and there was a report that the missing man had committed suicide in Portugal.

Many with strong reservations wondered why the family and friends would have allowed his death to pass unmentioned for six years, during which time the Mengele family suffered the badgering of the media. Joseph Mengele's lawyer in Germany, Fritz Steinacker, who defended a number of war criminals, had promised he would inform authorities when his client died.

Wiesenthal began to take the possibility seriously as he learned that unlike other instances this investigation had begun in West Germany and was based on information obtained from a raid on Hans Sedlmeier's home. The first report from experts indicated that the man who had lived with the Stammers and had been befriended by the Bosserts was indeed Mengele. David A. Crown, former chief of the CIA laboratory and Gideon Epstein, an analyst of the Forensic Document Laboratory at the Immigration and Naturalization Service of the United States, both handwriting specialists, said they were "thoroughly convinced beyond a shadow of doubt" that the papers collected from the Stammers and Bosserts were written by Joseph Mengele.

Matching the bones with the living being who swaggered through Auschwitz was more difficult. There was a paucity of records for comparison purposes. Much talk centered on a pelvic abnormality. Wiesenthal said Mengele had fractured a hip in a motorcycle accident. The dossier on Mengele indicated only a fender-bender incident in the summer of 1943, and Ella Lingens could not recall any period when Mengele was laid up with an injury. However, no one could locate a medical history that covered Mengele's war wounds or other desired details. The dental records, for example, were all World War II reports, and most of the original teeth of the corpse had been replaced.

On the other hand the forensic scientists could determine the precise height of the Embu body, which matched Mengele. The age at death also fitted the long-time fugitive. And although the details on the teeth were sketchy, the investigators could declare: "Skeletal evidence indicates the upper central incisors were widely spaced prior to their removal"—the trademark cleft noticeable in photographs of Mengele and remarked upon by many who knew him.

On June 21 the scientists issued a preliminary report that concluded: "It is further our opinion that this skeleton is that of Joseph Mengele within a reasonable scientific certainty." Perhaps the single most telling piece of evidence was a series of photographic skull-face superimposition analyses—matchups of the head and face pictures of young Joseph Mengele, the shots taken by the Bosserts, and the skull dug up at Embu. The comparisons covered twenty-four points, including such areas as the mouth, nose, chin, and eyes.

Although Menachem Russek seemed convinced, the Israeli government reserved its judgment until it could study a final report from the scientists. Most others accepted the findings. The confusion over the coroner's statement that he had seen a fifty-two-year-old drowning victim seemed cleared up when he agreed that he had based his knowledge on the information given to him by the Bosserts at the time of the drowning (at the time Mengele was a month shy of his sixty-eighth birthday). A dentist, Maria Buene Vieira de Castro, told the Associated Press she had treated a patient who identified himself as Dr. Muller in April of 1979, two months after Mengele's new certified death date. She insisted that Dr. Muller was the man newspaper pictures described as Mengele. Her treatment of Muller ended after he threw a tantrum in the waiting room and insulted a black patient. "He wasn't the type of person you forget," said the dentist, "gray hair streaked with blond, unsettling, piercing blue eyes." Interesting, except that Mengele's eyes were greenish brown.

The Bosserts hired Flavio Marx, the lawyer who prevented the extradition of Nazi Gustav Wagner and who also represented Sicilian Mafioso Tommaso Buscetta on the run in Brazil. Marx

268

says he negotiated a $100,000 deal with *Stern* magazine for their story along with the pictures, papers, notebooks, and some tapes of Mengele in their possession. (*Stern* says it paid less than $100,000.) Marx asked $20,000 from a British TV unit to interview the Bosserts but settled for $2,000 as the market value of Mengele fell sharply within a few weeks.

In Germany Rolf Mengele, almost immediately after the first word on the recovery of the body in Brazil, had come forward to say that it was his father. He said he would explain his involvement at a press conference. He did not attend, but his stepbrother Jens Hackenjos, twenty-eight, an architect and the son of Irene and the husband she took following her divorce from Mengele in 1954, along with his wife Sabine, conducted the session in a basement office. There they handed out a statement from Rolf in which he first affirmed his belief that his father had drowned and then said, "To all the victims and their relatives my own and our most profound sympathy." The condolences make no mention of his father's behavior, a position taken by the entire Mengele clan. Rolf explained the six-year delay in revealing the death in "consideration for the people who have been in contact with my father over the last thirty years."

Rolf then handed over to the editors of the German magazine *Bunte* some thirty pounds of photographs, letters, notebooks, and memorabilia. He said that any money from sales by *Bunte* should go to organizations dealing with Holocaust victims.

Neither *Bunte* nor *Stern* found a particularly ready market for their materials in the United States, where the asking price from television began at $600,000. Most who were privileged to examine the detritus left by Joseph Mengele came away feeling it was insignificant. Said one journalist, "The meanderings of an old man, virtually worthless if the man didn't happen to be Mengele. Mengele didn't seem to have known anyone of any importance in the Nazi hierarchy or to have gained any insight into the workings of the Third Reich. As historical material it is almost valueless."

Rolf, in his own behalf, told a *Bunte* editor, "I have not supported my father, but I didn't want to betray him." Those who worked with Rolf sifting through the materials on Joseph Mengele regarded him as ambivalent. He was described as helplessly dominated and manipulated by his tyrannical father in spite of their having only two meetings. The father-son code in the letters was seen as a way to enmesh Rolf ever deeper in the conspiracy to protect. Whenever the editors tried to tell Rolf details of his father's crimes he would insist these were still only "alleged activities." Rolf is not only the son but a lawyer.

Mengele's son veered toward a harsher judgment in an interview on Germany's ZDF–TV channel as he spoke of an unresolved conflict within himself: "On the one hand he was my father. On the other the charges against him, the horrid pictures of Auschwitz, were always present. I was very much relieved that the situation worked out this way [that he drowned] and not in any other way, such as a trial important though it might have been."

The interviewer asked how as a lawyer Rolf came to terms with his personal ties and his professional obligations. Rolf responded that he was glad he lived in a state of law where the penal code took this into consideration—in other words, the statutes excused him from the responsibilities he would otherwise have regarding a fugitive from justice. He did say that he felt a special moral obligation which may exceed the feelings of others because "in view of my descent, I am identified with these . . . incomprehensible events. This is also a motive for me to work together with all disciplines in order not to suppress the past but to overcome it and to recognize clearly not only the individual deeds but their mental and historical origins." It is interesting that in so saying, the son separated himself from those who wanted to make Joseph Mengele a lone-wolf psychotic monster and absolve the rest of his generation.

Rolf contended that in his letters and face-to-face confrontations with his father he could not communicate to his father his dismay that his mere presence at Auschwitz was "an unbearable thought. I was hoping to get an explanation from him. I was hoping that he would say that he had tried incessantly to get out of Auschwitz and that he had volunteered to go to the front. We did not even reach an understanding on this first point. Unfortunately I had to realize that in talking to me he did not speak of guilt, which might have brought about a feeling of regret."

In the excitement of the denouement, some curious aspects of the matter seem to have been overlooked. Was it only coincidence that the clues leading to the discovery of the body came six years after Mengele's death—the statute of limitations for aiding a felon in West Germany is five years.

First there was the letter from Luk in the spring of 1985. Then Dierckx went public two months later. How was it that the Hackenjos couple rented the basement office a full four weeks before discovery of the body?

Most odd are the events leading to the search of Sedlmeier's house. The official version says the former bagman and Mengele company executive was in his cups some time in 1984, boasting that he had supplied money to Mengele for many years. A university professor, at this writing unnamed, overheard him. But not until 1985 did this person report the conversation to West German authorities, resulting in the May 31 knock on the Sedlmeier door.

Further, Sedlmeier seems not to have made any attempt to hide incriminating materials. He had to know he was under suspicion, having been interrogated in 1971 by Klein and been named in a number of publications as a contact with the fugitive. Under these circumstances would his wife have idly retained

As Peter Gerhard, Mengele (third from right) enjoyed a backyard barbecue at his home in a São Paulo suburb. Norberto Glawe (third from left) had served as Mengele's helper and nurse after the war criminal suffered a stroke in 1976. The others in the photo are unidentified friends of Glawe.
Credit: Black Star

Gitta Stammer, Mengele's hostess and sounding board, faced the press after the discovery of his body in Brazil. For thirteen disputatious years she and her husband, Geza, harbored the fugitive.
Credit: Black Star

Wolfram and Liselotte Bossert, the husband and wife who helped Mengele for the last eight years of his life, watched as gravediggers exhumed what they said was his body.
Credit: Wide World Photos

Rolf Mengele (far right) visited his father (center) at the home of Liselotte Bossert (second from right) in São Paulo in 1977. Also in the picture are the Bossert children, Sabine (far left) and Andreas.
Credit: Wide World Photos

Dr. Jose Antonio de Mello, medical examiner for the state of São Paulo, holds the skull exhumed from the grave at Embu after Brazilian police were told that the man buried as Wolfgang Gerhard was actually Mengele.
Credit: Benedicto, Camara Tres, Black Star

Attendants carry the bones and rags suspected of being the remains of Mengele.
Credit: Camara Tres, Black Star

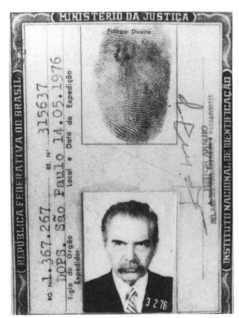

Notes on evolutionary theory that mentioned the work of Lamarck and Darwin were found in Brazil among the effects of a man later identified as Joseph Mengele. Handwriting experts said the script matched that of earlier samples of Mengele's handwriting.
Credit: Wide World Photos

Mengele substituted his photograph for that of Wolfgang Gerhard on this Brazilian foreign resident's permit.
Credit: Camara Tres, Black Star

X-rays of the skull taken from the grave at Embu were superimposed by computers upon photographs of Mengele to prove that the body was that of the long sought war criminal.
Credit: Black Star

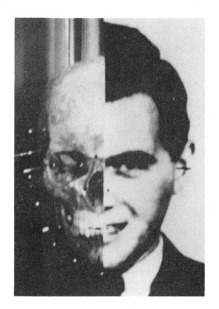

Using photographs obtained from Rolf Mengele, the cover of the German magazine *Bunte* featured a straw-hatted, smiling Mengele with Rolf's memoirs. The pictures proved to be less exclusive when *Stern*, using a set from the Bosserts who befriended Mengele, published a series at the same time.
Credit: Wide World Photos

Elsa Gulpian, who worked as a maid for the man she knew as Señor Pedro, holds a 1945 photograph of Mengele. He asked her to live with him in 1978 when she said she was quitting to be married.
Credit: Camara Tres, Black Star

photocopies of letters to Mengele and the families in Brazil? His scolding of his wife in the presence of investigators does smack of playacting. It is also worth noting that the alleged tipster on Sedlmeier never claimed a piece of the reward money.

The conspiracy that successfully sequestered Mengele for forty years (including six as a corpse) may very well itself have orchestrated the great discovery. As the summer of 1985 deepened there appeared little hope for prosecuting any of the participants. Rudel had died in 1982, Gerhard four years earlier. The Brazilian investigators seemed disinclined to pursue the investigation further, leaving the Stammers and Bosserts with only the vague threat of action by tax officials concerned with ownership of the Brazilian real estate. The Alvaranga house, originally owned by the Stammers, suddenly belonged to the Bosserts, as if after Mengele's death the assets were split up with the permission of the family in Günzburg.

Hans Sedlmeier seemed well protected by the expiration of the term of his jeopardy. He has been well rewarded for his services on behalf of the Mengeles, living as he does in a spacious home with an immense lawn and garden in a prosperous section on the outskirts of Günzburg. He has refused to cooperate with the police. "I did what I did and they can no longer charge me for what was done." Prosecutor Klein admits that Sedlmeier was always "very discreet" in his movements (a characterization that lends further suspicion about the clumsy behavior leading to his exposure).

He certainly offers no public apologies for his behavior. Reporters seeking an interview are treated to a barrage of epithets. The most printable statement defines his attitude: "I could tell you what Mengele did, what he did during Auschwitz, what he did after Auschwitz, but you wouldn't believe me. The newspapers won't print the truth because it's not in the interest of the Jews."

Even less forthcoming is the Mengele family—about a dozen blood relatives. The gesture of Rolf donating his father's memorabilia to *Bunte* with the proceeds to benefit Holocaust victims now seems rather less generous—it turns out that he retained book and film rights and at last report was asking half a million dollars for them.

A *Bunte* editor has remarked that within the Mengele family they all hate one another but remain united against the outside world. Such indeed describes the tribe which has made no statement explaining the support given the fugitive. The Mengele company prospered through its allegiance to Nazism, participated in the postwar recovery of Germany, and remains highly esteemed. "It was like a lightning bolt from heaven when I read that Sedlmeier did all this," said a pensioned employee. "But leave the family alone. The guys who are running the plant were born in the fifties. What do they know about their uncle? You can't sue them for Joseph. Only in the last few years did all this come up. But you still can't prove it all." . . . "The Mengeles have always been a good Christian family," said a Protestant pastor. "The company has a good reputation."

As they have in the past, the Mengeles seem to go on untouched. They experienced no real injury for steadfast support of Adolf Hitler and none for aiding and abetting the world's most notorious war criminal. The family's perceived obligations to the larger society are fulfilled by donating a fire engine to Günzburg volunteers, giving a car to the local Red Cross, financing a kindergarten and, to be fair, providing good jobs with good pay. The Mengeles thereby connect to the outside world by a cash nexus, just as they did with the family outcast, to whom, it must be said, they were never excessively generous. The Mengeles, after all, know the value of the mark.

Looking back, Gitta Stammer says, "I would say we were drawn into history without wanting to be. They [the Bosserts] entered because they wanted to." Her apologia strikes the author as somewhat disingenuous; certainly the Stammers failed to resist to any meaningful degree their involvement in what she calls "history." As with all positions taken by the principals, as well as with their memories of facts, the truth is frequently obscured. Whatever her feelings years ago, Gitta Stammer now smiles when she remembers being advised Mengele had drowned. "I didn't feel sad when I heard he was dead," she says.

The Bosserts, on the other hand, were devastated. Asked if he would shield Mengele if given the opportunity again, even though he faced possible prosecution, Wolfram says, "Yes, it's part of my character, my life. I've never in my life denounced anyone. I couldn't manage that, not after I developed a certain personal affection. I wouldn't be able to denounce this person."

And Liselotte Bossert has defended her friend with this remarkable statement: "He wasn't the one who sent people to the gas chambers. He only chose people to work." That last has come from so many Mengele defenders that it sounds as if a Mengele antidefamation league has been mailing out stock rebuttals. As far as his experiments, she says, "He did a service to humanity. Those people were condemned anyway."

Her husband takes the high road to avoid imputations that he became a mindless follower: "I looked on him," he says, "not with admiration, but I recognized he was a talented man, of great knowledge and wisdom."

CHAPTER

XVI The "Last" Nazi

"HE HAS THE STATURE OF ABSOLUTE EVIL . . . I have deliberately deviated from historical portrayals of this mysterious 'master.' It is in keeping with his character that he was never caught—presumably thanks to the pleasant way in which he promised children 'a tasty pudding' before sending them into the gas chambers . . . and asking new arrivals whether anyone felt ill as a result of the trip. Because this 'doctor' stands in such sharp contrast not only to his fellows of the SS but to all human beings, it seemed permissible to me at least to suggest the possibility that, with this character, an ancient figure in the theatre and in Christian mystery plays is once more appearing on the stage. . . . Seemingly human, the phenomenon of the DOCTOR is in reality comparable to no human being . . ."

So wrote Rolf Hochhuth in his play *The Deputy*, published in English in 1964. Hochhuth endowed Mengele with mythic, satanic proportions. Similarly, media reports of Mengele at Auschwitz and his post–KZ adventures created a larger-than-life, out-of-time image. Such magnification that blurs reality has characterized the likes of dramatic dealers in death from Genghis Khan and Vlad the Impaler to Hitler and Mengele. The same process made a near-legend out of Adolf Eichmann, until Hannah Arendt placed that poorly educated striver in the perspective of rigid banality.

Joseph Mengele was of flesh and blood, an actual person guilty of very real crimes. He was not a TV-type homicidal maniac who lived only for the pleasure of killing. He was not even, as far as one can discover, neurotically impaired by anxieties or phobias that prevented him from functioning either while he served the SS or during his fugitive years. There is no indication of sexual problems—a frustration for fundamentalist Freudians —that would distinguish him from most other "normal" men.

Robert Jay Lifton theorizes that torturers help cope with the brutish emotional aspects of their deeds through mental gymnastics he labels as "doubling," and thereby are able to create an alternate, acceptable self for the nasty side of their lives. But Mengele showed no signs of emotional trauma as a result of what he did at Auschwitz, nor was he so naive as to believe in a grand reconciliation after the war.

Ella Lingens, the Auschwitz prisoner doctor, declares: "I know of almost no SS man who could not claim to have saved someone's life. There were few sadists. Not more than five to ten percent were pathological criminals in the clinical sense. The others were all perfectly normal men who knew the difference between right and wrong. They all knew what was going on."

In his *History of the Holocaust,* Yehuda Bauer remarks: "The commanders and sub-commanders in the camps were in most cases not sadists, nor were they uneducated. Many of them such as the doctors and engineers were the products of the best Central European universities."

Elie Wiesel devastatingly understates the matter: "My feeling is that German culture in those times was not permeated enough by ethical demands. Therefore it was possible for an SS officer to kill hundreds of children a day and still be capable of admiring poetry, music and philosophy."

By all accounts Mengele was, in fact, "brainy." His judgments on politics and people in his fading years should not obscure the breadth of his education or his potential. Ella Lingens, who despised him, remarks that, at another time and in another place, he could have had a brilliant intellectual career. Reduction of all members of the Third Reich to the Eichmann status, the banality of evil, mitigates against blame and understanding of what happened in the twelve years and three months of the Third Reich.

An essay in *Time* magazine suggested that those who doubted Mengele died at Bertioga Beach were motivated by a sense of justice denied. People, said *Time,* felt cheated of the opportunity to inflict pain and suffering on the man who generated so much agony in his lifetime. Certainly those who bear the Holocaust scars on their bodies or in their minds may feel swindled of their *right* to see Mengele publicly writhing in the dock, then dangling from a noose (although West Germany has no death penalty). Mengele's death for many victims robbed them of the opportunity to work through and resolve their continuing grief. As long as Mengele roamed free as the personification of the perpetrators of the world's greatest mass murders, there was an opportunity to hope for a redress of pain.

Above all, Mengele's death denied the world a trial. More so than Eichmann, a bureaucrat removed from the killing ground and never a policy-maker, Mengele's trial might have served as a forum in which to reexamine and interpret what happened. Hanna Arendt sharply criticized the Eichmann trial in Jerusalem as fraught with testimony calculated to inflame but which had no direct bearing on the conduct of the prisoner. But justice can be more than a weighing of the scales against the individual facing his peers. It can also on rare occasions be a morality play that instructs as well as punishes or exonerates. Where the crimes have been committed in the name of the State, where the laws have legitimized what civilized humanity has long deemed obscene, certainly it is fitting to bear witness to the larger context. What Mengele did to the Jews, and others, was not illegal in Germany. It was only morally illegitimate, notes Rainer Baum in *The Holocaust and the German Elite,* but morally illegitimate in a different context only.

Hundreds of thousands of Germans from all ranks of the military, the medical, and scientific communities, the bourgeoisie—like the Mengele family—working-class men and women, all participated in the theory and implementation of the Final Solution as a legal action of the Third Reich. *Time*'s essay said Mengele "defiled science. . . . He defiled Germany." He did *not* defile the scientists of his day; they set the standards that Mengele enthusiastically followed. He did not teach or lead the hundreds of thousands of ordinary Germans who profited by the economic and professional exploitation of victims, including those who filled out the documents, who operated the trains, who manned the camps and drove the condemned into the gas chambers, and, above all, who stood silently consenting, as fellow human beings were violated, maimed, and murdered according to the tenets of the, then, eminently respectable "race science."

Even without the opportunity of trial testimony by witnesses, the hunt for Mengele has raised useful discussion about the current state of Nazism. Foremost is the question of whether groups like ODESSA are still plotting to preserve war criminals. The last days of Eduard Roschmann and the poverty of Wolfgang Gerhard, who died leaving only $100 according to his daughter, lessen faith in even the existence of an ODESSA. The people who conspired to hide Mengele do not appear to be sophisticated, well-trained operatives, the sort for a crack secret organization. Surely, for example, an ODESSA could have managed to provide Mengele with identification papers without the need for Sedlmeier to coax and bribe Gerhardt to rush from Austria back to São Paulo. Instead of a craftily constructed plan hiding Mengele, the desultory pursuit by law-enforcement agencies seems to have allowed him his freedom. (Had the wanted man been a member of the Baader–Meinhof terrorist gang or a volunteer in the Red Army Brigades, one wonders if less reticence would have been shown by authorities about close surveillance, for example, of the Mengele family.)

There has also been talk of *Kameradenwerk* (friendship efforts) as a blanket organization for the care and maintenance of ex-Nazis. Available evidence suggests that *Kameradenwerk* has never been a functioning group but only a term applied to efforts in general to help old Nazis.

Still, many question whether Mengele is dead. These, understandably, include numerous Auschwitz survivors, as well as those, such as some in the media, who long to keep a news story alive. A West German newspaper, for example, carried a short-lived story that Mengele was alive and dying of cancer in Paraguay; the alleged source was an anonymous Israeli agent. A finer piece of imagination appeared in the tabloid *National*

Examiner, which proclaimed Mengele was alive and well in Germany but transformed into a woman named Dr. Josephine Mendoza.

The hunters, as seen, came under closer scrutiny with the final chapter on Mengele. The Klarsfelds have acknowledged that in their line of work sometimes one does miss the mark. But if they erred, the hunters did keep the Mengele story alive. Some of the grumbling about them suspiciously resembles the comments of one R. Dew from the British Foreign Office during the war. Said he: ". . . a disproportionate amount of the time of this office is wasted on dealing with these wailing Jews." Had the cries been louder, perhaps something might have been done to save the millions who perished.

Still widespread is the troubling failure to distinguish between what Mengele and his colleagues did at the KZs and certain Allied actions in World War II. A Günzburger says of Mengele: "Maybe he did some bad things, some things which were bad for Germany, but what the Americans did at Dresden also wasn't so great." (Actually the British destroyed Dresden.) Alfonz Dierckx, the Belgian Nazi and Mengele chum, declared: "Nothing is said of Hiroshima, Nagasaki, Dresden and other German cities where women, old people and children were killed, thousands of homes were destroyed with pitiless bombing by the Allies." And another Günzburger, with his own self-serving historical perspective, put it: "Everyone knows he was inhuman but after forty years why make such a drama out of it."

True, the attacks on Dresden, Hiroshima, and Nagasaki killed and injured hundreds of thousands, including large numbers of noncombatants. But at least the *purposes* of the bombings were to eliminate manpower for arms factories, to destroy the will to support the war, and to convince leaders that further resistance meant total obliteration of their countries. There were functional tactical and strategic motivations. On the other hand, the *Einsatzgruppen* killings and the gas chamber exterminations had no relevance whatsoever to the successful prosecution of the war for the Axis powers. In fact, the mass murders were counterproductive, tying down as they did troops and equipment needed for combat and eliminating potential factory labor.

The moral obtuseness that equates the deeds of Mengele with strategic military operations that did, admittedly, inflict civilian loss reflects what Rainer Baum perceives as the crucial failing of the Germans—their "moral indifference." They would not—or could not?—recognize that what was being done in their name was an outrageous violation of moral behavior. With too few exceptions, as mentioned, they kept their mouths shut or "only followed orders."

Mengele's townsman who decries the "drama" forty years later avoids the real issue. "Everyone knows," he said, "that Mengele was inhuman" (which is arguable, since he still has his defenders).

But Mengele is not a case study in abnormal psychology, as some would have it, or an aberration to be fascinated by, written about but not to be taken in the context of history. To the contrary, Mengele, whatever his extreme characterological predispositions, was part of the mainstream of his nation and its prevailing moods, attitudes, and indeed scientific philosophies during the time of his heinous—by standards other than his and his mentors and millions of others in Germany and indeed beyond—crimes against humanity. He was never a pariah in his land. And as noted, he is not even that among many there today. The Holocaust and Mengele happened not because they were phenomena contrary to their time and place. Quite the opposite.

And as Elie Wiesel and others have been trying to tell us ever since, what happened once can happen again, and for the same reasons and with very likely the same victims. That is why the Holocaust must never be forgotten or forgiven. And that is why Joseph Mengele and his ilk must never be forgotten or forgiven.

Mengele's breed may be on the wane, and he can be said to be its last and most notorious representative. But the species is still abundant. Members of the German communities of South America show an affinity for the tenets of Hitlerism even though they may have formed no discernible, organized movement. Elsewhere in the world, in, among others, South Africa, in the no-man's land between Israel and its Arab neighbors, in the Soviet Union, in Cambodia, in Iran, home-grown elements of Nazism appear victorious. Add in the nurturing soil of world-wide moral indifference, sprinkle with one or two charismatic personalities slouching their way to their own Bethlehem, and the last Nazi will most surely not have perished at Bertioga Beach.

Partial Bibliography

Arendt, Hannah. *Eichmann in Jerusalem,* New York: Viking, 1964.

Aziz, Philippe. *Doctors of Death.* Ferni Publishing, 1976

Bauer, Yehuda. *A History of the Holocaust.* New York: Franklin Watts, 1982.

Baum, Rainer C., *The Holocaust and the German Elite.* Rowman and Littlefield, 1981.

Bower, Tom. *Blind Eye to Murder.* New York: Doubleday, 1980.

Cohen, Dr. Elie. *Human Behavior in the Concentration Camp.* New York: W.W. Norton, 1953.

Conot, Robert E.. *Justice at Nuremberg.* New York: Harper & Row, 1983.

Delbo, Charlotte. *None of Us Will Return.* New York: Grove Press, 1968

Ehrenburg, Ilya. *The Black Book.* Holocaust Library, 1980.

Eisenberg, Azriel. *The Lost Generation.* Pilgrim Press, 1983.

Fertig, Howard. *From the History of KL Auschwitz.* Panstwowc Museum (Oswiecim), 1967.

Fitzgibbon, Constantine. *Denazification.* New York: W. W. Norton, 1967

Friedmann, Dr. Philip. *This Was Auschwitz.* United Jewish Relief (London), 1946

————. *The Roads to Extinction.* Jewish Society of America (Philadelphia), 1980

Gilbert, Martin. *Auschwitz and the Allies,* New York: Holt, Rinehart and Winston, 1981

Harel, Isser. *The House on Garibaldi Street.* New York: Viking, 1975.

Harris, Whitney. *Tyranny on Trial.* SMU Press, 1954.

Hart, Kitty. *I Am Alive.* New York: Abelard Schuman, 1961

————. *Return to Auschwitz.* New York: Atheneum, 1982.

Hausner, Gideon. *Justice in Jerusalem.* New York: Harper & Row, 1976.

Hilberg, Raul. *The Destruction of European Jews.* Quadrangle, 1961.

Hill, Mavis; Williams, L. Norman. *Auschwitz in England.* MacGibbon & Kee, 1965

Hoess, Rudolph. *Commandant at Auschwitz.* London: Weidenfeld & Nicolson, Ltd., 1959.

Katz, Robert. *Black Sabbath.* New York: Macmillan, 1969.

Kessel, Sim. *Hanged at Auschwitz.* Stein & Day, 1972.

Kieler, Wieselaw. *Anus Mundi.* New York: Times Books, 1980.

Lengyel, Olga. *Five Chimneys.* Ziff-Davis, 1974.

Partial Bibliography

Levi, Primo. *Survival in Auschwitz*. Collier, 1973.
———. *If This Is a Man*. New York: Penguin, 1979.
Lingens, Dr. Ella. *Prisoners of Fear*. London: Victor Gollancz, 1954.
Linklater, Magnus; Hilton, Isabel; Ascherson, Neal. *The Nazi Legacy*. New York: Holt, Rinehart & Winston, 1984.
Mann, Peggy; Hersh, Gizelle. *Gizelle, Save the Children*. New York: Everest House, 1980.
Manvell, Roger; Fraenkel, Heinrich. *The Incomparable Crime*. New York: Putnam, 1967.
Mendelsohn, John. *The Holocaust, Selected Documents*. Garland Publishing, 1982.
Mitscherlich, Alexander; Mielke, Fred. *Doctors of Infamy*. Elek, 1962.
Müller, Filip. *Eyewitness Auschwitz*. Stein & Day, 1979.
Nauman, Bernd. *Auschwitz*. New York: Praeger, 1966.
Newman, Judith Sternberg. *In the Hell of Auschwitz*. New York: Exposition Press, 1963.
Nomberg-Przytyk, Sara. *Auschwitz*. University of North Carolina Press, 1985.
Nyiszli, Dr. Miklos. *Auschwitz, A Doctor's Eyewitness Account*. New York: Fawcett–Crest, 1960.
Perl, Dr. Gisella. *I Was a Doctor in Auschwitz*. International University Press, 1948.
Shapell, Nathan. *Witness to the Truth*. New York: McKay, 1974.
Shirer, William L. *Rise and Fall of the Third Reich*. New York: Fawcett, 1962.
Stiffel, Frank. *The Tale of the Ring*. Pushcart Press, 1984.
Vrba, Rudolph; Bestic, Alan. *I Cannot Forgive*. New York: Grove Press, 1964.

Index

Index

Index

Index

Index

Index

Index

Index

Index

Index